362.583

W9-CPF-249

LSTA Grant
2004

Voluntarism, Community Life, and the American Ethic

310 S. Peoria St. Ste. 512
Chicago, Il 60607 3534

Phone 312-226-6294
Fax   312-226-6405

PHILANTHROPIC AND NONPROFIT STUDIES

Dwight F. Burlingame and David C. Hammack, general editors

Thomas Adam, editor. *Philanthropy, Patronage, and Civil Society: Experiences from Germany, Great Britain, and North America*

Albert B. Anderson. *Ethics for Fundraisers*

Karen J. Blair. *The Torchbearers: Women and Their Amateur Arts Associations in America, 1890–1930*

Eleanor Brilliant. *Private Charity and Public Inquiry: A History of the Filer and Peterson Commissions*

Dwight F. Burlingame, editor. *The Responsibilities of Wealth*

Dwight F. Burlingame and Dennis R. Young, editors. *Corporate Philanthropy at the Crossroads*

Charles T. Clotfelter and Thomas Ehrlich, editors. *Philanthropy and the Nonprofit Sector in a Changing America*

Marcos Cueto, editor. *Missionaries of Science: The Rockefeller Foundation and Latin America*

Gregory Eiselein. *Literature and Humanitarian Reform in the Civil War Era*

David C. Hammack, editor. *Making the Nonprofit Sector in the United States: A Reader*

Jerome L. Himmelstein. *Looking Good and Doing Good: Corporate Philanthropy and Corporate Power*

Warren F. Ilchman, Stanley N. Katz, and Edward L. Queen, II, editors. *Philanthropy in the World's Traditions*

Thomas H. Jeavons. *When the Bottom Line Is Faithfulness: Management of Christian Service Organizations*

Amy A. Kass. *The Perfect Gift: The Philanthropic Imagination in Poetry and Prose*

Ellen Condliffe Lagemann, editor. *Philanthropic Foundations: New Scholarship, New Possibilities*

Mike W. Martin. *Virtuous Giving: Philanthropy, Voluntary Service, and Caring*

Kathleen D. McCarthy, editor. *Women, Philanthropy, and Civil Society*

Mary J. Oates. *The Catholic Philanthropic Tradition in America*

J. B. Schneewind, editor. *Giving: Western Ideas of Philanthropy*

William H. Schneider, editor. *Rockefeller Philanthropy and Modern Biomedicine: International Initiatives from World War I to the Cold War*

Bradford Smith, Sylvia Shue, Jennifer Lisa Vest, and Joseph Villarreal. *Philanthropy in Communities of Color*

David H. Smith. *Entrusted: The Moral Responsibilities of Trusteeship*

Jon Van Til. *Growing Civil Society: From Nonprofit Sector to Third Space*

Voluntarism, Community Life, and the American Ethic

Robert S. Ogilvie

INDIANA UNIVERSITY PRESS

Bloomington and Indianapolis

This book is a publication of

Indiana University Press
601 North Morton Street
Bloomington, IN 47404-3797 USA

http://iupress.indiana.edu

Telephone orders   800-842-6796
Fax orders   812-855-7931
Orders by e-mail   iuporder@indiana.edu

© 2004 by Robert S. Ogilvie

All rights reserved

No part of this book may be reproduced or utilized in any form or by
any means, electronic or mechanical, including photocopying and
recording, or by any information storage and retrieval system, without
permission in writing from the publisher. The Association of
American University Presses' Resolution on Permissions constitutes
the only exception to this prohibition.

The paper used in this publication meets the minimum requirements
of American National Standard for Information Sciences—
Permanence of Paper for Printed Library Materials, ANSI Z39.48-984.

Manufactured in the United States of America

Library of Congress Cataloging-in-Publication Data

Ogilvie, Robert S., date
  Voluntarism, community life, and the American ethic / Robert S.
Ogilvie.
      p. cm. — (Philanthropic and nonprofit studies)
  Includes bibliographical references and index.
  ISBN 0-253-34423-9 (cloth : alk. paper)
  1. Partnership for the Homeless (New York, N.Y.)
2. Shelters for the homeless—New York (State)—New York. 3.
Voluntarism—New York (State)—New York. I. Title. II. Series.
  HV4506.N6O35 2004
  362.5'83—dc22
                                        2003025347

1 2 3 4 5 09 08 07 06 05 04

Contents

Acknowledgments

The road to completion of this book was long, and there are many who helped me along the way. At Columbia, Lisa Anderson made me understand that one should not undertake the professional practice of the social sciences simply as an academic exercise, and she correctly warned me that to sustain myself through what could be years of unrewarded work, I should pick a topic close to my heart. Bob Shapiro and Tony Marx were there to guide me at every step. They were excited about my ideas and they were the ones who helped me craft a viable research project.

At Berkeley, Michael Teitz, Fred Collignon, Michael Southworth, and Randy Hester all played a critical role in supporting what I was doing and in bringing me into City Planning. City Planning is a hybrid field with one foot in academia and the other in the real world and teaching. Marcia McNally and Randy Hester gave me a context in which to think more broadly about the volunteers that I had worked with. Sandy Muir, also at Berkeley, helped me with this rethinking and with new reading and reflection in this context. I saw that one of the things that made the work of the volunteers in the shelters so interesting, from a sociological sense, was that those who had continued volunteering for all of these years, nearly 20 years in some cases, had done so because they had developed communities. Ed Weeks of the City Planning Department at the University of Oregon—along with a few other anonymous reviewers from a summer writing seminar that the *Journal of Planning Education and Research* (JPER) and the *Journal of the American Planning Association* (JAPA) organized in 2001—helped me conceptualize what the second phase of the research would have to look like in order for the book to take on the questions that I now wanted to tackle.

At the Partnership for the Homeless, there were many people whose friendship and eagerness to share insights about their work were essential. Bill Appel helped to write drafts of the survey, and he connected me to many shelter volunteer coordinators many times over many years. He also agreed to be interviewed, along with Brenda Griffin. Jim Jones and Virginia Brown were so open, helpful, and friendly, and Margaret Shafer and Peter Saghir were so giving of their time and insights. It is to all of them, and to the thousands of other volunteers at the Partnership, that I dedicate this book. I have gotten a great deal of inspiration from them and I hope that I can return a little.

During the time it took to complete the research and to write this book the support and feedback of my wife Stacey was critical. Her editing did a lot to make this book more readable. Writing and rewriting was made much easier by the good-natured patience of my son John—who let Daddy work when both he and I would rather have been playing. I thank and love both of them.

Of course, without editors books would not be possible, and at Indiana University Press Marilyn Grobschmidt and Richard Higgins have been my champions. They both understood what I was trying to say and their input has made my words better. I also thank Rachel Berney for her help drawing the table in chapter 7, and Jane Rongerude for her help preparing the index. Of course, all of the errors that remain are my fault.

Voluntarism, Community Life, and the American Ethic

Introduction:

Voluntarism and the American Ethic

Ethic: The body of moral principles or values held by or governing a culture, group or individual.
—*Random House Webster's College Dictionary, 2d ed.*

Ethic: (a) a set of moral principles or values; (b) a theory or system of moral values; (c) the principles of conduct governing an individual or a group; (d) a guiding philosophy.
—*Merriam-Webster's Collegiate Dictionary, 10th ed.*

When Alexis de Tocqueville looked at volunteers in civil associations in America he saw "a multitude of citizens who are regulated, temperate, moderate, far sighted, masters of themselves."[1] These people's *mœures*, as he called them, their *habits of the heart*, as he also called them, are what I refer to as the *American Ethic.* Then as now, this ethic is developed through citizen interaction in civil associations that have been charged with managing small common affairs. In *Democracy in America*, Tocqueville saw voluntary participation in the affairs of what he called "public associations in civil life" as being the source of such important qualities as feelings of reciprocity and loyalty to fellow citizens, a rich moral imagination, functional communities, a sense of potency in the face of social problems, and the feeling of being a useful member of society.

To Tocqueville, this ethic represented a unique answer to the challenge posed by the natural tendency of democracies toward excessive individualism. The difficulty that he saw with individualism is that when problems arise the inclination is toward centralized problem solving. This is a shortsighted response, in his mind, because it leads eventually to the erosion of the democratic conditions. The challenge, therefore, is to develop and maintain problem-solving capabilities that strengthen democratic conditions. This is the democratic balancing act, and in Tocqueville's analysis, through participation Americans were turned into democrats. True America was still characterized by individualism, but, in the words of Charles Taylor, it was a "holist-individualism."[2]

Exactly how voluntary participation in the affairs of public associations in civil life leads to ethical development in and among the participants is something that few have examined in detail.[3] Furthermore, the question of why some voluntary institutions seem to be ethical generators and others don't is one that has largely gone unasked. The point of this book is to explore these two unresolved issues in detail and to outline how to build institutions that can generate the American Ethic. Given that today many fear that the American Ethic is becoming a thing of the past, and that the country is worse off for it, this sort of investigation is timely. While I see plenty of evidence to support the contention that American voluntarism is in decline, or at least has become more individualistic, there are many examples of associations that are functioning as the sort of ethical generators that Tocqueville wrote about.[4] This book will focus on one of these examples: the Partnership for the Homeless and its volunteers in New York City.

The Partnership for the Homeless

The Partnership for the Homeless was founded in 1982. It is the largest nonprofit provider of services to homeless people in the nation. I worked there for four years as the director of volunteers. Of the many programs that the Partnership for the Homeless runs, the one that I found most remarkable, and the one that I will focus on, was the network of church-and synagogue-based homeless shelters.[5] As of October 2001 there were 120 of these shelters in all five boroughs of New York City, with a total of 1,239 beds. The shelters are all run by volunteers, about 11,000 of them.[6] It was while I was working at the Partnership—as those who work there refer to it—that I was first exposed to the American Ethic. Through an examination of the formation, growth, and operation of this remarkable institution and its equally remarkable volunteers, the answers to the two questions that I posed in the previous paragraph will be derived. For details on the formation of the American Ethic I will focus on the operations of two church shelters: Sacred Heart of Jesus in Glendale, Queens, and Fifth Avenue Presbyterian Church in midtown Manhattan.

The Partnership for the Homeless is a uniquely American story. It was bred by, and is supported by, voluntary citizen action in response to a dire social need. The organization was started by the late Peter Smith, who in 1982 convinced the priest at his church, St. Joseph's in Greenwich Village, to let him start a volunteer-run homeless shelter in the church basement.

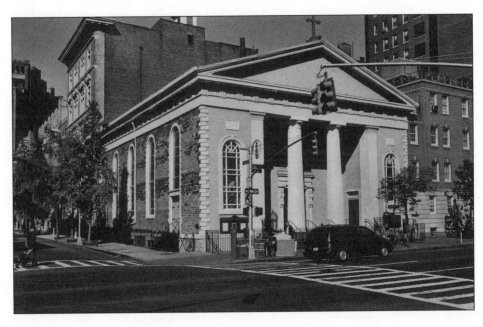

St. Joseph's Church in Greenwich Village.

The priest was skeptical that Peter would be able to get enough people to volunteer to spend the night in the basement with homeless people in order to open a shelter. The church had nothing to lose, however, so the priest let Peter use the basement to give his idea a go. Peter succeeded at St. Joseph's, and he used this shelter as a model on which to build the Partnership for the Homeless. I began my position as volunteer coordinator in 1991 and became director of volunteers shortly thereafter. As the director of volunteers I was responsible for recruiting, training, and retaining volunteers and for supporting the vast web of volunteer shelter coordinators in the church shelters who were doing the same thing. By 1991 there were 10,000 volunteers. While I personally recruited and helped recruit hundreds of new volunteers during my four-year tenure, and while I worked to train and retain many more, I am acutely aware that the participation of so many volunteers was the expression of something much greater than the work of a few people. It was in these roles that I became aware of the effect that participation can have on people.

The Partnership's shelters are a little-known parallel universe to the city of New York's Department of Homeless Services (DHS) shelters, which were spun off from the city's Human Resources Administration (HRA), the main provider of social welfare services, during Mayor Dinkins's administration. The two systems could not be more different. Where the city shelters are huge and impersonal, despite reforms in the late 1990s that reduced their size, the Partnership shelters are smaller and intimate. Where the city shelters are intimidating, the Partnership shelters are safe. Where the city shelters have been forbidden by law from denying service to anyone or from imposing behavioral requirements as a condition of residence (recent rulings from the state appellate court, if upheld, will change this), the Partnership's shelters are selective and will expel those who do not follow their rules. Because the Partnership and its shelters operate in so different a manner from the city shelter program, I begin the book with a description of the Partnership. Most Americans have never been to a homeless shelter, let alone volunteered at one, so very few people have any firsthand knowledge of what they are like and what it is like to spend time in close quarters with homeless people. Therefore, images that most Americans, especially those in big cities, possess of homeless shelters in their mind's eye are secondhand. These images are likely to be of big, dangerous, crowded places that homeless people are terrified of. Very few people could imagine volunteering in one of these places. Because the shelters that the Partnership runs are so different from this image, I will describe the look, the feel, and the operations of two of the church shelters so that a true sense of these places can be had.

The shelters at Fifth Avenue Presbyterian Church and at Sacred Heart of Jesus Church are my two examples of public associations in civil life in which citizens develop the psychological qualities that Tocqueville identified in *Democracy in America*. The parts of town where these shelters are located are as different from each other as two parts of one city could be, and the differences are clearly reflected in the two churches. I will point out these differences through the course of the book, but I will spend more time focusing on the similarities, which are much more striking. I have chosen these two as my examples because of their success and because of their similarity. The primary indicator of success that I use is the size of the volunteer corps, which I have found to be the most accurate indicator of the existence of a thriving association. If a voluntary institution is doing its job well, it will have a lot of volunteers, and if it isn't doing its job well, then it won't. The Sacred Heart shelter has been successful since its founding in March of 1982, and it has always had between 200 and 250 volunteers; it consistently ranks among the largest volunteer corps of any of the shelters in the Partnership's network. This shelter has always been very well run by a dedicated leadership group. The Fifth Avenue Presbyterian Church shelter also has a large volunteer corps, about 160, and the church itself has over 800 volunteers in a variety of social service programs. Since its founding in 1986, the shelter at Fifth Avenue Presbyterian has been open every night. What makes this shelter an interesting comparison case, however, is its resurrection from a near death experience. By 1999, the shelter program at Fifth Avenue Presbyterian Church was down to its last six volunteers and the church leaders were about to close it. The shelter program was saved by reorganization, after which the operations at Fifth Avenue Presbyterian began to unwittingly resemble those at Sacred Heart. It was because of this reversal of fortune and how it was brought about that I chose the Fifth Avenue Presbyterian Church shelter as one of my examples.

This book starts with the story of the development of this remarkable network of 120 church- and synagogue-based homeless shelters and their 11,000 volunteers. New York City has a long history of church-based social services and the development of the Partnership for the Homeless is described within the context of this history. A detailed description of how the homeless shelters operate at Sacred Heart of Jesus and Fifth Avenue Presbyterian follows. In the volunteers' own words I tell the stories of the phenomenal success of the Sacred Heart shelter and the near demise and resurrection of the shelter at Fifth Avenue Presbyterian Church. I do this by describing the main characters in each of the shelters and by explaining what the shelters look like, how they got started, what happens in them, what the volunteers do, what their capacities and limitations are, and what their successes and failures have been.

Once the setting is established, I then describe and analyze the community-generating functions that these two successful shelters perform. I refer to these two shelters as *community-generating institutions* and to the communities that they generate as *communities of practice.* These communities are generated, I theorize, by the volunteers doing work that serves important functions in their lives. These functions are integration, mediation, socialization, education, and the provision of space for moral development. Chapter by chapter I explain how the work that the volunteers do in the shelters enables them to perform these functions in their lives. Using the volunteers' voices at every stage, I explain how these people start volunteering in the shelters, how they become integrated in them, how the shelters mediate—that is, connect people to each other, to sources of meaning, and to sources of power—and how and why the two shelters I examine succeed at some aspects of mediation and fail at others.

Mediating institutions like these are critical incubators of the American Ethic and I look at one of the least-examined aspects of the work of mediating institutions: the moral development of the volunteers. Morality is a word seldom used in American social science, but moral development is a central aspect of what transpires in these church shelters, and it is a critical aspect of community generation. The conception of morality that I use is descriptive and can be understood as a sense of what we owe to each other as members of the same society.[7] In this conception, morality is in part socially formed, and social interaction with others within the structured environment of a mediating institution is one of the crucibles of the social formation of morality. I describe how the shelters function as the settings of real life morality plays, and I look at how the process of socializing volunteers into the shelter volunteer corps and educating them about the dos and don'ts in the shelters leads the volunteers to expand their conception of what is owed by members of a society.

Community is thought to be in decline in America today for numerous reasons. One of the central hypotheses in the writing about the decline of community is that the freedom afforded individuals in America is irrevocably in conflict with the responsibility required for the development of community.[8] My argument, however, is that these church shelters, with their voluntarist approach and their ability to figure out ways to integrate large numbers of people, are able to resolve this seemingly irrevocable conflict and generate functioning communities among their volunteer corps.[9] A critical part of my explanation of how they do this is my functional definition of *community,* which is based on Michael Taylor's conception of communities as being characterized by "shared values and beliefs, direct and many sided relations, and the practice of reciprocity."[10] My argument is that the two church shelters developed these characteristics that Taylor talks about not because they were trying to develop communities but because their leaders realized that they had to develop these characteristics in order to effectively perform their task of sheltering homeless people. Those in charge of the shelters had to figure out how to get people to volunteer, and they had to develop an organizational capacity to sustain themselves over a long period of time. In doing what was necessary for the operation of their shelters, the volunteers developed the ability to perform certain functions; by performing these functions the shelters developed into communities. This art of

8   creating such community-generating voluntary associations is the art of social architecture, and in the chapters that follow I spell out the elements of this art. I evaluate the successes and failures that the volunteers at these two shelters have had as social architects, and I outline some policy steps that can be taken to create an environment conducive to the well-being of institutions such as the church shelters of the Partnership for the Homeless.

1

The Partnership for the Homeless:

The Tradition of Churches Helping the Homeless in New York

The Partnership for the Homeless is as its name describes it. It is a partnership of those who work for the homeless of New York City—a partnership of the city of New York, churches and synagogues, church charities, private donors, volunteers, and paid staff. It was founded in 1982 by the late Peter P. Smith in a church basement in Greenwich Village. Its initial purpose was to shelter homeless people. It has since grown to encompass a number of other programs, including street outreach, rehousing homeless families, providing shelter and health care to homeless people with AIDS, and furnishing apartments for rehoused formerly homeless people. Nonetheless, sheltering single homeless in church and synagogue basements continues to be its main function, and this is the task that occupies the overwhelming majority of its 11,000 volunteers.

The story of the beginning of the Partnership for the Homeless is the story of Peter Smith's epiphany. Peter was a well-connected, politically active New York City attorney. He had been an associate in the Manhattan law firm of Shea & Gould, "Shea" as in Shea Stadium, and was described, even in that capacity, as a political operative.[1] Peter was deeply involved in Democratic Party politics in New York State. He was a campaign aide to Robert F. Kennedy when Kennedy ran for president in 1968, and when Kennedy was killed, it was Peter who organized the funeral train from Washington to New York. In 1977, the newly elected mayor, Ed Koch, appointed Peter to be his commissioner of general services. This appointment was, at least in part, payback for Peter's role in lining up support for Koch in Queens, through his close ties to Borough President Donald Manes.[2] Peter's mundane-sounding position was actually a crucial one, as it was this department that handled all city purchasing, leasing, and contracting. Some of Peter's notable accomplishments as general services commissioner were to help create Operation Green Thumb, a program that leased vacant city lots to community groups for gardens, and another program that leased apartments to tenants who were eventually given a chance to buy them for $250 apiece.[3]

Peter's tenure as commissioner of general services was cut short, however, when background probes uncovered his prior embezzlement of $70,000 worth of funds from a client while at Shea & Gould. Peter was indicted, convicted, disbarred, and sent to federal prison for four months.[4] Upon being sentenced Peter was quoted by the *New York Times* as saying "my life is over," but he certainly didn't act like that after his release.[5] When Peter came out of prison, it was with a new mind-set, one more focused on helping his fellow man.[6] He didn't immediately know how he would do this, but after returning to his home in Greenwich Village, like others he began to notice the increased numbers of homeless people living on the streets of New York. Unable to practice law and unappointable due to his criminal record, Peter needed to find a creative way to work himself back into public life.[7] Enter the homeless situation in New York.

I use the word *situation* as synonymous with *predicament,* because by the early 1980s that is what the city was in with the new homeless population. New York had always been known for its "Bowery Bums," older alcoholic men who lived on the street in the Bowery and other parts of the lower East Side of Manhattan who were portrayed with color by Damon Runyon, Joseph Mitchell, and other chroniclers of New York life. By the late 1970s, however, there were homeless people living in the streets in parts of New York where they had never been before. This was a different set of people than those portrayed by Runyon and Mitchell, and instead of being seen as local color, New Yorkers regarded them with a combination of confusion, fear, pity and loathing. A new word, *homeless,* was invented by the burgeoning advocacy groups to describe this new population, many of whom were deinstitutionalized mentally ill people. They were young as well as old, and men as well as women. New Yorkers were soon demanding action, loudly.

The New Yorker who demanded action in the loudest voice was Bob Hayes. In 1979 Hayes was a student at New York University (NYU) law school who had befriended a number of homeless people who lived on the streets near his apartment. It was in the name of one of these people that he filed a lawsuit, *Callahan v. Carey.* In this suit, Hayes contended that the Constitution of the State of New York compelled New York City to shelter any homeless man who requested shelter. Rather than spend a lot of time and money to fight this lawsuit, Mayor Koch signed a consent decree in 1981, which created the nation's first right to shelter ordinance. This initial consent decree was later followed by *Eldredge v. Koch,* which established the right to shelter for homeless women, and *McCain v. Koch,* which established the right to shelter for homeless families with children. New York remains the only city in the country in which such rights have been established. Mayor Koch later told me that he signed the decree because he mistakenly thought that the additional expense of sheltering more homeless people would not be that great.[8] At the time, the city of New York was already sheltering homeless people at its upstate Camp La Guardia facility, which is now run by Volunteers of America, and at facilities within the city, and the Mayor didn't think that the new ordinance would dramatically increase existing efforts. This turned out to be a serious miscalculation on his part—the DHS, the city agency that would be developed to take care of the vast homeless operations, would grow in 15 years to have an annual budget of about $500 million. This was a decision that Mayor Koch later said he wished he could make again.[9] To ensure that the city respected this new right that had been won for the homeless, Bob Hayes began the Coalition for the Homeless. The mission of the Coalition was to monitor the homeless services that the city was providing and to sue the city when it was deemed that the city was not living up to its obligations.

Complicating the city's ability to deliver on the right to shelter was the severe budgetary situation that New York City was in. Ed Koch had gotten elected in part because of the damage that the fiscal crisis had inflicted on the career of his predecessor, Abraham Beame, and the city now operated under the budgetary oversight of the New York State Financial Control Board, a state-appointed watchdog agency. Even if Mayor Koch had wanted to simply follow the paradigmatic Great Society formula of establishing a massive city agency to deal with this problem, which is what the advocates for the homeless through their use of the courts eventually forced him to do, this did not seem to be an economically feasible option. Neither was it a politically feasible thing for him to do. Mayor Koch soon realized that sheltering the homeless was going to be much more expensive than he first realized, and that homeless policy was to become a political football. He began to look about for some help. Enter Peter Smith.

With Smith working behind the scenes, one of Koch's early responses to this crisis was to challenge the city's churches and synagogues to do what they had traditionally done in New York and get involved in this pressing social welfare issue. Mayor Koch issued this challenge during a speech that he had been invited to give by Rabbi Balfour Brickner at Stephen Wise Free Synagogue on the Upper West Side. Rabbi Brickner had written Koch a letter asking him to come and speak to the congregation and invited guests on the topic of what they should do in response to the burgeoning homeless crisis. Recalling that day, Mayor Koch said that he told the congregation about what the city was doing to help the homeless, and that he told them that in spite of the fact that there were city shelters, there were still people who would refuse to sleep in them because they were too afraid. These were people who churches and synagogues needed to help. Koch went on to tell the congregation that the Catholic Church was already sheltering the homeless and he asked them why they weren't doing the same.

The rabbi, Koch noted, "was absolutely beside himself with rage at my making such a demand and said . . . something like . . . having people sleep overnight would be incompatible with the facility."[10] As Koch remembered it, however, this was a turning point. Despite the affront, the people who were there that day were so upset that they weren't doing as much as they could do that they and the rabbi ultimately decided that the Stephen Wise Synagogue would start a homeless shelter. To facilitate this, and the other church and synagogue

shelters, the city began to set some limitations, formulate some regulations, and offer some support.

In pushing for the opening of these shelters in the churches and synagogues, Mayor Koch was not advocating the start of something new as much as he was pushing for the reinvigoration of a venerable New York tradition of service to the poor by religious institutions. After getting over the shock of being publicly called out for their inaction by the mayor, the city's religious leaders began to respond to the mayor's call. This meant that in a small way the city could now share the financial, political, and moral burdens of taking care of the homeless with the religious community. But simply asking the religious organizations, which were not yet commonly referred to as *faith-based institutions,* to help would not get a large scale, church-based response to homelessness. For that to happen, an organization would have to be created that could mobilize the necessary resources, provide support, and link the church shelters into a larger system. This was the role that the Partnership for the Homeless was to play, and with the Mayor's backing, Peter Smith got to work creating this organization.

To educate people about this novel concept of running a homeless shelter in a church, Peter and the small staff of the Partnership began holding a series of what he called *Action Days.* On the itinerary for these initial Action Days were tours of the shelter at St. Joseph's, trips to the Bowery Mission, a church-based organization in the Bowery that had been working with homeless people since 1879, and lectures on the logistics of shelter operations. To spread the word further, Peter and his early employees went out to churches and synagogues at night and on the weekends to talk about their program and to recruit congregations. Employees of the Partnership for the Homeless continue this practice to this day. Following St. Joseph's, four churches and one synagogue opened shelters virtually simultaneously, and within six months there were 50 shelters operating.

How the Partnership Operates

From its very beginning, Peter Smith developed the Partnership for the Homeless as a nonprofit umbrella organization that drew support from a web of public and private entities. One of the first steps that

14   Peter took was to secure the support of the major religious charities in the city for this new organization. Because he was aiming to open the shelters in churches and synagogues this was a crucial step, and he received the support of the Federation of Protestant Welfare Agencies, Catholic Charities, the United Jewish Appeal, the Episcopal Diocese, the New York Board of Rabbis, and Terence Cardinal Cook. Cardinal Cook particularly did the Partnership a great service by sending out letters to every parish informing them of this new organization and urging them to get involved. To help oversee the new organization and to raise funds, Peter appointed prominent employees of Wall Street firms and of the major religious charities and institutions to the Partnership's Board of Directors. This enabled him to use them and their contacts to raise money and awareness. With the mayor's help, he secured funding from Wall Street firms seeking to meet the requirements placed on them by the Community Reinvestment Act of 1977. Building on the mayor's backing, Peter used his knowledge of the workings of the city to appeal to well-placed bureaucrats to get logistical and material support for his fledgling organization.

In conjunction with city officials, Peter began to formulate a program in which the city would cooperate with the Partnership to bus homeless people from central locations (later known as *drop-in centers*) to a church shelter each evening. At the shelter they would have dinner, sleep through the night, and have breakfast in the morning. The homeless people would be bused back to the drop-in center from the shelter in the morning and would remain there, or do whatever they did during the day, and in the evening they would get back on the buses and go back to the shelters. The shelters would all be run by volunteers, and the city's HRA would supply the cots, the linens, and other materials that the shelters needed. HRA would also supply the transportation for the homeless people to get to and from the shelters. At the drop-in centers, the homeless men or women could wash themselves during the day, get fed, and get the drug, alcohol, or mental illness treatment they needed. The drop-in centers would also be responsible for screening out inappropriate clients from the pool of those who were referred to the shelters. The Partnership for the Homeless would manage this whole system and try to expand it.

After St. Joseph's opened, within six months there were 50 shelters running in churches and synagogues throughout the five boroughs. The first office of the Partnership was on West 13th near St. Vincent's Hospital. This was where the paid staff of the organization, which performed the crucial intermediary coordination, facilitation, and information-sharing roles, worked. In the beginning it was a one-room operation on the first floor with about a dozen employees sharing two phones. The staff of the Partnership for the Homeless also sought out sources of funding, other than city funds, to run its operations. In 1983, the Partnership's second program, Project Domicile, was developed to offer assistance to families, usually women with dependent children, who were resettling in the Bronx or Brooklyn into affordable housing. Once these families were resettled, they would be taken to the furniture warehouse that the Partnership had opened in Red Hook to get furniture for their apartment. This warehouse, which was later to evolve into Furnish-a-Future, was used to hold furniture donated from individuals, hotels, and businesses. For the first year after they were housed, the Project Domicile clients would be visited by volunteers who would make sure that they were managing their new lives well. Despite the Project Domicile program, developing new shelters and running the existing ones was the main task of the employees of the Partnership in the early years.

Bill Appel, the director of the shelter program, described the steps of the shelter opening task as cold calling, going on site visits to do reconnaissance to see if the site looked viable, and then working with the pastor and the congregation to open the shelter. In order for a church to be a viable shelter site, it needs to have both a willing congregation and an appropriate physical plant. This combination of qualities is fairly difficult to come by, with the willingness of the congregation being the prime limiting factor. Bill Appel estimated that there are 1,000 churches in Brooklyn alone, yet there are only 25 shelters there. Very few congregations are willing or able to open homeless shelters in their churches because, as Bill noted ruefully, "there are a lot of churches that are strictly open for worship."[11] Among those that are interested, their physical plant has to be appropriate according to certain city-mandated criteria. In order for the Fire Department, the

Health Department, and the Department of Buildings to certify a church room as safe to house people overnight, the physical plant has to be solidly constructed; the area used for the shelter has to have at least two ways in and out and needs proper ventilation; the roof has to be at least eight feet high; and there has to be proper lighting, emergency exit lights, hot and cold running water, and heat. There also has to be one toilet for every six people. In addition to these requirements, the Partnership was also looking for churches that had kitchens and showers. In many cases, the Partnership helped pay for upgrades at churches that didn't meet these standards. Because space is tight in New York, most of the available rooms in these churches are small. This is one of the reasons that the shelters are small; fire codes are another. In New York City the pre-1996 fire codes for rooms that people slept in had a dividing line at 20. Below 20 there were fewer fire and building safety requirements that had to be met. Renovations to physical plants were very expensive and the ability of the Partnership to pay for upgrades was limited. Any money that the Partnership spent on improving the physical plants of churches had to come from private sources, as it was not possible to use government funds for this purpose. These facts limited the amount that the Partnership could spend, so the shelters were limited to 19 or fewer residents. These facts have also limited the number of churches that host shelters. By Bill Appel's estimate, if the Partnership could afford the renovations, another 80 to 90 church shelters could open.[12] In 1996, following the decline in arson in New York, the Fire Department shifted their focus to prevention rather than reaction, and as a part of this new focus they inspected the church shelters and revised their regulations to drop the limit for spaces without sprinklers to 15 people. The older shelters that were started under the old limit were allowed to continue to operate as they were, but any new ones had to abide by the new limits.

The city agency that worked most closely with the Partnership in the beginning was HRA through its DHS. DHS has since been spun off and is now an independent agency. They support the Partnership and the shelter system logistically as well as financially. The financial support comes in the form of funding to the Partnership to pay for

some salaries and some of the expenses of running the shelters. Fuel
reimbursements of up to $5,500 per season are available to the churches that can prove they incur extra heating costs by staying open at night to shelter homeless people. DHS also pays for the buses and the drivers to take the homeless people to and from the shelters. They also fund all but one of the drop-in centers. DHS supplies the cots for the people to sleep on, a two-week supply of clean bed linens (which they also launder), and other material for the shelters.

In most of the shelters, when the homeless clients (or guests as they are called at many of the shelters) arrive in the evening, usually between 6 and 7 P.M., they have dinner. They also have breakfast before they leave, usually between 6 and 7 in the morning. In many of the shelters the volunteers buy and cook the food themselves, but in others, the food is paid for through a combination of funds. Some of the money comes from DHS, some from the Federal Emergency Management Agency (FEMA), and some from the Hunger Prevention and Nutrition Assistance Program (HPNAP) of the New York State Department of Health, which used to be known as the State Nutrition Assistance Program (SNAP). The rest is made up by private donations and other grants. The Partnership and the churches themselves solicit private donations to supplement the salaries of Partnership employees and to supplement the costs of running the shelters. Many of the larger churches have their own paid social service staffs, which are integral to the functioning of the shelters in their churches.

While some of the original drop-in centers, like the Holy Names Center on the Bowery and the Moravian Coffee Pot, which used to be located at the First Moravian Church in Manhattan, are no longer in operation, there are currently nine drop-in centers throughout the city. These are the Bond Street drop-in center in downtown Brooklyn, which is run by the Salvation Army; the Grand Central Partnership, which is run by the Business Improvement District of the same name in the basement of St. Agnes Church on East 43rd Street; the Neighborhood Coalition on East 77th Street; the Olivieri Center, which is run by Urban Pathways, a nonprofit organization, on West 30th Street and is for women only; the Open Door, which is run by the Port Authority and is on West 41st Street near the bus terminal; Project Hospitality

18   in Staten Island; Peter's Place, which is run by the Partnership for the Homeless at St. Vincent de Paul Church on West 23rd Street and is for the elderly; the Living Room in the Bronx; and the John Heuss House, which is run by Trinity Church on Beaver Street in Lower Manhattan and is for the chronically mentally ill. Eight of these outreach centers are contracted by DHS to nonprofit service providers and one center is funded through the federal Department of Housing and Urban Development (HUD). Each center does its own private fund-raising as well.

The drop-in centers are the point of entry for homeless people who want to get referred to services other than those offered by the city shelters. Each center can hold about 100 people, and while the people can stay overnight and sleep in chairs, by city decree beds are not allowed. This stipulation was crucial in overcoming resistance in many of the residential neighborhoods in which drop-in centers are located. Beds would have connoted permanence, whereas chairs, and the title "drop-in," signify temporariness. For the city shelters there are separate intake centers, but the drop-in centers, and the institutions that they refer people to, are a separate universe from the city shelters. Homeless people hear about them through word of mouth or from one of the seven citywide mobile outreach teams that operate around the clock. These outreach teams are usually the first resource for a homeless client. The teams, which are all contracted out by the city, include those run by the Partnership for the Homeless, the Salvation Army, Grand Central Social Services, Metropolitan Transportation Authority (MTA) Connections (this group works in the subways), and the New York Police Department's Homeless Outreach Squad. The outreach process is often a slow one, as it can take weeks for a bond of trust to develop between the street outreach worker and the homeless person. Once the outreach worker is able to gain the trust of the homeless person, he or she refers the homeless person to a drop-in center. Different people get sent to different drop-in centers, depending on their age, health condition, and mental status. Once there, a wide array of services is available to them. The services available at the Bond Street center illustrate this range. Services include: three daily meals; entitlement assistance; recreation activities; therapy and referrals for therapy; educational and vocational training; instruction in independent living skills; workshops on budgeting and money management; comprehensive medical services, podiatry, and dentistry; nutritional guidance; substance abuse treatment and counseling; and detox referral. When the drop-in centers themselves can't handle a person's needs, they refer out to a partner organization that can. This is especially the case for medical care and HIV care. At Peter's Place, for example, St. Vincent's Hospital sends a medical team, comprising an M.D. and a nurse practitioner, three times a week, and Project Renewal, a nonprofit that does outreach and provides medical and mental health service to the homeless, sends a psychiatric team.

Drop-in centers are critical for the operation of the church and synagogue shelters. Before any homeless person is sent out to a church or synagogue, the staffs at the drop-in centers and at the supporting agencies perform psychiatric evaluations, conduct medical tests for communicable diseases, such as HIV and tuberculosis, and observe behavior at a variety of times and in a variety of social situations. Critical behavioral factors that the staffs at the drop-in centers look for are signs of drug and alcohol use. No one who uses drugs or alcohol is permitted in any of the church or synagogue shelters, and anyone who begins using drugs or alcohol after being admitted to these shelters will be kicked out. (Those who are in treatment programs can be admitted to the church shelters, but active users are forbidden.) The observation and treatment process usually takes at least a week, so a homeless person usually spends at least a week in a drop-in center before going out to one of the church or synagogue shelters.

Despite this elaborate observation and treatment process, in most years during the winter when all of the church shelters are open, almost everyone from the drop-in centers gets sent out to a church shelter. The centers develop relationships with certain churches so that the same drop-in centers send the same people to the same churches night after night. With these permanent relationships, the staffs at the drop-in centers get to know the various church shelters that they work with and they can match the homeless clients and their conditions to the proper church shelters. As one example, shelters in bigger churches that have professional social service staffs can handle clients that a shelter at a smaller church cannot.

The staff of the Partnership for the Homeless is integral to the development and maintenance of the relationships between the shelters and the drop-in centers. The Partnership staff visits the drop-in centers twice a year to see what the needs of their client populations are, and they make regular phone calls to see how many drop-in center clients need accommodations each night. While the Partnership staff is doing this, they stay in constant communication with the churches and synagogues to see how they are doing and to obtain the right number of shelter beds to meet the need. If the shelters don't have enough beds, the homeless clients stay at the drop-in centers until beds are found for them. Because most of the church shelters have maximum lengths of stay and because people from the shelters are constantly being housed, beds open up all the time. At the same time, the Partnership staff tries to make sure that there are not too many beds available; they have found that having empty shelters gives volunteers the impression that the homeless problem isn't that bad and that their services aren't needed. Empty beds are lethal to volunteer retention, so the staff does whatever they can to avoid them. For the 2001–2002 season the bed capacity of the Partnership's system was 1,239.

The largest shelter, at Transfiguration Church in Brooklyn, sleeps 19 and the smallest, at Washington Square Church, sleeps 4. Some, like Transfiguration, Fifth Avenue Presbyterian and Brooklyn Heights Interfaith are open every night, while many others open three to five nights a week. A few shelters open as little as one or two nights a week. This makes the Partnership's job of matching homeless clients with these shelter beds quite complicated. Often, church shelters will operate in pairs, as what the Partnership calls *sister churches,* with one being open on the nights that the other isn't. An example of this is in Queens, where Sacred Heart of Jesus and Ascension Lutheran operate in tandem to provide shelter to the same 10 men, seven nights a week. Each of the sister churches usually has its own separate set of volunteers, and each has its own rituals. They will, however, host the same homeless clients. Each shelter organizes its own volunteers and divides up their duties however it sees fit. Some are very hierarchical, with the pastor, or more likely the pastor's wife, as the sole decision maker. In these cases, this person usually does most of the volunteering, and the volunteer corps is very small. Some of the shelters with small volunteer corps have extraordinarily heroic volunteers who dedicate large chunks of their lives to taking care of their shelter guests. Claudine James, the former coordinator of the shelter at Union United Methodist Church in the Brooklyn neighborhood of Crown Heights not only cooked dinner for eight homeless men four nights a week for many years but she also brought the dinner over to the shelter and served it. This model of shelters run by extremely dedicated older women is common in the Black neighborhoods, but it is rare in the wider network. Most shelters divide up the work among larger groups of volunteers who share the decision making and the work. Most shelters depend almost entirely on the congregation of the host church or synagogue for volunteers, while a few in churches in commercial districts of Manhattan depend more on external sources of volunteers such as neighboring businesses and volunteer referral agencies. Some of the large Manhattan church shelters have volunteer coordinators who are part-time paid staff. All of the other shelters are wholly volunteer-run. Most of the shelters are the sole projects of their host churches. A few, however, are hosted by a consortium of neighboring churches and synagogues. The Brooklyn Heights Interfaith shelter, for example, is a cooperative effort of volunteers from Church of the Assumption, Congregation Mount Sinai, First Unitarian Church, Grace Episcopal Church, Plymouth Church of the Pilgrim, and St. Ann & the Holy Trinity Episcopal Church. In all of the shelters, recruiting and retaining volunteers is a pressing concern. However, some of the shelters do this so well that they are able to staff spin-off shelters in neighboring churches and develop additional volunteer-run programs out of the shelter. In contrast, other shelters have shut down due to a lack of volunteers.

The clients are bused to and from the shelters on yellow buses, used as school buses during the day, that are owned and operated by Advanced Busing. This service is paid for by the DHS. These buses are also used to take people to and from city facilities. DHS has two employees whose job it is to work with the Partnership, the bus companies, and the churches and synagogues to coordinate homeless transportation. One handles the logistics of the program operation and the other manages the contracts. Because of the city's reporting requirements and the many components of this system, the job of coordination is time consuming and detail oriented. The reporting requirements of working with the city have turned the Partnership, in Bill Appel's words, into "a paper factory." Every aspect of its operations has to be in writing and anything out of the ordinary has to be reported. So, if the buses are early or if a shelter is going to close one night because of a special event, a report has to be written and faxed to DHS for their files. The shelters that close down in the summer usually do so between April and June, and they generally reopen by October. For these shelters, the Partnership submits a request for opening each fall and each spring they submit a request for closing. These shelters close not only to give the volunteers a break but also because there is less demand for shelter beds during the warmer summer months. The Partnership would rather close the shelters down in the summer and reopen them in the fall than dispirit the volunteers with the sight of empty shelter beds.

When Peter started the Partnership in 1982, he envisioned it as a temporary program, one that would be in place for a few years until federal, state, and city government picked up the reins and solved the homeless problem. This is how Peter sold the churches on the idea; they were assured that if they got enough volunteers, in a few years they would be able to return to normal. An early credo of the Partnership was that they were trying to work themselves out of a job. With hard work and missionary-like zeal, Peter built an organization out of nothing. By the time he died in 1991 there were 152 shelters in operation and the annual budget was approaching $5 million. Today the budget is approximately $7 million. Despite the best efforts of the Partnership employees and volunteers, in the years since the founding of the Partnership, homelessness has not been solved. Nonetheless, despite the initial promise that they would soon be able to go back to normal, the churches haven't quit. Neither have the volunteers. Bill Appel estimates that of the churches and synagogues that have opened shelters, 80 percent are still operating, and with many of the same volunteers. Why this is so is what makes this story interesting.

While the idea that Peter Smith had in 1982 of churches hosting homeless shelters sounded novel to many, it really wasn't. The tradition of churches helping the poor and the homeless is an old one in New York, and I found this out shortly after I started at the Partnership, when I volunteered to spend the night in one of the church shelters. This was in August 1991, and at the time there were 152 shelters; 6 in synagogues, the rest in churches. There were approximately 10,000 volunteers, but despite being the agency's volunteer coordinator, I only had the vaguest idea of what the volunteers did. I thought I should find out, and so did Mary Randall, the volunteer coordinator of the St. Paul's Chapel homeless shelter, a member of the Partnership for the Homeless. St. Paul's was a year-round shelter, and in August a number of Mary's regular volunteers were on vacation. The job of finding a replacement had fallen to her, and she was having a difficult time finding anyone in her regular volunteer corps. Mary was quite insistent, and she asked me to volunteer in such a way that I felt I had no choice; she was letting me know that in her opinion, the only way that I could be effective in my new job was to know what volunteering in the shelters was actually about.

Though the Partnership was only nine years old at the time, the parish of which St. Paul's is a part had a history of helping the poor in New York that was nearly as old as New York itself. It was appropriate, therefore, that I should familiarize myself with a church shelter in this setting. St Paul's chapel occupies an entire city block. It is bounded by Broadway to the east, Fulton Street to the south, Church Street to the west, and Vessey Street to the north. Within sight is New York's City Hall. The World Trade Center stood across the street. St. Paul's is a beautiful old Georgian chapel designed by Thomas McBean, built in 1766. The chapel, and its graveyard, is one of New York's historical treasures. It is the oldest public building in New York City to have been in continuous use.[13] A thanksgiving service was held here for George Washington on April 20, 1789, following his inauguration, and Washington was a customary worshiper on Sundays. The chapel was also the sight of the funeral of President James Monroe. St. Paul's is part of the Trinity Episcopal parish. At the time I had no idea of the eminent history of Trinity parish, nor did I know the extent to which its work with the poor exemplified the work that American religious congregations have done with the poor since the beginning of European settlement on this continent.

In 1696 New York Governor Benjamin Fletcher gave his approval for the Anglicans in New York to buy land for a new church. This land was granted in 1697 by King William III, who chartered Trinity parish at the same time. Over time the land grant made the parish very wealthy. As of 2000, Trinity parish owns 24 commercial buildings in Lower Manhattan. With a total of approximately 6 million square feet of office, retail, and manufacturing space, Trinity is one of the largest commercial landlords in New York City.[14]

With this wealth the parish has, from its very beginning, been a strong supporter of educational and charitable work in New York. The Charity School, now the Trinity School, was founded in 1709. This was followed by the establishment of a school for Indians and slaves. In 1754, the parish granted the land that enabled the founding of King's College (now Columbia University). As New York urbanized in the nineteenth century and as poverty in New York became more abject, especially in some of the infamous slums that were hallmarks of the era, Trinity parish opened an outreach center on the Bowery in 1857 to assist needy families. This was followed by the establishment of a mission house in 1879. This precursor to the settlement house movement contained a girls' vocational school, a home for aging women (now St. Margaret's House), cooking and nutrition classes for immigrant women, a workingman's club, and a relief bureau.[15] It was as part of this long-standing tradition that the parish established St. Paul's shelter in 1982. Six years later, in the next step in their work with the homeless the John Heuss House, a drop-in center, was founded. This 24-hour facility is the only one of the six drop-in centers in Manhattan that is specifically for the mentally ill.

In addition to these facilities and services, the parish established a grants program in 1972. This program has made grants throughout New York and around the world, particularly in Africa. Among its more notable New York investments is its involvement, begun in 1989, with the Nehemiah plan to fund the construction of 512 homes in the South Bronx. This has been followed up by a second phase in which the parish is helping to build 242 one- and two-family homes.

In this parish, St. Paul's Chapel is overshadowed by Trinity, its bigger and grander sister church. The current Trinity Church, which is the third Trinity Church built on the site, is a Gothic revival edifice designed by Richard Upjohn, the co-founder of the American Institute of Architects. It was consecrated in 1846 and sits imposingly at the head of Wall Street. In its graveyard are crypts containing the remains of some of the "old guard" of colonial and revolutionary New York. Alexander Hamilton is buried there and the sight of his crypt at Christmas time covered with red poinsettias is not soon forgotten. St. Paul's Chapel, in comparison, is a humbler building. The steeple isn't as tall; the graveyard, though historic, doesn't have massive crypts; and the sanctuary doesn't hold as many people as Trinity Church. St. Paul's historical significance dwarfs that of its sibling, however.

Unlike a newer church building, St. Paul's does not have a basement, so the 10 to 14 homeless men who spend the night here sleep up in the balcony that encircles the sanctuary. The volunteers sleep on cots at the back of the church at the base of the steeple. St. Paul's has a lot of volunteers who work on Wall Street in the law firms, brokerage houses, and investment banks. Very few of them live in the neighborhood, as at that time very few people lived below Chambers Street in Lower Manhattan at all. Though people had begun moving into nearby Battery Park City in 1982, the city of New York had yet to begin its program of tax incentives for the conversion of empty office space to residential use in Lower Manhattan.[16] Most of the volunteers, like most of the people who work in the district and most of the people in the congregation, were people who commuted to work in Lower Manhattan from uptown, the outer boroughs, Westchester County, Long Island, Connecticut, and New Jersey. For a lot of these people, the history of the church made it an attractive place in which to volunteer.

Despite the historical attraction, I was a bit apprehensive when I agreed to volunteer. Having gotten me to volunteer, however, Mary reinforced my commitment by arranging an orienting tour of the chapel. I did that one afternoon during the week and learned how to lock the gate, where I was to sleep, and where the homeless men who spent the night were to sleep. And that was it. My next step was to show up at 6:30 P.M. on Friday night so that I would have some time to spend with the other volunteers before the homeless clients arrived. The fact that there would be another volunteer there was very reassuring to me and it made me a lot less worried about spending the night at the shelter. I had no idea what it was going to be like, and I didn't think that my short orientation to the church had prepared me to handle an emergency, if there was one. Since there was another volunteer there, I figured that he could handle problems if they came up. As it turned out, matching new volunteers with veteran volunteers was the regular approach at the Partnership. This was done to share the work, to have more people in authority present, and to orient new volunteers to their tasks. I don't recall the name of the other volunteer now but he, like Mary Randall, was not a social service professional. Rather, he was a person whose concern about homelessness in New York motivated him to volunteer to spend his Friday night with 10 homeless men and one other volunteer at a church in Lower Manhattan.

The night turned out to be entirely uneventful. The clients showed up shortly after 7 P.M. and they made their own dinner in the pantry at the rear of the church. All of them had their own favorite places to sleep and they pulled mattresses and bed sheets to their favorite places on the balcony and settled down for the night. As volunteers, one of our main responsibilities was to lock the front gates and the front doors of the church so that tourists and vagrants wouldn't wander in through the evening and night. After we did that, there was nothing else to do, really, except go to bed. Or, in my case, wander around the cemetery for an hour or so looking at the old headstones and marveling at the fact that I was locked into one of Manhattan's historic sites, looking up in the twilight at the World Trade Center, and that I was in charge. As I wandered through the graveyard I was struck by the layering of history in the place, by the fact that here in this historic building, with two subway lines rumbling underneath and two of the tallest buildings in the world across the street, we were taking care of the needs of people, just like this place always had. This made me wonder about the historic roots, precedents, and significance of the new job that I had just taken on.

Trinity parish is not alone in having a long and distinguished history of social service in New York. Rather, the history of church-based outreach to the poor is as old as New York. Long before the current homeless crisis and long before Mayor Fiorello La Guardia created the nation's only municipal welfare state in the city of New York, the churches and synagogues of the city were taking care of the poor, sick, needy, and homeless. The current homeless crisis in New York is only the latest of many such crises in the city's history.[17] As Kenneth Kusmer has noted, "vagrancy and street begging have a long history in America," with surges in homeless populations happening in the 1840s and 1850s, during the depression of the 1870s when the word *tramp* was coined, and continuing on through every other depression that the city suffered.[18] While each new homeless crisis provokes a rediscovery of homelessness by journalists and academics, the churches have always been there taking care of, and in many cases ministering to, the homeless.

In the early seventeenth century the first system of poor relief in the city was established by the Dutch Reformed Church. For the better part of the century this was the only system of poor relief in the New Amsterdam colony. In 1683 poor laws were finally passed. These shifted some responsibility for poverty relief to the counties, but the poverty relief system was now administered by the wardens of the Anglican Church. As the city grew in the eighteenth and nineteenth centuries and as immigration, urbanization, and industrialization transformed the nature of poverty in New York, the common council, the forerunner to today's city council, responded. Construction of the first city-run alms house was authorized in 1734.[19] In addition to taking care of those in the alms house, the city also supported many "outdoor" poor, the precursors to today's homeless.[20] Later on in the eighteenth century other forms of nonreligious and nongovernmental charitable organizations were formed. In New York these included the Humane Society (1787), which was formed to aid imprisoned debtors, and the New York Society for the Prevention of Pauperism.

Despite the new role for the common council, the churches remained the major providers of charity. As urban poverty grew in the nineteenth century, so did the debate over what form this charity should take. This debate over how best to do good, and who were the worthy recipients of the good deeds, was an ideological as well as a programmatic debate. The churches of New York and their members were deeply involved in both aspects of this discussion. On the subject of who the worthy recipients of good deeds were, for some there clearly was a difference between who was worthy and who wasn't. For others, all were deserving. Among the Protestants of the early nineteenth century, as Michael B. Katz notes, there was a missionary focus to their work and volunteers were pressed into service to bring the word of God to the poor and illiterate.[21] The hope was that with Christianity and some hard work, the poor would improve their lot in life. As the volunteers got to know the poor, however, they began to lose their optimism and as Katz notes, by the mid-1830s they "began to blame the poor themselves for their misery."[22] The tendency developed to equate poverty with moral failure, and the remedy was moral uplift of the poor done through scientific charity. To this end the Association for Improving the Condition of the Poor was founded in 1843 by religious leaders. They developed the district visitor system, a system of more than 300 well-off men who volunteered to do home visits to people in need. The hope was that the poor would learn to emulate the characteristics of the wealthy. This organization was among the first to posit a connection between filthy living conditions and morality.

Unlike the Protestants, the Catholics saw their social reform role as one of charity and not of social change. Leery of Protestant proselytizing, especially when it was directed at Catholics, the Catholic churches began "carrying out the corporal works of mercy to the poor, the hungry and the homeless."[23] To the Catholics, poverty was not necessarily the result of moral failings, and their response to poverty was much less judgmental and less condemning. The principal

Catholic relief organization was the St. Vincent de Paul Society, which was founded in France and came to the United States in 1846.

As to how the good deeds should be done, the leading Protestant organizations soured on volunteers by the mid-nineteenth century and started to create professional organizations. At this point in American history Protestant churches, especially the Presbyterians and the Episcopalians, were much wealthier than the Catholic Church and they could afford to create organizations with paid staff. As the nineteenth century segued into the twentieth, the organizations developed more of a "secular emphasis on 'urban moral and social control.'"[24] This meant that the Protestant volunteers remained but played a subordinate role to the professionals. As the nineteenth century progressed, filthy slums, overcrowded and disease-ridden tenements, and other features of poverty in industrial cities developed in New York while the church agencies considered what their response should be. Moral uplift would require missionaries, while social control would require political action and institution building. Individual parishes, as well as various Protestant and Catholic denominations, did a bit of both. They raised funds, built buildings, and created social service institutions throughout the city. This is how settlement houses such as the Neighborhood Guild, the first settlement house in the United States, were formed, as well as other famous institutions like the New York City Mission Society (1827), the Association for Improving the Condition of the Poor (1843), which was formed to "morally uplift and help the deserving poor," the Hebrew Benevolent Society (1860), the New York Catholic Protectory (1863), and the Bowery Mission (1879).[25]

Throughout this era, the Catholics continued their focus on charity, and their example was akin to mutual self-help. With the failure of scientific charity, the approach of the Protestant agencies shifted from moral uplift to social welfare. The Charity Organization Society (1882) led this shift. They later merged with the Association for Improving the Conditions of the Poor to form the Community Service Society (1939). As the church-led social welfare reform movement of the nineteenth century gave way to the Progressive Movement at the turn of the twentieth century, the New York religious community continued to play a central role. The difference now was that the institutions they developed were bigger and richer, and they increasingly served as umbrella organizations to fund and direct the service-oriented institutions. It was during this era that institutions such as Catholic Charities (1920), the Federation of Jewish Philanthropies (1917), United Jewish Appeal (1939), and the Federation of Protestant Welfare Agencies (1922) were formed. Volunteers were still engaged in working with the poor, but the agencies that the church charities funded were increasingly professional. The role of the volunteers was now secondary.

It was during the La Guardia administration that the city of New York got seriously into the business of providing social services to its citizens. It was during these years, 1933–1945, that New York began to construct, on the foundation laid by the churches, what has been described as the nation's only municipal welfare state. The La Guardia years were only the opening phase of the building of the municipal welfare state, but at no time did the old religious charities go away, and at no time did the tradition of New York City churches helping the poor decline. Catholic Charities, for one, never stopped sheltering the homeless, and the church charities and the new city agencies developed a tradition of working together. During the protest era of the late 1960s and early 1970s, New York saw the rise of the National Welfare Rights Organization, which sought to change welfare laws by signing up so many people as to break the system. This very nearly did break the system in New York, where one million people signed up for welfare. Even during this era, the tradition of cooperation, though strained, continued.

2

In the Church Shelters

It was this tradition of cooperation between the churches and the city that Mayor Ed Koch, in an era of fiscal restraint, appealed to and hoped to strengthen when he made a speech at Stephen Wise Free Synagogue on the Upper West Side in 1982. And it was in the spirit of this tradition that Peter Smith, a Catholic, stepped forward to coordinate the church and synagogue effort. With his challenge to the city's religious community, Mayor Koch was appealing not just to the ancient churches that had a tradition of social service, like St. Paul's, or the radical synagogues that had been founded in activism, but also to the humble neighborhood churches in the outer boroughs, the vast majority of which had never done anything like this before.

For parishes like Trinity, or for other well-to-do Manhattan churches like Fifth Avenue Presbyterian or St. Bartholomew's that had histories of social service, what Koch was asking wasn't very earth shattering. But for other parishes and synagogues, however, especially the younger, humbler ones in the other boroughs, he was making quite an astounding and controversial request. Most of these churches, of course, did nothing. Aside from the multitude of storefront churches and those whose physical plant would not able to pass code, for the hundreds that had the physical capacity to open a shelter but didn't, disinterest, worries, and fears carried the day. A few that wanted to open were unable to overcome neighborhood resistance. These were only a few, however, and in the others, the congregations simply did not want to deal with people whose problems were foreign to them, people whom they did not want in their churches. In contrast to this massive nonresponse, in addition to the big churches that traditionally provided social services, a few dozen congregations that had no history of social services opened shelters. Their actions and stories are a testament to dedicated people in their midst who mobilized others to face the unknown because they were asked to do something to help people in need by people whom they trusted. The actions of these people are examples of the American Ethic. In many of these cases, the eagerness with which the congregations and the neighbors rallied was a surprise to all. Nowhere was anyone more surprised by the eagerness of the reaction than at Sacred Heart of Jesus Church in Glendale, in Queens.

The Shelter at Sacred Heart Church in Glendale, Queens

Sacred Heart had never been involved in social service provision before Mayor Koch's request. While Trinity parish is close to the Bowery, the lower East Side, and the other places where, to borrow from Jacob Riis, the "other half" have traditionally lived, Glendale couldn't have been farther. A civil service enclave, meaning that many of the residents work for the Fire Department, the Police Department, the Sanitation Department, or another city agency, Glendale has the feeling of being worlds apart from Manhattan. This feeling of apartness is neatly expressed by locals who refer to Manhattan as New York, so as to let you know that they live somewhere else. There are some who will even tell you, proudly, how many years it has been since they have been into New York, and in some cases it is very many. Like many other similar neighborhoods in New York, however, this feeling of apartness was destroyed on September 11, 2001, when a number of firemen in the parish were killed in the World Trade Center.

Unlike the city as a whole, the majority of Glendale residents own their own homes, which are attached or semi-detached. It is likely that they or their parents moved up, literally and figuratively, from Ridgewood, a neighborhood just to the west on the Brooklyn-Queens border, when the area was still mainly potato farms. To use an old term, Glendale, unlike the rest of Queens, has remained White ethnic with Germans, Irish, and Italians predominating. This is because houses in the neighborhood rarely go on the market. Instead they are usually passed down to offspring, or they are sold through word of mouth to adult children of neighbors. While the potato farms may be long gone, the cemeteries that surround Glendale have taken their place as green buffers against the rest of Queens and Brooklyn.

By New York standards, this is a new parish. It wasn't established until 1929, and when Jim Jones and Harold Brown opened a shelter for homeless women in the church basement, the parish had never before had on-site social services for homeless people. Sacred Heart had always been an active parish, hosting their own school, Boy Scout and Girl Scout troops, a senior center, and a youth program. They had just never had anything like a homeless shelter at their church before. In fact, there weren't any homeless people in the neighborhood. Neither were there any homeless people at the nearest subway stations, at 71st Avenue and Queen's Boulevard in Forest Hills or on the M line that runs south from Ridgewood. Unlike Trinity parish, which is one of the wealthiest parishes of any denomination in the United States, Sacred Heart parish is quite humble. It isn't poor by any means, but certainly doesn't own expensive real estate that was given to it by British royalty nor does it have its own grant program like Trinity parish

Sacred Heart Church in Glendale, Queens.

does. Rather, Jim Jones, chair of the Parish Council and co-founder of the shelter, describes Sacred Heart parish as blue collar, working class. I would add Middle American.

By the standards of Catholic parishes Sacred Heart, with 2,000 families, is fairly small. The church was built in 1929 and it was meant to be a temporary church. The plan was to build a bigger church on empty land behind the temporary church as the parish grew. The parish never grew, however, as the boundaries became set and other parishes were created that surrounded Sacred Heart, leaving it no room to grow. The temporary church, a red brick structure with a three-story white steeple, thus became the permanent church.

In the New York City context Glendale is conservative. This conservatism is reflected in the voting patterns, conservative democratic or liberal republican, and in the local resistance to previous proposals by the city to site facilities for low-income people nearby. The first example of such resistance occurred in the fall of 1971 when Mayor John Lindsay proposed the building of low-income housing in nearby Forest Hills. A bitter, racially polarized showdown ensued and it was only the ability of the mediator who was called in, the then-unknown Queens lawyer Mario Cuomo, that got the neighborhood to accept any sort of low-income housing project at all. The same sort of neighborhood resistance greeted Mayor Dinkins's attempt, nearly 20 years later, to site one of the smaller (40–50 beds) homeless shelters that the city was planning to build to replace the large armory shelters.[1] Mayor Lindsay managed to get a scaled-down version of his project built, while Mayor Dinkins got nothing. Neither of them got reelected following their respective showdowns with this part of town. The conservatism is also reflected in the local insularity. One of the shelter volunteers proudly told me that she had not been to New York, which was how she referred to Manhattan, since 1968 and that she had no intention of ever going again. She may be extreme, but she was not unique. Conservative though they might be, the people of Sacred Heart parish are good Catholics, and in good Catholic spirit, they responded to the call for help.

It was in this local context that Harold and Virginia Brown and Jim Jones decided to try to open a homeless shelter in the basement of

their church. It began innocently enough with Harold, in his capacity 35
as a member of the Parish Council, receiving a letter in the mail from
Cardinal Cook telling him about the organizational meeting, the "Action Day," that the Partnership was going to be having at NYU. At this
time the Partnership was comprised of little more than founder Peter
Smith and a few other volunteers out of the original shelter site at St.
Joseph's Church in Greenwich Village. It was operating out of a second-floor walk-up space above a store on Sixth Avenue near Peter's
house in the Village. This was 1982, and as Jim Jones noted, homelessness was becoming "the in thing, the in political thing to do."[2] To
spread the word about this new organization Smith was putting together a series of Action Days, and the one that Jim and Harold were
invited to was at NYU. Rather than look at this idea of opening a
homeless shelter in their church as a challenge, Jim and Harold looked
at it as on opportunity to finally put the time that they spent at the
church to good, productive use.

For years, Jim and Harold had alternated as presidents of the Sacred Heart Parish Council, and as Virginia noted, during all of that
time they had not had any power in that position. Parish councils
were a reform made in Catholic churches following the Second
Vatican Council, known more commonly as Vatican II, which was
called by Pope John XXIII in 1959 and which convened from 1962 to
1965. Parish councils were an innovation meant to democratize the
Catholic parishes and to get parishioners more involved in the running of their parishes. They were set up as consultive bodies to advise,
offer their opinion, and assist the pastor in the care of the parish. Despite attempts to make the Catholic Church more democratic, the traditional autocratic rule of the Catholic priest over his parish still continued, and as Jim and Virginia noted, in reality the Sacred Heart Parish
Council resembled a public relations campaign, as no self-respecting
priest would willingly give up the power that he had. The priests were
supported in their autocratic attitude by canon law, which gave no
legislative or decisive power to the parish councils and which vested
the governing powers of the parish solely in the hands of the pastor.[3]
Vatican II was a big step for the Catholic Church, with the changing
from Latin masses to English masses. But despite the ostensible

In the Church Shelters

democratization of the parishes, as Jim noted the priests still did everything, and everyone else simply did what they were told to do. The de jure granting of consultive authority to the parish councils, however, created a situation in which the parishioners expected more openness but nothing compelled the priest to deliver it.[4] To American Catholics, who were accustomed to democratic decision making in other realms of their lives, the parish councils seemed like little more than a public relations exercise. The council, in Jim's view, was supposed to come up with ideas and programs for the parish that looked good, and if the priest liked them he would approve them. At Sacred Heart there were a lot of programs, as it is a very active parish. Most of the time, however, the Parish Council did very little.

So when the letter from the cardinal mistakenly got delivered to the Brown residence instead of to the church, Virginia looked on this as a gift from God. "God must have been looking over our shoulder," she said, and after opening the letter without realizing what it was, she recalls saying to Harold that this could be an opportunity for him and for the others on the Parish Council to actually do something for a change, to make up for all of those nights they had spent in meetings accomplishing nothing.[5] Virginia and Harold's children were young then and Virginia said to her husband that if he and Jim didn't even bring this up in front of the council, she was not going to sit home every night with the children when he was over there or at the Knights of Columbus playing games or having beers. With this pressure, Harold showed the letter to Jim and they both decided to follow up on the cardinal's suggestion and go to the Action Day. Jim still doesn't know why Harold decided that they should go to the meeting. Although they had been on the Parish Council together for years, Jim says that Harold was a very private person, and he hardly talked. It helped that the Partnership for the Homeless seemed to have no ulterior motive, and that it had the imprimatur of Terence Cardinal Cook. Because no one else from the council wanted to go to the meeting, they decided, along with Virginia, to go themselves.

At that first Action Day, they were taken to see the shelter that was already operating at St. Joseph's. They were also taken on a field trip to the Bowery Mission. After seeing the St. Joseph's shelter in operation, they felt that this was something that their church might actually be able to do. Following the visit to St. Joseph's, as Jim said, "we did our homework." This homework involved a visit to Catholic Charities to learn about what might be involved in running a church shelter, a meeting with some nuns who had experience working with homeless people to learn the practical ins and outs of running a shelter, and another field trip to a Partnership shelter, this time at Grace Episcopal.[6]

Armed with this knowledge, Jim and Harold proposed the idea of a homeless shelter to the Parish Council. Recounting the meeting, Jim said, "We were very surprised that they really were not—they weren't gung ho—but they weren't opposed."[7] This is a group that Jim and Virginia described as "a mix of liberal and conservative and this and that," and they noted that "there was really only one . . . who was against it."[8] The vote on the council was 34 to 1 in favor of opening the shelter. The opposing person wasn't vehemently against it, according to Virginia, and he and his wife shortly became volunteers after Jim asked them, "Why don't you try it." After getting the agreement of the Parish Council, Jim and Harold went to see the parish priest. To their surprise, he did not oppose the idea. As Jim noted, "I don't know why he didn't [oppose the idea]. He was a very conservative pastor; he was very tight with the money." Jim ascribed the lack of opposition to the fact that he and Harold had done their homework. He thinks, however, that the real reason was not so much that the pastor supported the shelter but that "he was retiring and he didn't really care. He said, bring it on the new guy."[9] The pastor could have stopped it, but as Virginia noted, "he didn't try." With this "consent" in hand, the next step was to get up in front of the altar during service one Sunday in the fall of 1982 and tell the congregation that they were thinking of opening a shelter.

Jim and Harold told the congregation that they would like volunteers to help them run a homeless shelter in the church basement, which was then unused and in disrepair, for one month on a trial basis. They said that it would be modeled on already-existing church shelters that people could go and visit for themselves to see how they operated. They also told the congregation that the Cardinal supported the idea. This shelter, they said, would take five homeless women who would be bused in from Manhattan, and their plan was to open it five nights a week. If this worked out, they would like to try to open on a larger scale the next winter. The last thing that they said was that none of this would happen unless the congregation approved.

The initial reception from the congregation was positive and enough people volunteered for the shelter to open for five nights a week for one month in the spring of 1983. That one month went so well that afterward, as Jim noted, "People said, 'Gee, why don't we keep going,' and we said no, we promised one month, and we'll stick to our promise."[10] During that fall Jim and Harold spoke at all the masses, and they told the congregation their plan for the next winter. Recalling one of those speeches Jim said,

> We were all surprised that people applauded that we were going to do this. Harold and I, on the spur of the moment, figured we'd stand outside the church with a basket and see if we could collect some money, and we collected hundreds and thousands of dollars without even trying. People were very generous, and we had our first meeting and 125 people showed up, and nobody objected to it except . . . she lived across the street and she was afraid that when we released them [the homeless guests] in the morning that they were going to roam the streets of Glendale. We had said that if we got 50 volunteers we would go with it, and we were just overwhelmed.[11]

This, in itself, was a remarkable response in this small, insular, conservative Catholic parish, but what made the response even more remarkable was that most of the people who volunteered for the shelter were people who were not otherwise active in the parish. In fact, both Jim and Virginia noted that they had never seen a lot of these people before in all of the years that they had been attending Sacred Heart. In Jim's opinion these were people who became active in the shelter because "it hit them at the right time and they wanted something to do that was meaningful."[12] Prior to the coming of the shelter these members of the parish had all, in his opinion, "felt sort of alienated, that there was nothing there that they were really involved in anymore that was worthwhile." The shelter gave them an opportunity to change all of that.

While the Parish Council approved the plan, the priest did not object, and the congregation was in favor, what really got the shelter going were the efforts of a few individuals—particularly Jim and

Harold, who did the homework and convinced the Parish Council, the priest and the congregation, and Virginia Brown, who refused to get up and speak in front of the congregation but who has become what Jim called "the fire" behind the whole organization. Getting Virginia to play this role was difficult, and Jim and Harold were both nervous about her. Harold refused and the task fell to Jim. Virginia acquiesced but given how the job has, in her words, "snowballed" over the years, she told me, "I said yes once, and I don't know if I'll ever say yes again." From Jim's point, getting Virginia on board from the beginning was essential and he confessed, "We never would have survived early on [without her] . . . because you need somebody to do all of that work."[13] "That work" entailed all of the administrative work that was essential to the running of the shelter, work that someone who had a full-time job would be very hard pressed to do. This is work that Virginia could do because she was at home.

Throughout the history of volunteering in American, women have traditionally played a large, if not dominant, role. Before paid employment was available to women, volunteer work was one of the few ways in which American women could use their time and develop their talents outside of the home. It was women, and the institutions that they started, who supplied much of the impetus behind the reforms of the Progressive Era, and women constitute most of the volunteers at the church shelters that the Partnership runs. Though women's groups such as the National Organization of Women are on record as opposing volunteerism, the tradition of female-dominated volunteering continues, especially among the older generations who never had paid employment out of the home. American women have traditionally been the bulwark of the American Ethic, and they certainly are the bulwark of the Partnership for the Homeless.

Securing Neighborhood Cooperation in Glendale

With the history of local resistance to prior attempts to build low-income housing around Glendale, securing neighborhood cooperation should have been difficult. Even if the local history had been different resistance might be expected, as siting social service facilities in any American city has become a highly politicized process. In New

York, as in other places, the standard procedure was to follow the path of least resistance, with the Forest Hills incursions of Mayors Lindsay and Dinkins being the exceptions. When it came to siting the city-run homeless shelters, financially strapped New York simply looked for the cheapest available space that it could find. These spaces were the empty armories that it owned around town, and the city opened homeless shelters in the armories that were in neighborhoods that were not well organized enough or politically powerful enough to resist. Hence there were armory shelters in poor neighborhoods like Washington Heights and in working-class neighborhoods like Flushing, while armories like that of the Seventh Regiment on the wealthy Upper East Side were spared homeless shelters. The armory shelters had already developed such a bad reputation by 1982 that upon looking back, one would think that Jim and Harold were crazy to think that they would be able to open a homeless shelter in their neighborhood.

With homelessness becoming so highly politicized, the crucial first step in securing neighborhood approval for the opening of the Sacred Heart shelter was to remove the shelter from the political process. The fact that the religious leaders put their imprimatur on the shelter was quite influential in helping Jim and Harold. So was the fact that the Partnership was seen as a legitimate organization with no agenda other than to help people. What helped the most, however, was the deliberate way in which Jim and Harold, with the cardinal's letter in hand, went through a series of steps in which they educated themselves, informed the parish leadership of what they were up to and what they learned, asked the parish leadership for permission, and asked the congregation for their endorsement of the idea. While they didn't ask the congregation for permission, by asking for their endorsement, starting slowly and asking them to volunteer to run the shelter, Jim and Harold were giving the parish control over the enterprise. This made all of the difference in the world in securing an overwhelmingly positive response. In Jim's analysis, securing the priest's assent was a critical step because, as he noted, "the Catholic mentality is if the pastor says that you're going to do it, you're going to do it. Nobody ever speaks back."[14]

Despite their efforts to keep the operation apolitical, the political apparatus of the city, in the form of the local Community Board, tried to insert itself into the shelter formation process. In an effort to get city hall closer to the people, 59 community boards had been created in 1974 by city officials who intended them to be "mini city halls," places where citizens could go to vent about neighborhood services and local issues and hopefully get some action. The members of the community boards were appointed by the borough presidents and the boards "were given an advisory role in land use decisions and serve as a forum for the expression of community interests relating to a range of issues."[15] At roughly the same time as Jim and Harold were getting the priest's acquiescence, their local Community Board got wind of what was going on and called Jim and Harold and said that they wanted to get involved in the formation and running of the Sacred Heart shelter. As Jim remembered it, the Community Board contacted them when they first started and they said, "Oh, gee, we got to get involved. We got to get involved in this. You got to let us know."[16] Though the borough presidents appointed the community board members, they relied in part on the city council members for advice on whom to appoint. As a result, the community boards quickly became de facto extensions of the political operations of the city council members. In response to the Community Board overture, "Harry and I said, get out of here," Jim recounted. "We're getting this thing in our church, and we're not letting you know beans. . . . I think they . . . would have brought a lot of politics into it."[17] Virginia added to this rationale by noting that "that was one of Peter's [Smith] rules, really . . . that you really . . . weren't political. You were there to help someone and that's all there was to it."[18] Jim continued the train of thought by adding, "because we just felt that they [the Community Board] would just want to take control of it [the shelter], and make it their organization and get whatever political mileage out if it they could, instead of dealing with the issue."[19] So they shut the Community Board out.

In addition to being sure that they and the rest of the volunteers would be in control of the shelter, the other benefit of moving forward without the involvement of the Community Board was that they were able to operate anonymously, or at least relatively anonymously. Anonymity has been an important tool for the church shelters, which usually operate with the mind-set of the less scrutiny the better. "This way," Jim noted, "if nobody knows we are there . . . it's in the basement, and if you really didn't know we were there you could pass by that church and you wouldn't even know that 20 people were inside the basement of the church."[20]

Bill Appel and Brenda Griffin of the Partnership emphasized the importance of anonymity for many of the church shelters with two examples. One was of a church shelter in the Bronx that Bill visited shortly after he began working at the Partnership and the other was of a church in Staten Island that tried to open a shelter but failed. As the coordinator of the shelter program, Bill tried to visit all of the shelters every few years and when he arrived at the shelter in the Bronx, he met the volunteer coordinator there to find out if everything was working all right. One of the questions that Bill asked was whether or not they were having any problems with the schedule of the buses that took the homeless people to and from the church. As Bill remembered it this volunteer coordinator turned to him and said "Bill, the men arrive in the dark and they leave in the dark and that is exactly how we like it, if you know what I mean."[21] The man then showed Bill the place where the bus turned off the street and into an alley and picked up and dropped off the men. This comment about the men arriving and leaving in the dark really stuck with Bill, especially, as he said, because the volunteer coordinator didn't mean it facetiously. The man went on to say that there was opposition in the neighborhood to the presence of homeless shelters but that they had been in operation at that point for two years and nobody knew that they were there.

After Bill told me this story I told him and Brenda that there were a number of volunteers I had interviewed at Sacred Heart who told me that the homeless shelter there been operating for years before they had any idea that it was there. Both Bill and Brenda nodded and said that this held true for a lot of the church shelters. I asked them if this was by design, and rather than answering the question directly Brenda told me a story about a church in Staten Island that was planning to open a shelter and went public about it. The congregation in

this church was apparently gung ho; they had already done their inspection and everything was wonderful, and then someone put a
story about the shelter in the local newspaper. As a result, said Brenda,
"the next thing we know . . . the people in the community had picket
signs out . . . and they never opened the shelter."[22]

For these shelters this use of free, small, and anonymous spaces in
church basements, which was born of necessity, became a virtue.
Neighbors who did not attend the church and were just walking by
would not notice any difference and wouldn't be able to tell that a
shelter was there. This was not the only time that the Partnership was
to benefit from such a transposition of necessity to virtue.

Dodging the community board, securing the assent of the priest
and the parish leadership, educating themselves, and getting the endorsement of the congregation were still not sufficient to get the Sacred Heart shelter open. The volunteers still had to be trained and
organized, and potential opposition from the rest of the neighborhood had to be dealt with. Even in an insular Catholic neighborhood
like Sacred Heart, there are bound to be neighbors who don't belong
to the church, and whose approval was not directly sought. These
were the sort of people who had squelched the shelter in Staten Island
and who could have done the same in Glendale. In Glendale, however,
no word of the shelter was mentioned in the local newspaper. Instead
people learned of it much more slowly through word of mouth. This
way neighbors learned about every step of the proposal and the planning of the shelter. Fortunately they put up no resistance, although a
few people in the neighborhood stood outside their houses and
looked out on the first nights when the buses arrived with the five
homeless women. It seems that the depoliticization of the shelter had
the same effect outside of the congregation that it did inside. The
people in the congregation and in the neighborhood turned out to be
very generous and gave great support to the shelter from the very beginning. One hundred and twenty five people showed up at Jim and
Harold's first meeting after the end of the trial month, and the only
dissent was from a lady who lived across the street who was afraid that
if the shelter opened there would be homeless people leaving the shelter in the morning and roaming the streets of Glendale.

While different neighborhoods have different reactions to social service facilities in their midst, the difficulties that churches near to Sacred Heart had when trying to open homeless shelters of their own demonstrated the importance of the slow, deliberate, and consultative process that Jim and Harold used in the noncontroversial opening of the Sacred Heart shelter. In the years following the opening of the Sacred Heart shelter, Harold and Jim developed a "traveling road show" in which they would go around to other churches in Queens when a church wanted to open a shelter and they would tell of the experiences that they had opening and running their shelter. Jim noted that virtually all of the churches that they went to opened shelters. Included in the group were Ascension Lutheran, Grace Lutheran, Resurrection Ascension, St. Matthias, St. Andrew Avalino, St. Kevin's, and Sacred Heart Bayside. Most of them followed a similar procedure to that of Sacred Heart and they opened without any local complaint. The exceptions were what Virginia referred to as "the fiascoes." These were at Sacred Heart in Bayside and at St. Kevin's in Flushing.

At Sacred Heart Bayside the priest, who thought that his church should also open a shelter, got up in front of the congregation one Sunday and announced that the church was going to open a homeless shelter that week. This was met by anger from the congregation, but in the end the shelter opened because, as Jim noted, nobody had the courage to stand up to the priest. At St. Kevin's in Flushing, the problem was slightly different. That church was near a city shelter, the Flushing Armory. The people from the neighborhood had experience with homeless shelters and they didn't like what they saw. So when a shelter was proposed for St. Kevin's people protested, and at the meeting at which Harold and Jim had been invited to talk, people came with signs and placards opposing more homeless shelters. Jim and Harold were able to assuage opposition by telling the congregation about their experiences and by answering the questions that people had about the shelter. As it turned out, most of the protesters were not from the parish but instead were residents of the neighborhood. This meeting let everybody have a good say, it let them get all of their anger out, and in the end the church still opened the shelter.

After that first trial month, Sacred Heart Glendale got a new pastor, and while the old pastor, Father Stonebridge, didn't stop the shelter from opening, the new pastor, Father Hartmann, was strongly in favor. He said yes right away, Virginia noted, "because he always said, if I had an aunt who was in that position, or an uncle, I would want somebody to help her, or help him."[23]

Getting the Shelter Running and Setting the Rules

In their tours of the other church shelters and of the Bowery Mission, Jim and Harold learned that the rules they adopted and the structure they created would be crucial to the success of their shelter. Fortunately, they both knew about organization from their days in the air force and the marines, and from their respective climbs up the ranks of the corporations that they worked for. As Jim notes, "we set it up where everybody would have responsibility, and we had a hierarchy so the people would be able to report to somebody."[24] So job descriptions were written and the work was divided up in a way that will be explained in detail in chapter 3. With the Community Board out of the way, with the priest not opposed, and with the Parish Council and congregation in favor, the Sacred Heart shelter opened for its first season in the fall of 1983. Though Jim and Harold had done their homework, the reality of running a homeless shelter was not something that could be practiced, and they were faced with a constant stream of situations that would require astute management if the enterprise were to survive and thrive in Glendale. The fact that they were able to manage these situations in the trial month gave the shelter an enormous amount of credibility in the eyes of the congregation and the neighborhood. The first situation happened on the first night of the trial month.

A few hours before the first bus was to arrive, Jim and Harold, who were very nervous at this point, went to talk to the son of a couple in the parish who is a priest and had dealt with homeless people. They thought he could give them some last minute pointers about what they should expect to happen, which would thus calm them down. "So Harold and I went down to talk to him," Jim noted, "and he said,

'Well, who is going to search them for guns and take their drugs away' … and Harold and I turned to each other and said, 'What guns? What knives?' So we were very shook up."[25]

That was just hours before the opening, so on the first night, without the knowledge of the volunteers, a nervous Jim and Harold went down to the church basement and took the knives out of the kitchen drawer. For an extra measure of protection, they then took a carving knife and put it under the pillow of one of the volunteers. But in their nervousness they forgot to tell her. As a final touch "we turned down the lights in the basement to make it sort of homey."[26] To complete the scene, it rained that night.

And what a night it was. The bus from the drop-in center at the First Moravian Church in Manhattan pulled up in the early evening, and as Jim narrated:

> Who should walk in but five Black ladies, in this lily-white neighborhood. And we are looking at these ladies walking across the church basement and we were thinking, what the hell did we start? Harold and I were scared. We called the shelter every half hour until 11:00 to make sure they were still alive. And the volunteer, when she went to bed, didn't know there was a knife under her pillow, and put her hand under the pillow, and felt the knife and must have flipped [laughter]. And one of the ladies was so wet, she decided to dry her clothes. The volunteer said, "I'll help you dry your clothes." She turned on the oven and put her clothes in the kitchen, and set off the smoke alarm.[27]

It was at this time, with this woman running around stark naked, smoke pouring out of the kitchen, the smoke alarm going off, and a volunteer with a knife in her hand, that the pastor chose to come to the basement and visit the new shelter. Virginia added further context by reminding me, "You have to realize that when we started in '82, we weren't getting people that were finally getting in the system. We were getting all the people that came out of the hospitals. So these people had very big problems."[28] The troubles she meant were the severe mental disorders of people who had been discharged from mental institutions several years earlier, who had spent the intervening years living on the streets of New York City rather than in the community mental health facilities that the State of New York had promised but had never delivered.

Sacred Heart managed to get through that first night because the volunteers and the priest had been prepared for the fact that they were getting psychiatric patients. The hidden benefit to such a chaotic first night was that surviving it unscathed was a great confidence booster for all involved. As Jim recounted, he and Harold both thought, "If we could get over that night, we can get over anything."[29] And soon, by word of mouth, it got out that these homeless people weren't so bad, and that volunteering at the shelter wasn't such an intimidating thing to do. What turned out to be the real difficulty that Jim and Harold faced out of that trial month was convincing the volunteers that they should stick to their initial plan and shut the shelter down until the next winter. The volunteers were so excited by that first month that they wanted to keep going through the rest of the winter, but Jim and Harold stood firm, as they didn't think that they were ready.

Getting through the initial period was the critical part, as Virginia remembered, because there was concern to assuage and skepticism to overcome. But, as she noted, "when they saw nothing was going to happen" and, as Jim added, when the congregation and the volunteers saw that "they weren't going to be knifed, that they weren't going to be killed" and "the ladies, even though they were psychotic, they were funny," things began to come together. In Virginia's mind, the crucial early step that led to the success of the shelter was the rule designed to make sure that the shelter volunteers didn't feel guilty about how they handled a problem:

> If [the volunteers] were having a problem that was getting out of hand, no matter what time it was, they could call Jim, or my husband or myself, and we would come down. We never wanted one of the volunteers to be responsible for calling the police or calling . . . an ambulance or something, because it would end everything. So they always felt that the phone was right there and they could call somebody and they would come down and take over, that they didn't have to feel guilty about it."[30]

The early awareness about the importance of rules and structure was quickly honed by the daily experiences of running the shelter. Jim, Virginia, and Harold learned, among other things, that the work had to be parceled out into pieces that the volunteers could reasonably do; that they needed to be flexible if the demands being placed on the volunteers were too great; that there had to be a means for ensuring follow-through on commitments and for providing backup for volunteers who couldn't follow through; and that there had to be a method of training for proper behavior, a process for disciplining inappropriate behavior, and rewards for the right sort of behavior. The monthly meeting of the organizational committee and the constant oversight of Jim and Harold in the initial days, and Jim and Virginia currently, are indispensable to shelter operation. The monthly meeting is when the schedule is set and it is through the schedule that the work is parceled out, responsibility is divided up, and a support structure is put in place for the volunteers. As Virginia noted, "you have to divide up the pie."[31] This is also when changes are made to the schedule so that it works better for the volunteers. I will talk more about this in depth later on.

Their experience taught Virginia, Harold, and Jim that even with the best organization someone needs to be in charge, someone who in a pinch can come down and take control to keep situations from spinning out of hand. That someone was all three of them. For the long run, they realized that there had to be a way of building a common sense of purpose and belonging and of reminding people about their mission.

Finding a Job for Everyone

Through building this common sense of purpose and belonging, the Sacred Heart shelter has become a de facto community center; that is, a site of ethical generation. Unexpectedly, the shelter has become a place for the kids in the neighborhood to go to after school because their parents know that Virginia, or one of the cooking volunteers, will be there and that this is a safe place for the kids to be before the parents get home. Virginia likes this because she can put the children to work, folding bed sheets, usually under the supervision of one of the older girls. There is one child in particular, a seventh grader, who Virginia has found can control the other children, and she is the one who is put in charge. This has become an unexpected source of voluntary assistance for the shelter.

Though the shelter doesn't start operation until October, Virginia has a significant amount of clerical work to do in the summer, and this past summer she had some of these same children helping her. During the summer she sends out postcards to all of the volunteers, with her return address on the front and a stamp on the back. Written on the postcard are the different volunteer jobs available and the days and the shifts. All the volunteer has to do is fill out the card and send it back. Most of the volunteers pick the same jobs and shifts that they had the previous year, but others ask for new assignments. Some of them write back and say that they are sorry but they won't be able to volunteer at all. Virginia or Jim will call those people to see if they can find another role for them. Virginia has found that people are very responsive to these calls because she thinks it shows the volunteers that they are not being taken for granted and that their time and efforts are considered important enough to retain. This, and the fact that they make a point of never turning a potential volunteer away unless it is for a disciplinary reason, are the main reasons why the volunteer return rate at Sacred Heart is almost 100 percent and why they have at times had so many people wanting to volunteer that they have had to restrict some people from volunteering in two successive years so that others could get a chance.

In order to never turn away volunteers, Jim and Virginia have found that they need to create roles for senior citizens as their veteran volunteers age. It was as part of this creation of new roles that Virginia and Jim made up volunteer job descriptions in the first place. They wanted to make sure that everybody knew the responsibilities, they wanted to cover all of their bases, and they also hoped that when people saw all of the job descriptions, those who were thinking of quitting would realize that there was something worthwhile there for them to do. To retain their new volunteers Jim and Virginia have had to learn to restrain those who are very eager to take on large responsibilities too quickly. The restraint is partly for fear of burning the new volunteers out and partly because the new volunteers don't yet know what they are doing. It is also partly out of a desire to establish adherence to the procedures of the shelter, one of which, as Jim noted, is that you do it their way or you don't do it at all. To work in the new volunteers, they are normally paired with a veteran who will work with them and teach them the ropes. Though Jim and Virginia have a job description for each task, they are not sufficient for educating the volunteer as to his or her role.

Early on Jim, Virginia, and Harold realized that organization, job descriptions, and adherence to procedures were all necessary for the long-term health of the program. Given that Glendale was a fairly tight little neighborhood to begin with, where people know each other and where the same families have lived for generations, I thought that these preexisting conditions, for lack of a better term, might be the reason why so many volunteers came out and continued to come back out to the shelter. I asked Jim and Virginia about this. I wanted to know whether they attributed the size and enthusiasm of the volunteer corps to the Glendale community, to the extent that the neighborhood was actually a community, or did it have more to do with the way they organized the shelter? They both concurred that the shelter organization was the primary reason, though Virginia gave the community a secondary role. In fact, "there is always something to do while you are here. If you volunteered and said no I can't do setup, I can't do overnight, I can't do this, then we said, 'Well, can you do this?'" Offering someone something important to do, never turning them away, and working to make the task fit their ability and schedule were all important in helping to build group affiliation at the shelter, and that keeps people coming back.

To assure that the volunteers would come to see themselves as a group and that they would keep their minds on the task that they were asked to perform, Jim, Harold, and Virginia decided early on to have a prayer service at the end of every season. Reflecting on the benefits of this service, Jim noted that it helped to "refocus everybody's attention as to why the hell they were doing this. We're not doing it because we get in the papers, we're not doing it because somebody pats you on the back, we're doing it because this is actually what you are supposed to be doing." It also served as a way for people to meet one another. Without it, people who volunteered in the mornings would never have met people who volunteered at dinner,

and people who volunteered only on Mondays would never meet
those who volunteered only on Thursdays. This service brought them
all together and they would talk to each other and reminisce. To make
sure that people did come together, two rules were made: one, you
couldn't save seats for your friends, and two, you had to sit at long
tables.[32]

Harold Brown died in 1992, but Jim and Virginia remain in charge
to this day. Because of their leadership, the Sacred Heart shelter is one
of the most successful shelters in the Partnership for the Homeless
network. They began with 50 volunteers for the first trial month, grew
to 125 volunteers for the first full season, and nearly 20 years later
they continue to get 250 to 300 volunteers per year. They continue to
succeed in moving homeless people from the streets to apartments
and jobs. One of the things that makes the Sacred Heart shelter so
interesting is that it has taken root in a type of neighborhood and in a
part of New York that is thought to be hostile to endeavors such as
this. This has surprised many, Virginia included, who noted that
people in Queens generally are afraid of homeless people. While the
volunteers at Sacred Heart may have been afraid in the beginning,
from Virginia's viewpoint, they aren't any more.

> They [the volunteers] are nice to the people. And then after dinner they sit. It is
> like you are sitting here now, talking to me. After dinner is finished they will go
> out and say do you want to play checkers, or do you want to play dominoes or a
> game of cards or just sit on the couch and watch TV with them. And if you
> would have told me that ... the people in Glendale would have behaved in that
> manner, I would have never believed you. Because they are like Bertha, who
> never went out of Glendale, who has never been in New York. And that is what
> most of the people are like, they have their families, their ties. Their children
> might have moved away but they are going to be here for the rest of their lives.
> But they are very good, you know, they want to help these people.[33]

This spirit of wanting to help people and of feeling comfortable
helping in the basement of the neighborhood church is a classic expression of the American Ethic. Looked at this way, Sacred Heart
Church is just the sort of place where one would expect to see this
ethic expressed. By the early 1980s, however, many people were surprised that these Queens conservatives were working in such numbers to shelter the homeless. Equally surprising was the fact that at the
same time the Queens conservatives were putting together a thriving

shelter in their little church, some big, rich, liberal Manhattan churches were struggling to try and keep their homeless shelters open.

The Demise of the Riverside Church Shelter

One of the 20 percent of the churches that wasn't able to keep its shelter open was Riverside Church in Manhattan. This is despite the fact that Riverside Church boasts one of the largest congregations of any church in Manhattan, is very wealthy, and is renowned for its commitment to issues of social justice. The Riverside Church shelter was the one closest to my apartment and it was there that I began volunteering after I had finished my dissertation research, had begun writing, and had quit working at the Partnership for the Homeless. This was in November of 1994 and the first thing that I learned about this shelter was that it might be closing because it did not have enough volunteers. The first night that I volunteered, I was teamed with the shelter coordinator. Here as at Sacred Heart, at St. Paul's, and at almost all of the other church shelters, new volunteers are always teamed with one of the more experienced veterans for their first few times. That night we cooked dinner, and I stayed and chatted with the men after dinner. I went back and cooked dinner the following week, this time with my youngest sister, who was visiting New York for a week. That went well, and because I had a lot of free time in the evenings and lived only three blocks from the church, I was planning to make volunteering there a steady thing, though perhaps not every week. This didn't happen, however, because two nights later the shelter closed.

Many people come great distances every Sunday to attend Riverside Church, both to hear Dr. Forbes's sermons and to hear those of famous guest speakers like Rev. Jesse Jackson and former UN Ambassador and Atlanta Mayor Andrew Young, to name just two. Riverside Church is one of those Christian rarities, an interdenominational church that maintains affiliations with the governing councils of a number of different Protestant denominations. It has an international reputation for its longstanding commitment to social justice, and it was one of the first shelters to become part of the network of the Partnership for the Homeless. Unlike many of the 150 churches in this network, Riverside Church never needed to look to the Partnership for the

Homeless, or the city of New York, for money to pay the heating bills or to buy food. The church and its volunteers could afford it all.

Needless to say, the news of the impending closing of the shelter, when delivered by the Reverend Erik Kolbell, Riverside Church's minister for social justice, was stunning. I cannot say what shocked me more, the fact that this congregation could not get enough volunteers or that this church had a minister for social justice, but it soon became apparent that these two facts were symptoms of the same pathology. Rev. Kolbell, who invited me to be part of a committee that was charged with exploring potential ways to regenerate the shelter program, was one of the eight pastors on the staff of Riverside Church. The operations at Riverside are so large and complex that they have a programs minister—programs being pseudonymous with administration, as I later found out. Because of the various layers of bureaucracy that are involved in decision making and authorization, it takes months for anything to get done. This kept the individual congregants—potential volunteers all—far away from the decision-making process. It also seems to have kept them far away from developing the feeling of personal responsibility or ownership that is so important for the growth and the success of the shelters. Because the church seems to have so much money (how else can you account for their ability to pay the salaries of eight ministers?), the average potential volunteer may have felt that his or her little contribution would not make any difference and it probably was not needed anyway. The minister for social justice has a special shelter committee that reports to him but does not have any decision-making authority, such that potential volunteers may reason that with all of these people busy at work on the shelter program, their small contribution would not be noticed or missed by anyone. Since the Riverside Church shelter closed in early 1995 it has remained closed.

The Revival of the Fifth Avenue Presbyterian Shelter

The shelter at Fifth Avenue Presbyterian could easily have gone the same way as the one at Riverside Church, and it almost did. Fifth Avenue Presbyterian is also a large, wealthy church that is also renowned for its commitment to issues of social justice. Located in midtown

54   Manhattan, at the corner of Fifth and 55th, Fifth Avenue Presbyterian is in a commercial district with some of the world's highest rents. Rockefeller Center, the Museum of Modern Art, Trump Tower, the southern edge of Central Park, the Plaza Hotel, the St. Regis Hotel, the Peninsula Hotel, and too many luxurious shops to mention are all within a quarter-mile radius. The splendid church, a massive red-stone Gothic structure built in 1875, fits right into this milieu. Its interior woodwork, made of solid ash, was designed by the New York firm of Kimbel, whose work is displayed in the Metropolitan Museum of Art.[34] This is the fourth building that this congregation has had since its founding in 1808.

There are six pastors on the staff of Fifth Avenue Presbyterian, and the church has had a hand in founding such organizations as the New York Bible Society and the American Bible Society. Members of this congregation helped to established New York City's first free schools, later to be the New York City Public School System, the Presbyterian Board of Home Missions, and the Board of Foreign Missions.[35] This tradition and Senior Rev. Thomas K. Tewell's interpretation of Christianity, which centers on service to others, helps to explain the church's plethora of volunteers. Rev. Tewell regularly tells people in his Sunday sermons that they need to get concrete in putting their beliefs about service into action and that signing up for the homeless shelter, or for Meals on Heels, or for some of the other service projects is a good way to do this. The membership is 3,200, and over 800 volunteer in numerous social service programs. One hundred and sixty currently volunteer in the homeless shelter. Others volunteer with programs such as Meals on Heels, Habitat for Humanity, the AIDS Walk, AIDS Momentum, God's Love We Deliver, the Hospital Relief Programs, English as a Second Language tutorials, the Bowery Mission, and the Prison Outreach program. In a reversal of the normal pattern, this church sends volunteers to volunteer referral centers such as New York Cares, which in turn refer them out to other volunteer opportunities.

In a church with this sort of service history, opening a homeless shelter was not a controversial move that had to be handled with great care. When the Partnership for the Homeless approached the church in 1986 about opening a shelter, the board of deacons of the church

Fifh Avenue Presbyterian in midtown Manhattan.

In the Church Shelters

took up the request, and like any other request they "shepherded the idea through" the appropriate committees. Being Presbyterians, Margaret Shafer, the church's associate for outreach, noted, "we do everything in very, you know, very careful sort of deliberate ways. We have committees and approvals. I mean we are very big on that sort of stuff."[36] The Presbyterians are also very different than the Catholics in that they have a tradition of a more inclusive decision-making and governance process in their churches, therefore there wasn't the pent-up desire on the part of the congregation for something meaningful to do. While there are a significant number of residential buildings on the street that runs between Fifth and Sixth Avenues in this part of Manhattan, there was virtually no neighborhood hostility toward the opening of the shelter. Because the congregation had much more experience with this sort of program, it wasn't that controversial to them either. The main worry that the congregation had about opening the shelter was for security of the church building itself. As time went on and there was no property damage, the fear for the security of the building has dissipated, and it has been replaced by concerns over smoking and worries about the health of the homeless guests.

Rebuilding the Volunteer Corps at Fifth Avenue Presbyterian

The shelter at Fifth Avenue has been open every night since the fall of 1986, and despite the church's active tradition and the shelter's current vitality, the volunteer pool had dwindled to six in 1999. It only stayed open because the volunteer coordinator spent almost every night there. This was the same position that Riverside Church was in in late 1994, but Fifth Avenue Presbyterian took a different approach. Rather than shut the shelter down, the session, which is the governing board of the church, reassigned responsibility for the shelter to Margaret Shafer, and asked her to revive the shelter. This she did, and she began by persuading the existing volunteer coordinator to retire. Her next step was to hire a new volunteer coordinator whose job was to recruit volunteers, train them, create jobs for them, and get the shelter thriving again. She expressly forbade the volunteer coordinator from volunteering more than a few times a month. This, she told me, was because "if the coordinator gets lazy about bringing other people in and just stays [him- or herself], then you lose your pool really quick."[37]

In making the volunteer coordinator position a paid one, and in hiring an aggressive volunteer coordinator with a mission to save the shelter, Fifth Avenue Presbyterian escaped Riverside Church's fate. Unsure initially of what to look for in a volunteer coordinator, Margaret at first hired a seminary student who held the position for three months and who had 25 volunteers working at the shelter by the time that he gave up the position. It was the next volunteer coordinator, Peter Saghir, who in a year built the size of the volunteer corps up to 135. Margaret credits Peter, whom she described as "a terrific good looker, and a very appealing young guy, with lots of energy," with rescuing the program.[38] He is now a student at Brooklyn Law School and was succeeded by a new volunteer coordinator, Kathleen McGuffin, who continued to build. Kathleen recently resigned the position to care for a sick family member, and she has been succeeded by Cheni Khonji.

Peter had been a volunteer at Fifth Avenue Presbyterian for three years, first in the Meals on Heels program, then in the Habitat for Humanity program, then in the Homeward Bound Program, and finally in the homeless shelter before taking on the job as volunteer coordinator. A graduate of the acting program at NYU, Peter began attending services at Fifth Avenue Presbyterian in 1997. He says that the thing that attracted him to the church was the emphasis that they put on reaching out into the community. "They really, really stress volunteer work and community service," he noted, and Rev. Tewell emphasizes from the pulpit that an important aspect of the Christian ministry "is really about helping people, and love, and equality."[39] This was a vision of Christianity that Peter appreciated and after attending Sunday services at Fifth Avenue Presbyterian for a year he became a member of the church. For the three years that he was attending Fifth Avenue Presbyterian before he became shelter coordinator, Peter volunteered at the church an average of once or twice a month. This is a common level of commitment at this and the other churches. He actually began volunteering with the homeless outside of Fifth Avenue Presbyterian, with an organization called Common Ground. Common

Ground is a supportive housing organization in New York that owns three residential hotels for formerly homeless residents, and they incorporate all of their residents into a program that includes services such as job training and vocational tutoring. Peter's job there was to tutor people on computers and to conduct mock job interviews. This is where he first began working with homeless people and it was seeing the effect that this hands-on work could have on people's lives that attracted Peter to the programs that the church had for the homeless.

Peter's first volunteer work with the homeless and Fifth Avenue Presbyterian was with the Homeward Bound program. This program was the creation of a seminary student who, for his master's thesis, devised a six-week-long program in which the shelter residents at the church had two sessions per week to train them for housed life in the real world. In addition to teaching prosaic but necessary self-sufficiency skills such as budgeting, how to cook for oneself, and how to buy food, these training sessions also brought in doctors to talk about general health issues and a legal aid lawyer to talk about what the men, many of whom had committed minor crimes, could do to clean up their records or to work around them. Peter had only just begun working to build up the Homeward Bound program when he saw an announcement in the church bulletin that the shelter needed a new coordinator.

At first he was reluctant to apply for the job, as he didn't know if he had the time to do it. He did apply, however, and he became the shelter coordinator in August 2000. Although the job of shelter coordinator is officially listed as 15 hours per week, Peter thinks that it is actually more like 25 hours per week. Not included in the 25 hours are nights that he slept over at the shelter.[40] Upon being hired, Peter's main priority was to recruit more volunteers. To do this Peter was faced by different challenges than Jim, Virginia, and Harold were at Sacred Heart. While Peter didn't have to overcome the same degree of uncertainty and fear that they did at Sacred Heart, he had to compete with all of the other programs in the church that were trying to recruit volunteers as well.

When he began, Peter was handed a list of 25 names of people who had volunteered at one time or another, not all of them still active. To rebuild the volunteer corps, he started cold calling the names on the list, none of whom he knew, to see if they were still interested in volunteering, and if so, in what capacity. From this basis he began to compile an email list of people who were volunteering or who said that they were interested in volunteering, and he started slotting these people into the three positions that he needed to fill: food host, early evening host, and overnight host. His greatest initial concern was over getting enough overnight hosts to cover all of the shifts. He figured that he could do the early evening slot if it was needed, and that he could scrounge food somehow. There was no way that he would stay over every night, however, so he really had to work on this slot.

Rebuilding the volunteer corps this way was a slow process and in the first few weeks Peter had to sleep at the shelter two to three nights a week. To reach out beyond those who had volunteered in the past, Peter began putting notices in the church bulletin asking for new volunteers for the shelter. He followed this by asking Rev. Tewell to announce from the pulpit the need for more shelter volunteers. At the same time, Peter began having shelter open houses following the services in which Rev. Tewell made the announcements, so that people could come and see what the shelter was like. It was these moves that really began to increase the number of volunteers.

Rev. Tewell, Peter notes, was very helpful and a request to mention the shelter and its need for volunteers from the pulpit would invariably result in a much longer announcement about the good work that the shelter was doing and why it was important for the members of the congregation to volunteer in it. The people in the congregation trust and respect Rev. Tewell, Peter noted, and his announcements would get a lot of people to go to an open house. The open houses that followed would typically last an hour to an hour and a half. Peter made sure that all of the open houses were scheduled for right after services, because, in rebuilding, he said that one of his guiding principles was that "in general people want to do what is convenient for them" and that the more convenient he could make it for people to volunteer in the shelter, the more likely it would be that they would. Sometimes he spiced up the open house by inviting a guest speaker. Often the speaker was Emily Dunlap, the church social worker, who would discuss some of the causes of and solutions to homelessness.

In the Church Shelters

Peter's next step was to get the other voluntary groups in the church to make volunteering in the shelter one of their projects. The first group that Peter got to volunteer was one called Focus, which is a social group for singles in their 20s. Peter got them to take responsibility for a week. Next it was the Advocates for Peace and Justice, and he had them volunteer for a week also. And then he got the Couples Club to volunteer. From there he began incorporating those members of the other clubs who were interested in continuing at the shelter into his own shelter volunteer pool. Within a year he had built the pool of active volunteers up to 135, and he had an email list of over 200. Except for about 5 people, they were all from the congregation. I asked Peter why this was so and if he focused on the congregation because he found that to be a more reliable source. His reply was that he never really considered going outside the congregation. Although he knew that the church would have been happy to let anybody come in and volunteer, he thought that he was supposed to draw the pool from the congregation.

Of the 135 volunteers, 55 assumed overnight host responsibilities. People were now volunteering about once a month, which Peter thought to be the ideal time commitment. When people first began volunteering he would ask them to work twice a month for the first month or two, "just to touch base again," he said, "and plant your face in the guys' minds."[41] After that the volunteers could work as much as they wanted to, but Peter suggested that if they worked more than once a month they might burn out and if they did less than once a month the guys in the shelter wouldn't remember them. He also encouraged the volunteers to pop in any time in the early evening to say hello and socialize. Avoiding burnout among the volunteers was, Peter noted, his biggest focus, as this was one of the major problems that he faced when he first became volunteer coordinator. Peter also focused on creating more of a social atmosphere in the shelter, on turning it into what he called a community center.

To make sure that all of the volunteer slots were filled, Peter created a calendar on his computer with three slots per day, and he would fill in these slots with names as people volunteered for them in response to his emails. His email list, on which he had the addresses of

everyone who had volunteered since he had been there and everyone
who had come to an open house, was his secret weapon. "Even if
somebody had only volunteered once," he noted, they stayed on the
email list, and if they wanted to be taken off, as far as I was concerned
they could let me know and I would be happy to take them off."[42]
Otherwise they stayed on, as "just because somebody is not in contact
with me every month, I am not going to necessarily rule them out as
not being another volunteer."[43] He would begin by sending out one
email just before the beginning of the month in which he would greet
everybody, bring them up to date on what was going on at the shelter,
list all of the dates that were available for the three different positions,
and ask people to respond if they were interested in any of them. The
volunteers would then send back messages saying which slots they
wanted to sign up for, and Peter would put their name in the slot and
send back an email saying that they were confirmed. In the middle of
the month he would send out a second email that listed the dates that
were still available for that month and he would get the responses
back, slot them in, and confirm them. Generally, Peter only had to
send out two emails to get everything full, but occasionally he had
to get on the telephone to fill a few vacant spots. He was careful not
to "barrage people at the shelter with emails" and he used the phone
as often as he could. Usually he didn't send out any more than two
mass emails a month. Cancellation on commitments was usually
worse around Christmas and New Year's because of all of the holiday parties and out-of-town visitors, and there were two or three
people who became notorious for canceling, but beyond that, cancellation wasn't a major problem. When someone did cancel, however, Peter would get on the phone and try to find somebody who
usually was available on that night, or who hadn't volunteered in a
while, or who liked to volunteer at the last minute. Fortunately for
him, there are a number of last-minute, reserve volunteers at Fifth
Avenue that he could call on; they tend to be those with demanding,
professional jobs.

As a hedge against cancellations, Peter called all of the volunteers
for the upcoming week on Saturday afternoons to remind them that
they had signed up and to maintain personal contact with all of them.

This was his way of making himself available to the volunteers if they needed to ask anything and it gave him an opportunity to socialize. Socializing, in his mind, was important as preventing burnout for retaining the volunteers. "Something that I wanted to do," he said, "was to create a family, a community-style atmosphere."[44]

Because Fifth Avenue Presbyterian was not in a residential neighborhood, this atmosphere, which developed spontaneously in Glendale, had to be manufactured at Fifth Avenue Presbyterian. To this end, Peter took two steps. One was to update the volunteers on the condition of the shelter guests every time that he sent out an email and the other was to have events. The birthday parties were the first of the events, and Peter started holding those on the last Tuesday or Wednesday of each month. These started out as being for the homeless men in the shelter, but they soon grew to include the volunteers as well. On these days, volunteers would decorate the shelter with balloons and streamers and they would have cake and ice cream, sing "Happy Birthday," turn the TV off, put the tables in a circle, and just sit there and talk. At first these parties were kind of stilted, as the homeless guys weren't too enthusiastic, but after two or three months this caught on, and the homeless men themselves often help with the decorations. Usually a dozen volunteers drop by, in addition to the ones who are on duty that night, with half of them being a core group that comes every time and the others surprises.

The thing that was great about this, in Peter's mind, was how it changed the homeless guys and how it helped them open up. For the first few times, he noted, "I . . . initially forced them to, almost, because . . . it felt like they needed a little extra push to get some of them involved."[45] Now that they have gotten used to it, it has become something that they look forward to. Following the success of the birthday parties, the volunteers started to do a monthly bingo night, which has also been a success. For this they went out and bought trinkets, prizes, and a bingo wheel, and again about a dozen volunteers commonly attend bingo night as well. This in turn has been followed by a movie night, when they get popcorn, turn out the lights, and watch old movies.

All of these events are opportunities for the homeless men to interact with the volunteers and the volunteers to interact with the men and to get to know each other better. They are also opportunities for people to have some fun. Peter noted that one of the things that he envisioned when he took the volunteer coordinator job is that the shelter could turn into a social group, or a social event. "Volunteering for the homeless," he felt, "does not have to be a miserable, depressing, bad, serious, chip on the shoulder kind of thing," and social events are a way to make sure that it doesn't become that.[46] With the social events people began to interact and see volunteering at the shelter as something enjoyable, as a fulfilling experience, rather than something heavy and serious. "And, you know, the volunteers are happy, the guys are definitely happy, and it sort of . . . all feeds off of each other."[47] The result is that the homeless men and the volunteers have become "like a little bit of a community, the volunteer community of the shelter."[48]

The shelter is located in what used to be a storage room in the church basement, and it houses 10 elderly men, all of whom are bused from Peter's Place's drop-in center. The youngest shelter guests are in their 60s, and most are in their 70s and 80s. Many of these men are very frail due to their age. Several of them have been sent to the hospital from the shelter, two have left the shelter to go into nursing homes, something that the members of the church arranged for them, and one of these two died at the nursing home in his sleep. This issue of frailty and mortality is one that the volunteers at Fifth Avenue Presbyterian are forced to confront "more often than anybody is comfortable with," according to Margaret Shafer.[49] With shelter guests this old, however, the dynamic that has developed at the Fifth Avenue Presbyterian Church shelter is different than at Sacred Heart. Peter likened the men in the shelter at Fifth Avenue Presbyterian to 10 grandfathers with whom the volunteers got to spend the night and got to become friends.[50] With these grandfathers, one of whom got the nickname Grandpa, the volunteers developed "the kind of responsibility that you have when you accept somebody into your home and your family that is really very frail."[51]

64 Just like at Sacred Heart, the shelter's cots and linens come from the city and the other furnishings were donated by the volunteers. Unlike Sacred Heart, Fifth Avenue Presbyterian only uses three shifts of volunteers each night. The first are the food hosts, who at any time in the day before the men arrive bring food over to the shelter. The men eat dinner at Peter's Place, but there is always food for them at Fifth Avenue, prepared as in Glendale by the food hosts, who volunteer specifically for that purpose. The second shift is that of the early evening hosts, who welcome the men at 6 P.M. and stay until 8 P.M. to

Fifth Avenue Presbyterian homeless shelter.

provide the evening snack and conversation. At about 8:30 P.M. the overnight hosts arrive and they are there until the men are picked up by the bus, between 6:30 and 7 A.M.

Again like at Glendale, the majority of the volunteers are women, and a significant majority of them are church members. The bulk of the volunteers are single, under 35, middle management business-

女

women who moved to New York after college to work. They live
spread out through Manhattan, Brooklyn, or Queens, with a few coming from points further out. Due to the frequent hospitalizations of
the shelter guests, a team of volunteers has been set up to do hospital
visitations. When the shelter resident nicknamed Grandpa died, the
church held a memorial service for him and he was buried in their
cemetery plot. The volunteers in the Homeward Bound program take
the men shopping just before they go into their apartments to buy
sheets and towels and sundries, and this is paid for by a fund of money
donated by the congregation, called the can opener fund.

Because most volunteers are young and the homeless men are elderly, there is an intergenerational affection that has developed. Because virtually all of the volunteers are single, as Margaret noted, there
is an eagerness for friendships and the shelter, unlike most places in
the big city, provides a nonthreatening atmosphere in which to develop them. As at Sacred Heart friendships develop among the volunteers, but at Fifth Avenue Presbyterian they are also plentiful between
the volunteers and the guests. Margaret noted that the homeless
guests do a lot of storytelling and this has become an integral part of
their shelter. Most of the men are happy to tell their life stories once
they begin feeling at home, and the storytelling has had a very powerful effect. One of Rev. Tewell's common sayings is that everybody is a
child of God and everybody matters, irrespective of their background.
As Margaret notes, the shelter volunteers, like the church congregation,
are middle to upper middle class, and aside from the shelter, they don't
generally intersect with the homeless population in any other part of
their lives. What the shelter provides, she notes, is a place in their lives
where they can feel safe and secure about carrying out the vision that
they have for the way the world ought to be. It is a setting in which
people can intersect and build relationships. This is why the 14-year-
olds in the confirmation class are required to serve at the shelter.

The Homeless on the Steps Program

One of the features of the Fifth Avenue shelter that is significantly
different from the Sacred Heart shelter is the large role that the Fifth
Avenue shelter guests play in the running of the shelter. At Fifth Avenue

it is the guests who do most of the setting up and cleaning up each evening. The principal role of the early evening volunteer host is to bring the dinner, get the guests to sign their names on the manifest to send to the Partnership for fuel reimbursements, and then visit with people to make them feel comfortable and be ready in case of any emergency. The volunteers have a walkie-talkie to keep in contact with the security guard, whom they can ask to call the police or an ambulance. A further avenue of participation for the guests is the homeless ministry program, which is directed at the people who were sleeping on the steps and around the church at night. Because of the neighborhood it is in, Fifth Avenue Presbyterian Church has long had homeless people sleeping outside at night. These are a different population of homeless people than the ones who are in the shelter. They are people who haven't yet been cajoled by an outreach worker into going to a city facility or to a drop-in center, or who have been to a drop-in center and were referred by that center to an institution that they didn't want to go to. The Fifth Avenue Presbyterian congregation felt that because they had a homeless ministry, it should be extended to all of the homeless people who were making use of the church, not just to the ones who came from the drop-in centers.

The program for the Homeless on the Steps, as they are referred to, is one that to the surprise of many has proven to be quite controversial. No one at Fifth Avenue Presbyterian proposed that the homeless people who lived on the street around the church should be brought into the shelter. Instead, they proposed a halfway step in which the volunteers would go out and feed them and try to cajole them into going to the drop-in centers, where they could begin treatment and assessment that would lead to admission to the church shelters. At first the men in the shelter were strongly opposed to this idea. This surprised the volunteers, but it fit a pattern seen in other shelters. Margaret Shafer likened this opposition to new baby syndrome. She thought that the homeless men in the shelter, who had been there for a while, feared that they would be forgotten as the attention of the volunteers turned to the new baby, the people on the street.

An incident at Madison Avenue Baptist Church in the winter of 1993 (see chapter 5) makes me think that the opposition from the men in the shelter was for a different reason. What I noticed at Madison Avenue Baptist is that the shelter guests who have been through the screening and evaluation processes of the drop-in centers, and who are trying to stay sober and drug free, feel that they have accomplished something. They know that they are in a situation that is far better than if they were still on the streets or in a city shelter, and they do not like to see other homeless people who have not proven themselves, and who are not necessarily making the same effort to stay clean and sober, getting the same treatment.

However, one night at Fifth Avenue Presbyterian a volunteer brought in a lot of food from a party, much more than the men in the shelter could eat, so the volunteer and the men took it out and fed the people who were out around the church. A few weeks later, when it was really cold, the men in the shelter decided to make a big pot of chili, which they brought out and served to the men sleeping on the steps. From this a wake-up program developed, in which one of the men from the shelter helps some volunteers every morning to wake the street homeless up at 5:30 A.M. to get them to clean up their cardboard and move along. They bring out pots of tea and coffee, and they visit with the men on the street. This movement at Fifth Avenue, in which the shelter guests play a service role, has grown to include another group of shelter guests who now serve lunch to Fifth Avenue's Habitat for Humanity volunteers up in the Bronx.

Not all of the neighboring hotels and shops are in favor of this program and it may have been their opposition that led to the city's attempt to ban the Homeless on the Steps program. In the fall of 2001 the Police Department conducted a series of nighttime raids, and they threatened to arrest homeless people who continue to sleep on the steps of the church. The church asked for meetings with the city to try to stop these raids, but the failure of talks led to a lawsuit brought by the church and the New York Civil Liberties Union against the city in late 2001 to force an end to these raids. I will talk more about this incident in chapter 4, but for now a temporary restraining order issued against the city is allowing the outreach program to continue. Now 10 people are allowed to spend the night on the steps, and the church, its outreach volunteers, and the men from the shelter who run the Homeless on the Steps program are free to build relationships with these people and try to get them to drop-in centers. Margaret Shafer estimates that so far they have gotten 77 homeless people off the streets and into drop-in centers and treatment.[52] As Rev. Tewell noted, "We know that having people sleep outside our building is not a long-term solution."[53] In their minds, it is better than nothing, however.

Personal Relationships and Everyday Heroism

What knits the volunteers at Fifth Avenue together are the personal relationships that have developed, along with the feeling that they are doing a good thing. And doing good is clearly important at Fifth Avenue. It is the sort of place where congregants take great pride in being what Margaret referred to as "do-gooders," but as she noted a benefit of the shelter is that being a "do-gooder" comes at a low cost when compared to what people think the cost of volunteering in a homeless shelter is. One example that she gave me of this was of the many young professional volunteers who continually tell her about conversations that they have with co-workers who are amazed and impressed that they volunteer in homeless shelters. "The public image of this," she observed, "is that this is a really heroic thing to do." While that might be true, Margaret went on to note that "because they [the volunteers] feel safe and secure about doing it, it is an easy kind of hero to be." The effect of these sorts of reactions, according to Margaret, is that "there is a status, in the best sense of the word, that people get by doing this."[54]

What distinguishes the relationships at Fifth Avenue from those at Sacred Heart is that at Fifth Avenue there is a much greater degree of connection between the homeless men and the shelter volunteers, and between the homeless men and the church congregation. While the homeless spend only the night at the Fifth Avenue Presbyterian shelter, like at all of the other shelters, at Fifth Avenue Presbyterian they have, as individuals, become members of the community, rather than being only the reason for the existence of the community. But that isn't the only difference in the communities of the two places.

Fifth Avenue now has an alumni group of former homeless guests, and the church keeps track of them and invites them back for birthday parties and other events. One of the alumni is now a shelter volunteer, and six have joined the church as members of the congregation. Three of the alumni who have joined the church are on church committees, including the low-income housing policy group and the shelter steering committee. Two other men who currently stay at the shelter have joined the church, and they both usher. They get all their church mail sent to them at 7 West 55th Street, which is the address of the church, and as Margaret said, "the first day one of them ushered, I sat there and I thought, you know, most people in the congregation don't know [that these ushers are homeless] and I know that he is ushering and there are three more guys sitting in the row in front of me who I know to be homeless and I said this is getting close to the kingdom of God."[55]

This church, like all of the others, is not supposed to proselytize, and Margaret insists that while the church doesn't, the men likely proselytize each other. One man started because he had grown up going to church and thought it would be nice to attend this one. He convinced a couple more to attend with him, and they did, and it grew from there. This, Margaret said, is how it should be. "There ought to be this feeling of belonging and being a part of things, and those who want a home and family have found one. And this congregation has been very accepting, you know, when they know [that the shelter guests have joined the congregation and that they are ushering], they are thrilled and when they don't know it doesn't matter."[56]

One of the immediately distinguishing features of this huge program the Partnership runs is that it is very intimate. Despite the 1,230 beds and the 10,000 volunteers, with settings that are so small and so dispersed, it is very easy for people get to know each other and form relationships. The intimacy is a gift of the setting. In these small, homelike shelters, the volunteers and the homeless clients are offered the rare opportunity to form a community. Both of these shelters are examples of what Peter Dobkin Hall calls *community organizations*.[57] In Hall's conception, a community organization is one that is rooted in a location and is "'of, for and by' the communities they serve." He contrasts these to community-serving organizations, which are not

70 rooted in a place and are "run by credentialed professionals, . . . pursuing agendas set by constituencies other than those being served" or other than those who are doing the serving.[58] Community organizations provide opportunities for their members to participate, and they are locales for the practices and deliberations among people that can develop and maintain communities. I will refer to this type of organization as a *community-generating* institution.

The fact that an organization is a community organization is necessary, but not sufficient, for it to be community generating. There have to be certain types of practices within the community organizations in order for them to generate community, and in subsequent chapters I will talk in greater depth about why the organizations that were formed at Sacred Heart and at Fifth Avenue Presbyterian became community generating.[59] At Sacred Heart, Jim, Harold, and Virginia set up the type of organization that led to their shelter becoming a community-generating institution shortly after its inception in 1983. It has remained one ever since. At Fifth Avenue Presbyterian Church, the type of organization necessary for the shelter to become a community-generating institution was created after August 2000 when Margaret Shafer hired Peter Saghir to reorganize what had been a failing organization. While Peter's organizational approach differs from Jim's and Virginia's in some significant ways, there are striking similarities. In both instances, the volunteer coordinators have created robust volunteer corps in which the volunteers not only give of themselves but also receive. In both shelters the volunteer coordinators have created organizations that are capable of performing important functions in the lives of the volunteers who join them. Therein, I believe, lies their community-generating success.

3

Why People Volunteer in Church Shelters and Why They Keep at It

In no country in the world has the principle of association been more successfully used or applied to a greater multitude of objects than in America.[1]

Social actions are always part of larger systems and processes of intersubjective understanding and this raises the question of the role of the acting subject (human agency) in the processes by which the action is contained.[2]

There can be no communities without members, so the first function that a potentially community-generating institution needs to perform is the integration of individuals into a collective. To set the stage for integration, there has to be a task for the potential members to perform. Peter Smith took care of this when he created the Partnership for the Homeless. This chapter examines whether or not simply giving people a task is enough to satisfy the integration function, or whether they have to be actively brought into membership. At first glance it didn't seem to me that setting the stage alone would be sufficient, because volunteering to take care of homeless people didn't seem like something many people would find appealing.

Finding out why people volunteered, therefore, was my first step toward understanding how the shelters integrated people into their membership. When I first began my research I expected simple responses, like "I felt that I should," or "it seemed like the right thing to do," or "to help people in need." In fact, I asked people why they began volunteering primarily because I thought it would be a good conversation starter. That it proved to be—and more so.

One of the first volunteers that I interviewed was Joe Pace. He was a young lawyer for a Wall Street mutual funds firm who volunteered monthly at St. Paul's Chapel, the same chapel where I had first volunteered. When I asked him why he volunteered he began his answer as follows:

> In terms of why I got involved in the program, it is difficult to say. I just saw the ad [for the Partnership for the Homeless]. . . . I was raised in the United Church of Christ and my wife and I currently belong to a Dutch Reform Church out in Long Island. My wife happens to do a lot of volunteer work as well.[3]

Joe's desire to follow his wife's example, the beliefs that were instilled in him when he was young—especially the belief that he should "give something back to the community . . . rather than just availing [himself] of everything that society has to offer"—combined with the ad that he saw in the subway from the Partnership all played a role in his decision to begin volunteering at the shelter at St. Paul's. Joe also remembered that as a child he had done some volunteer work. His parents encouraged this, but never actually volunteered themselves. Later, as an adult he volunteered at Syosset Hospital, which was near his home on Long Island. After starting work in Manhattan, he began looking for a volunteering opportunity in the area when he saw an ad in the subway for the Partnership.

Joe considered himself a relative newcomer to New York City. He didn't know very many people, and in that sense he was relatively unencumbered in his actions. He had grown up on Long Island, in what he called "Lilywhitesville," and went to college at Franklin and Marshall in Lancaster, Pennsylvania, in Amish country. He described Lancaster as being very sheltered, and he did some volunteer work there. From Lancaster, the next step was Brooklyn Law School. "It was a culture shock for me," he noted, "simply because there was homelessness and poverty and just diversity around you, which I was not accustomed to."[4]

Brooklyn Law School is in Brooklyn Heights, where Joe lived while in law school. Brooklyn Heights, New York's first suburb, is a residential neighborhood immediately across the East River from Lower Manhattan. Filled with three- and four-story nineteenth-

century brownstones, Brooklyn Heights is connected to Manhattan
by the Brooklyn Bridge, over which many of its residents walk every
morning to work. Its famous promenade, cantilevered out over the
Brooklyn-Queens Expressway with its unimpeded views of Lower
Manhattan, the Statue of Liberty, Ellis Island, and much of the rest of
New York Harbor, has been designated a special scenic view district.
Brooklyn Heights is one of the most beautiful and among the most
expensive neighborhoods in New York. In 1965 it became the first
historic district to be so designated in New York City. This neighborhood was not accustomed to having homeless people living on its
streets.

By the time Joe entered law school in the early 1980s, however,
homeless people had become fairly common in Brooklyn Heights. He
recalled that upon encountering them, his first impulses were revulsion and fear. Following that, he said, was "a certain element of compassion that goes along with it."[5] In particular, Joe remembered an
experience walking home from a study session on a very cold night
during exams that had a profound effect on him:

> I came out and it was really cold, five degrees, and there was one of the regular
> homeless guys . . . underneath the alcove of a building, but outdoors, and he
> looked like he was absolutely freezing to death. . . . I had a comforter or some-
> thing that I didn't need and I brought that back and gave it to him. . . . That kind
> of left an imprint on me, in terms of how could someone possibly live like this?
> And here we are, powerless as individuals to do something about it. . . . But
> maybe I can do a small part. . . . What really got me going on the Partnership for
> the Homeless was that I had this experience in law school, and the other thing
> was that I was so frustrated and angry at being constantly bombarded or ex-
> posed to the plight of the homeless and really developing a callousness. . . . So in
> the whole process of becoming callous, I said to myself, . . . OK, you might as
> well not just be bitter about it . . . do something about it.[6]

As is clear from Joe's account, because he hardly knew anyone, he
was not pressured into volunteering. He started volunteering because
he wanted to. It is equally clear, however, that he volunteered because he
thought that he should, because of how he had been raised, and because of the example that his wife set. It is also clear that he volunteered
at St. Paul's because it was a voluntary opportunity that was presented
to him at an opportune time in his life and because it fit, in that it
presented him with an opportunity to overcome feeling powerless

and callous. A further point was that the Partnership for the Homeless presented a convenient place to volunteer in a safe environment. This was particularly important because, as Joe noted, he tends toward what he called "low impact voluntarism." He did not want to feel that "life or limb was in any way jeopardized" and for this reason he said, "I don't think I would feel terribly comfortable doing an overnight in a mass shelter, a big city shelter like an armory."[7]

In addition to feeling comfortable at the St. Paul's shelter, Joe also liked the flexibility that their volunteer program offered. The shelter was near his office, and he could work his volunteering commitments around his demanding work and travel schedule. He volunteered once or twice a month, either for the dinner or overnight shift. Occasionally Joe missed a month because of work demands, but he made that up in the following months. One of the things that he liked the most about volunteering at St. Paul's was the feeling that he was "contributing something and making a difference, however small, in the lives of these guys who were going through the program."[8]

While Joe's background and immediate experiences made him inclined to seek out a volunteer position, he would not have started volunteering at the Partnership if it weren't for that advertisement in the subway. In the late 1980s and early 1990s, the Partnership ran a series of advertisements in the subways and the buses and on billboards around New York, asking for volunteers. The Creative Coalition, a public service organization of people in the arts and entertainment industry, volunteered to record and produce television and radio spots for the Partnership to raise awareness and get volunteers and donations. The Partnership also frequently used free public service announcements on television and radio. As director of volunteers, I went to the Home Shopping Network affiliate WHSE in Newark and recorded a series of five-minute commercial spots for the Partnership that WHSE aired free of charge during the night. All of these had the effect of broadening the recruiting reach of the Partnership to people that it had never reached before, in the hopes that some of them would be moved to volunteer or give money. St. Paul's shelter, like others in Manhattan churches or synagogues that were not in residential areas, recruited many volunteers this way. This sort of out-

reach was particularly effective: once these newcomers became volunteers, they spread the word about volunteering at the Partnership
in the old-fashioned way—by talking to people they knew.

Word of mouth from neighbors, friends, and co-workers is how
the vast majority of volunteers, especially those in residential areas,
found out that the church and synagogue shelters existed and that
they needed volunteers. This is how Pat and Gene Durant, who were
much more encumbered than Joe, discovered that there was a shelter
at their parish church, Sacred Heart of Jesus in Glendale, and why
they began volunteering there. The Durant family lives six blocks
from the church and they are members of the church. They began
volunteering at the shelter in 1986. Pat noted that the shelter had been
operating for four years in the church basement before they knew it
was there. Pat and Gene had become very involved with the school
and sports programs at Sacred Heart after their daughter started
school there and began playing sports. Pat coached sports teams and
Gene was the president of the home school association. Gene was also
the shelter's Wednesday coordinator. Pat notes that their high level of
involvement led some people to think of them as martyrs; "but that's
not the case at all; we're here because we want to be."[9]

Pat says that he began volunteering because he felt that he should
be doing something. He first began volunteering with the sports program a few years before we spoke, when his daughter started school.
His reason was "just to be involved" in his daughter's life. His daughter, who was 10 years old when Pat began volunteering, had been
playing basketball for about four or five years, and Pat was her coach
that year for the first time. "I just like to be involved with the kids,"
he said. "I know that I have enough knowledge about myself to
know that I am not going to steer them wrong. I'm not out there to
win every game, I don't berate them, I give them confidence and that's
the sports part."[10]

As a night foreman for the New York City Sanitation Department,
Pat worked the midnight-to-8 shift in Crown Heights and other
neighborhoods in Brooklyn, and he came in regular contact with a lot
of homeless people living in empty lots in what he called "cardboard
huts." He had long felt that he should try to do something to help

homeless people, but as an individual, he didn't know what he could do. "You don't want to take them into your house," he said; "you can't do that, . . . you know, I have my family."[11] He was also skeptical about the effect that simply giving the people money might have: "You can throw money around as much as you want but I felt like this was an opportunity to do hands-on interaction with people at a personal level and give them what they needed. And I wanted my daughter, who comes with me, to appreciate what she had."[12] So when Pat and Gene heard about the shelter, they began volunteering there.

As the Wednesday night coordinator, Gene called on her husband often, and he did the dinner shift every Wednesday with his kids. Occasionally, if the scheduled volunteer cancelled and Gene couldn't find a replacement, Pat would stay until midnight. In the environment of the church basement, he was able to help people whom he otherwise would not be able to help. Speaking to this point Pat said the following:

> I'm not going to go, get on the train, just pick a stop and get off and bring somebody home with me. I can't do that. But that same person that has an opportunity to get into this program, I can come here, I can help them here. And basically, that's it. That's it. I don't feel as if this is a ticket to heaven. I don't feel as though, like we mentioned before, I don't feel as if we are being martyrs down here. We have a lot of laughs down here. Sometimes it's tough, to turn around after working and say, oh we've got to go there tonight and maybe stay until midnight.[13]

In this environment, Pat was also able to give his kids a valuable lesson in life. As it was with Joe Pace, Pat and Gene's decision to start volunteering was the result of a mixture of their desire to do something to help homeless people, requests for assistance by the people who ran the shelter, the presentation of an opportunity to volunteer that looked appealing to them, and the opportunity to fulfill a need that they had. Joe, particularly, had wanted to get rid of the callousness that he was developing toward the homeless and to overcome his feelings of powerlessness. They all wanted to do something to help people who were in dire need, and they liked being able to do it in the church environment. Moreover, both Pat and Gene wanted to play a larger role in their daughter's life, and they wanted to expose her to life experiences that went beyond Glendale so that she would appreci-

ate what she had. The volunteer programs at the school and at the
church allowed them to do all of these things.

Others on Why They Began Volunteering

At this point it is worth remembering that an act is defined as voluntary only when "(1) its moving principle is in the agent himself, and (2) he is aware of the particular circumstances in which the act is done."[14] Given this, any theory of why people volunteer that does not have what philosophers call *agency* as part of its core is hard to imagine, and for many theorists of social action, agency seems to be indelibly linked to self-interest and free will.[15] Indeed, many of the volunteers that I surveyed expressed these sorts of free will motivations when they recounted why they began volunteering at their shelter. For many of them, the decision to volunteer seemed to have been a straightforward one, and while the words that they used to describe the decision differed, the underlying cause seemed the same—it was the exercise of their agency. Of the 100 people whom I interviewed, 55 of them said that they began volunteering for reasons that could be interpreted this way—they just decided one day that they should do it. Some of their actual answers are as follows:

> I felt I should.[16]
>
> To help those who needed it.[17]
>
> To help the homeless and contribute to the success of the shelter.[18]
>
> Because I've been fortunate in life and I wanted to give something back.[19]
>
> I had extra time and I realized that there were a lot of people who could use my help. I had heard about the shelter program at the church from someone who volunteered there, so I decided to start volunteering.[20]

It is at this level of individual agency that volunteering is almost universally understood and referred to in the American popular conception, and from the responses that I got from many of the volunteers as to why they began volunteering it is evident that individual agency played a part in the decision. In making their decision to begin volunteering, Pat, Gene, Joe, and all of the other volunteers I interviewed did something that is considered to be typically American.[21] When Herman Melville spoke of the thousand individual threads that connect our lives, and when the senior George Bush spoke of a thousand points of light, they were both speaking to this level.

With very few exceptions, however, these volunteers exercised their agency within a social and institutional context. Most of the respondents who cited reasons for starting to volunteer that seem to be of their own free will also acknowledged that without the right context they would not have acted. This fact that context is so important—even for the exercise of agency—points to the issue of the degree of encumbrance of the volunteers.[22] This concept of encumbrance, its opposite unencumbrance, and the degrees that exist in between these two poles is one that I am going to use to categorize the different approaches to understanding social action. While agency can easily be thought of as the action of an unencumbered self, the volunteer responses also show that it is exercised within a context and often in response to pressure and expectations. In fact the new volunteers, who had a much fresher memory of exactly why they began volunteering, were much more likely than the veterans to acknowledge the role of expectations, recruitment, and other encumbrances in their decision to volunteer.[23] The volunteers I interviewed and surveyed were encouraged to volunteer in many subtle and not-so-subtle ways. All of these amount to encumbrances and one of the chief encumbrances of these volunteers is the religious congregations to which they belong.

Given the location of the shelters, it is no surprise that a lot of these volunteers felt a religious calling to volunteer. Peter Cache, who volunteered at the Brooklyn Heights Interfaith shelter, said cash donations to the homeless weren't enough and "I want to be a better Christian." Steven Romeo noted, "I am grateful for life and that God has given me so much, and I am glad to have the opportunity to give back."[24] George James said, "I believe that the work of the shelter is an important part of the effort to deal with the homeless problem that we have in NYC and it is an important part of my religion."[25]

For 45 of the volunteers I interviewed, these requests from others, along with social expectations, social pressure, and institutional requirements seemed to be the main reasons that they were volunteering. For example, Marie Ranga, who volunteered at Our Lady of Good Counsel in Manhattan, said "there was an appeal during Sunday mass by Michael Tuckett, the director of the program at our church, and in December 1993 I decided to start."[26] Other replies included

Because someone at the church asked me to.[27]

Because it was part of a school internship.[28]

Because of a plea from the program coordinator.[29]

At the prayer (charismatic) meeting there was a call for people to help at the church.[30]

To fulfill a high school requirement.[31]

[It was] a church activity.[32]

This role of others in recruiting people to volunteer was reflected in comments such as those made by Terri Anderson, who volunteered at St. Bartholomew's at Park Avenue and 50th Street. She said that she began volunteering because it was something that she had always wanted to do and that she was recruited by a co-worker who volunteered.[33] John Bartha, who also volunteered at St. Bart's, said, "I was looking to do something, and someone at work put up a flyer about the homeless program at St. Bart's."[34] Dan Marina at Our Lady of Good Counsel was "moved to do so by a call from the church pulpit for volunteers." Sourabh Chatterjee said that he had "thought about it [volunteering] for a while" and that the volunteer coordinator at St. Bart's, who worked with Sourabh, had recruited him.[35] Sometimes membership in another institution was what put the future volunteer in a position to be recruited. Elmer Jang observed that he started volunteering at St. Paul's "because Pat Burton Eadie [the director of the shelter program before Bill Appel, later the vice president of the Partnership, and a member of the congregation at St. Paul's] asked me to. I am a member of the Downtown Glee Club and we used to rehearse at St. Paul's Chapel—Pat asked me one night and I have been doing it ever since."[36]

But even for those who emphasized that they were recruited, it was never just this one factor that got them going. Invariably, other personal reasons contributed to the decision. Donna Shane's son was a volunteer, and when she witnessed the impact that volunteering had on him she decided that she wanted to volunteer herself. In addition, she had suffered a nervous breakdown, and the parish had been so supportive that she wanted to give something back.[37] This combination of experiences, observations, and feelings of obligation, when combined with the right opportunity presenting itself, motivated Donna to start volunteering at the homeless shelter. No one of these factors in isolation would have been sufficient; she could easily have chosen some other way to satisfy her internal normative decision to give something back to her parish. She could have become a leader of the Girl Scout troop or visited homebound elderly. Either of these might have seemed easier and more pleasant than spending the night with 15 homeless people, none of whom were from her parish and none of whom shared her socioeconomic background.

Given what most New Yorkers know about homeless shelters, the fact that any New Yorker would volunteer in one is remarkable. This particular type of volunteering requires a strong institutional effort. When Clara Spence said that she volunteered in order "to come into closer contact with disadvantaged people [and] to overcome unsubstantiated fears," she was recognizing that she was afraid of homeless people before she began volunteering and this common fear is one that makes volunteering to work with the homeless seem like a fearsome task. It is because this fear is there and has to be overcome that a major organizational effort is needed to get people to volunteer to work in homeless shelters.[38] While she is unusual in recognizing that her fears were "unsubstantiated," she was perfectly ordinary in having them, given the experiences that every New Yorker has had with homeless people in public places and the media portrayal of this population. I was a part of the organizational recruitment effort and know how significant a role it played in getting people to volunteer in the shelters.

Without an effective organizational effort, few would volunteer in the shelters, and this vast network of shelters would not exist. Despite the importance of this organizational effort, individual agency and free will cannot be overlooked as motivations to volunteer. In fact, it seems that these impetuses to volunteer are entwined, and neither can be disassociated from the other. As individual agency is exercised within the framework of a set of social and institutional requests, obligations, and expectations, the decision to respond to these expectations and obligations is ultimately that of the individual volunteer. So while the volunteer coordinators made a great recruitment effort, and while they were supported by the Partnership for the Homeless, New York Cares, the Mayor's Voluntary Action Center, and others, individuals had to make up their own minds and decide how to respond. This layering of factors came across in many of my interviews with volunteers who said that although volunteering was their decision, they made it in light of expectations and requests.

Assessing Volunteer Motivations with Survey Data and Theories of Social Action

Given the complexity of the motivations that the volunteers expressed in our conversations about their reasons for volunteering, I began to read more widely about social action as a way of reflecting more closely on what I had heard and of developing a better conception of why people volunteered. In this effort I looked to the following sources: survey data from a nationwide sample of volunteers that sought to understand why they started volunteering, journal articles that deal with the topic of why people volunteer, and social theories that try to account for individual action.

The survey data comes from the Independent Sector, which conducts biennial surveys of the state of volunteering in America. In their 1999 survey of 2,500 American adults, the Independent Sector found that most people learned about volunteering in one of three ways: by being asked, through participation in an organization, or through a family member or relative, and that 56 percent said that they volunteer for an average of 3.5 hours a week.[39] Their 2001 survey found that 44 percent of American adults volunteered with formal organizations, that 69 percent of this group volunteered on a regular basis, and that they averaged just over 24 hours per month of volunteering time.[40] This difference in the number between the two years was caused largely by differing methodology. Whereas the 1999 survey included informal volunteering, which accounted for 14 percent of the volunteers, the 2001 survey didn't. As for why people volunteered, the 1999 survey found that the percentage of people who volunteered without being asked was 22.3 percent, that 49.1 percent of Americans reported being asked to volunteer, and that when asked, 89.5 percent of Americans volunteered.[41]

These findings—which are the closest that an analyst of volunteering in America today can come to finding nationwide facts about the phenomenon—raise some interesting philosophical questions about the motivations for volunteering. For example, because 22.3 percent of those who volunteered did so without being asked, are they the agents? Did they just decide one day to exercise their power and go out and make the world a better place? What about the other 77.7 percent of volunteers who needed to be asked? Was there no individual agency involved in their decision to volunteer? What role did American culture play in prompting some of these people to go out and volunteer unbidden or in making the others predisposed to react positively to appeals for volunteers?

Jon Van Til answers some of these questions in a review that he did of all 20 of the articles that had been published in the *Nonprofit and Voluntary Sector Quarterly* that dealt with the question of why people volunteer. Van Til summarized his findings into the following five propositions:

> the motivation of volunteers is a multifaceted process;
>
> volunteers weigh their options deliberately;
>
> the realm of voluntary action is itself complex and many faceted;
>
> concern for others persists as a motivating force; and
>
> the motivation to volunteer is constrained by broader social realities.[42]

Van Til's assessment of the literature on why people volunteer supports the position that broad social realities and obligations both constrain and motivate voluntary action. In fact, he prefers to use the term *voluntarism*, rather than *volunteering*, as a way of capturing and expressing the tension between the simultaneous self-oriented, unencumbered action and the other-orientation, encumbered action of volunteering. This is a simultaneity that Robert Bellah and his co-authors recognized in their *Habits of the Heart* with its subtitle *Individualism and Commitment in American Life.* In his assessment of the voluntarism literature, Van Til says that while the voluntarism literature recognizes that "it is clear that volunteering is affected by deeper forces of structure and change, the literature reviewed barely begins to address these questions."[43]

This is a problem with the voluntarism literature because my conversations with the volunteers made it clear that digging deeply into this question of the relationship between individual agency and deeper forces was critical to a good understanding of why people volunteered. Though volunteering is defined as the free, uncoerced gift of an individual's time and talent without giving money, and while it is natural that agency should be closely associated with volunteering, agency is not the only explanation for volunteering. An explanation for how the context in which volunteers find themselves affects the exercise of their agency is not well developed. For example, are those who volunteered without being asked, a group that I will categorize here for sake of argument as agents, acting in a strictly unencumbered way, or is there some aspect of their agency that is in reaction to an encumbrance? What about those who volunteered because they were hounded into doing it? Is this an action that stems solely from encumbrance? They could have said no to the person that was hounding them, but they didn't. Why not? Are the 77.7 percent of Americans who the Independent Sector says volunteered because they were asked to the encumbered ones and are the other 22.3 percent unencumbered? Clarifying all of this would be essential for developing an effective strategy for recruiting and retaining volunteers.

Further insights into questions such as these are found in the ongoing philosophical debate about social action that Ira J. Cohen frames as being between utilitarianism and romanticism.[44] According to Cohen, this debate between the romantics and the utilitarians has long dominated action theory and it has gotten more contentious in recent decades. Prior to the twentieth century, utilitarianism was dominant and it made the motivation for action seem very simple. Lately, however, romanticism has been gaining ground. Cohen outlines the utilitarian vs. romantic debate as follows:

> Most utilitarians included some variant of the idea that actors behaved so as to maximize their advantages and satisfy their wants, or to minimize their losses and reduce their discomfort. Romantic philosophers rejected this utilitarian position, arguing that utilitarians neglected the social meaning, cultural morality, and personal passions that all actions expressed or implied. The differences

between utilitarians and romantics condensed into debates around several, long-lasting, philosophical questions. Is social action inherently moral or amoral? Is it motivated by individual self-interest or communal obligations? Is action freely willed by the individual or determined by cultural socialization and/or the available material resources?[45]

These are all interesting questions, but it is the last two that provide a good link to the increasingly complex discussions between the heirs of utilitarians and romantics in American political theory over the motivations for action. Although this discussion has fragmented into many different positions, I am going to squeeze some of the major voices in these debates into a three-way debate between what I call the liberal-individualists (liberals), the holist-individualists, and the civic republicans. Although the primary interest of most of these theorists of social action is in explaining political participation, not civic participation, and while there are certainly discrepancies among those in each category, they are bound together by common visions of the role of encumbrance in prompting social action.[46]

These three schools of thought can be plotted along a continuum between encumbrance and unencumbrance, with the civic republicans at the encumbered end, the holist-individualists in the middle, and the liberals, the most direct heirs of the utilitarians, at the unencumbered end. This mapping is based on Michael Sandel's assessment that the liberals view American society as consisting of unencumbered selves.[47] Sandel, one of America's leading critics of liberalism, assails this vision as being overly simplistic, and while this may be so, liberal insights cannot be ignored for understanding a type of social action that has agency as a central element. According to the liberal view, especially as portrayed in Robert Nozick's *Anarchy, State and Utopia,* people move through life freely joining and leaving associations. Their lives, relationships, and interactions with others are on a contract basis. Tradition matters little, and people cooperate or form communities either for instrumental reasons or sentimental reasons. As befits their utilitarian lineage, liberal-individualists contend that if people cooperate for instrumental reasons, they do so because cooperation is a necessary burden for achieving their own private ends. The vision of society that arises from this is one of private society. If, on the other hand, people cooperate for sentimental reasons, they do so due to a shared goal, and once that goal has been attained, the so-cial contract on which the cooperation was based is voided and the community ceases.[48] Self-interest, as long as it doesn't harm others, is seen as the highest moral plane. If there is a role for government it is "to secure and distribute fairly the liberties and economic resources individuals need to lead freely chosen lives."[49]

While this approach has been judged useful in many areas, it is a bit thin for understanding why people volunteer in church basements to help homeless people. Such a contractarian approach argues that people do what is in their self-interest and nothing more. This is the argument of the rational choice theorists, and from this perspective social life is but an agglomeration of rational, individual actions or, put more succinctly, "a matter of maximizing the satisfaction of the individual's preferences."[50] In this approach, which has come to domi-nate American political science, people are deemed to act as rational individuals in a goal-oriented manner, sometimes within the context of institutional constraints but oftentimes not.[51] Some liberals even argue that altruism, arguably the most selfless form of social action, is actually an expression of the self-interest of the altruist.[52] In the case of the volunteers in the church shelters, this explanation—of their behavior as being an expression of self-interest—seems to be stretch-ing it a bit, as there are many simpler and potentially more rewarding ways for them to attend to their self-interest than by volunteering in the church basement. There are also other ways of explaining these peoples' actions that are more credible, explanations that account for such motivations as guilt, faith, obligation, love, charity, reciprocity, caring, and altruism, motivations that are trivialized by the liberal view of the world and that offer the potential for greater understand-ing of volunteerism than self-interest does. While I don't mean to imply that self-interest is not a contributing factor in the actions of some volunteers, it is unlikely to be the sole factor or even necessarily the primary factor.

In between the poles of encumbrance and unencumbrance is the holist model. This approach to understanding social action retains a role for agency as a motivation for action, but it also pays attention to the role of social encumbrances in motivating social action.[53] For example, a holist could believe that individuals act for the benefit of a group that they belong to rather than just for their own benefit, or that individual interests can be broadened over time through interaction with others so that what were contending interests in the beginning merge into complementary interests. Alexis de Tocqueville, foremost among this group, pointed out that Americans often volunteered and joined local associations to advance the public interest because they had to and because they had learned that this was important. People in America, he noted, "attend to the interest of the public, first by necessity, afterwards by choice; what was intentional becomes an instinct and by dint of working for the good of one's fellow citizens, the habit and the taste for serving them are at length acquired."[54] So what may have started out as self-interest becomes something larger than that—it becomes an instinct to care for the public interest. Once this instinct is developed, it becomes a motivation for action itself and it is passed on through the culture. By acquiring the habits of acting in the public interest, what Tocqueville referred to as *habits of the heart,* individuals become more community minded, and their self-interest is developed by the reciprocal influence of interacting with the self-interest of others to the point where it could be considered "self-interest rightly understood."

In his focus on self-interest and selfishness, Tocqueville remains an individualist, albeit of the holist sort. The notion that people might sometimes act because they feel obliged to others, or that they might not be selfish, are factors that an individualist is hard pressed to account for, even a holist one. To Tocqueville, there are ties between individuals, but they are there because the individuals have learned to want them, and these ties do not bind very strongly. A person could still be an unencumbered self if he wanted to be, but he recognizes that it would be to the social and civic detriment, so he chooses his encumbrances. He isn't obliged to be encumbered; he just thinks that it would be a good idea if he were. Behavior is still subjectively oriented.

This is the essence of the holist approach to understanding voluntary social action, and it is an essence that is shared by the civic culture theorists, the most prominent modern day adherents to the holist view.[55] In Gabriel Almond and Sidney Verba's schema, the American

civic culture is a participant one, which means that there is an interactive relationship among citizens' sociopolitical opinions, their political activity, and the sociopolitical institutions that they participate
in. According to this view, in America citizens create and run many of
the sociopolitical institutions, but these institutions in turn create an
environment in which the values and attitudes of the citizens are
molded. Understanding social action in America, according to this
approach, therefore requires an account of the role of the civic culture
and of the sociopolitical institutions in inculcating this culture, and it
requires an understanding of how individuals influence the creation
of sociopolitical institutions and are in turn influenced by them.

Despite its emphasis on culture, the civic culture approach, true to
its individualist nature, does not overlook the role of the individual as
the dominant social actor, and it does not neglect agency as a key aspect of social action.[56] What this approach to individualism emphasizes, however, is people's willingness to act out of a concern for the
welfare of others. It recognizes that individual's actions can be motivated by communal needs and it does so in a manner that is not peripheral to the model itself.

There are flaws to holism, however, and one that was noted by
Richard Dagger is that this model doesn't account very well for obligation as to do so would push the conception of why people act further
toward the social direction than Tocqueville and others seem willing
to go. So to the question of why people act in the interest of the neighborhood or the congregation, the holist answer seems to be that initially they do so because they have to, but after a while they become
civic minded—which is to say that they develop a genuine regard for
the needs of the community. This genuine regard for community is
still a selfish one, but it is an enlightened selfishness, a selfishness that
is acted out within a framework of encumbrances, what Tocqueville
called "self-interest rightly understood." While Dagger considered this
to be a flaw, I am not so sure it is, as some of the volunteers did indeed
seem to be acting this way.

Another criticism, this one directed more at the civic culture theorists, is that culture of any kind is an effect rather than a cause of
action.[57] The materialist variant of this criticism is that culturalist

approaches ignore material conditions, such as wealth or poverty, as the source of social traits. Furthermore, the civic culture school, which Almond and Verba developed as part of a political development theory, has been criticized for lionizing a particular version of middle-class American attitudes as a template for how countries and their people ought to be.[58] Of these two criticisms the second has more power than the first, as the first amounts to a reductionist understanding of what culture is. The charge that the civic culture approach is biased in favor of a certain way of living is a more complicated one. While it may hold true if you look at civic culture as a political development theory, as an action theory that looks at why Americans volunteer it is less powerful and beside the point. Furthermore, the materialist approach itself, which in effect purports to be able to describe how people act without needing to know the details of the encumbrances of people's lives, presents an even more flawed model for understanding social action.

The approach that puts the most emphasis on encumbrance is civic republicanism, which is otherwise referred to as communitarianism. Civic republicans see people's selves as tending "to be defined or constituted by various communal attachments (such as family, religious, or traditional), so close to us that they can only be set aside at great cost, if at all."[59] Man, Charles Taylor noted, "is a social animal, indeed a political animal, because he is not self-sufficient alone, and in an important sense is not self-sufficient outside a *polis.*"[60] Vast areas of our lives, according to this view, are governed by unchosen routines, by social attachments, and by habits that were involuntarily formed during our upbringing. Michael Sandel expresses the civic republican view when he claims that we think of ourselves not just as ourselves but "as members of this family or community or nation or people, as bearers of this history, as sons or daughters of that revolution, as citizens of this republic."[61] To the civic republicans, social attachments count more than self-interest, or at least they would if our overly individualistic laws and politics hadn't become so skewed as to weaken our social attachments and cut us all adrift.[62]

A bridge between communitarianism and the civic culture school is civic voluntarism. This approach differs from communitarianism in that it is more about description that prescription and it can also be seen as an updated civic culture, one which places a greater emphasis on the effect that resources have on action. One of the leading civic voluntarists is Sidney Verba. In his newer work, Verba and co-authors Kay Lehman Schlozman and Henry Brady explain the fact and the quantity of American voluntarism by claiming that voluntary action is a result of a combination of sufficient resources, psychological engagement with politics, and connection to recruitment networks.[63] The resources that they emphasize are time, money, and civic skills, and they trace the generation of these resources to "the fundamental involvement of individuals in major social institutions."[64] To them, the experiences that people have in their family, at school, and at work and their "voluntary affiliations with non-political associations and religious institutions" are "a function of their socially structured circumstances" and this is what affects the amount of an individual's resources.[65] Psychological engagement is exemplified by such things as an interest in helping others, a sense of efficacy, the subjective feeling that one can make a difference, "the civic values that imply that participation will be accompanied by the psychic gratification of having fulfilled a duty," and the group consciousness that makes people perceive that their fate is linked to others.[66] Recruitment comes in the form of requests for participation, which they note usually come at church, at work, in organizations, and from friends, relatives, and acquaintances. Those who are asked to participate "might have intended to act anyway, but the request was the triggering act."[67]

Civic voluntarists observe that from the beginning of the American nation, the state, though initially small, played a vital role in initiating the American habit of volunteering, and along with the holists, they believe that voluntarism in America has historically been plentiful because we have developed an institutional context that encourages it.[68] While there is disagreement over the question of whether it was public or private institutions that encouraged this civicness, over whether American civicness impeded the group of the state, and over whether increased state capacity and role in recent decades has damaged voluntarism, the important point for the question of why people volunteer is that voluntarism in America developed within an institutional context that was supportive of it. By the time Tocqueville arrived here, necessity and context were hard to separate. In many of the towns that he visited, people did indeed need to volunteer in the public interest, but this necessary volunteering had a profound cultural impact. The free institutions that the volunteer created "remind every citizen, in a thousand ways, that he lives in a society. They every instant impress upon his mind the notion that it is the duty as well as the interest of men to make themselves useful to their fellow creatures."[69]

Like all of the other schools of thought, civic voluntarism has its critics, and they note that its cardinal sin, which is the inverse of that of the rational choice theorists, is that people are more encumbered in their model than they really are in American society. While the civic voluntarist approach is valuable for its ability to incorporate a broad swath of motivations for actions, they don't pay enough attention to self-interest and they devalue agency as an explanation for voluntary action. Given the variations for the reasons that people volunteer, and the complexity of their own descriptions of those reasons, it seems that a good understanding of why people act this way requires a theory of social action that incorporates the best elements of these three approaches. It has to recognize agency as an important factor, it has to recognize the importance of resources and the institutional setting and support, and it has to recognize the importance of social bonds, obligations, and learned behavior. It also has to account for the motivating potential of guilt, faith, obligation, love, charity, reciprocity, altruism, and caring.

Among the volunteers I surveyed, different ones emphasized different reasons for deciding to volunteer, but the totality of their answers made it clear that for them, volunteering is a multilayered, intersubjective, normative phenomenon.[70] What I mean by this is that not only are those who decide to volunteer somewhere in the middle of the continuum between encumbrance and unencumbrance, but that their decision-making process is one with more than one phase.[71] As Talcott Parsons explained it, the decision to volunteer has two

phases: communication, which happens between the would-be volunteers and the voluntary agency, and the decision, which is what
happens within the volunteer's head.[72] Either could come first, depending on the individual case, and both are essential. In each phase
norms are engaged: substantive norms, or motivations, are engaged
in the decision phase, and procedural norms, or orientations, are engaged in the communication phase.[73] In trying to understand why
people choose to volunteer in a church or synagogue homeless shelter, and in trying to get more of them to do so, one should structure
the appeal so that both sets of norms can be engaged.

For some, such as Joe Pace, the decision happened first and the
communication followed. For Pat and Gene, it was the opposite. For
each, as well, different sets of norms were engaged at different times.
When Joe says, "in the whole process of becoming callous, I said to
myself, well you know if you are going to become callous and pissed
off about the situation, is there anything you can do about it," we are
hearing him describe the decision-making process that he went
through, one that, in his mind, was grounded in the fact that "I've
always had it instilled in me, since I was young, that [you should] give
something back to the community, give something back to society, if
you can, rather than just availing yourself of everything that society
has to offer."[74] At this point Joe is talking within the context of a clus-
ter of values and traditions that he was raised with. His parents and
his wife had set an example for him that he wanted to follow. On top
of that, his reaction to the environment that he was living in—his
revulsion at the condition of the homeless people in the city around
him and his dismay at his growing callousness—motivated him to
look for ways, albeit low-impact ways, to help the homeless and to
blunt his callousness. All this made Joe ready to act, and what was
needed to get him to act in this particular way was the communication that took place between him and the Partnership. What triggered
the action was the advertisement that he saw in the subway, which
was in effect a recruitment poster, and this ad represented a direct
appeal for help, an opportunity to give back to society in return for
the benefits it provided him. The Partnership's appeal resonated with
him. Together, the communication and the decision, the substance

92   and the procedure, got Joe to volunteer and to stay overnight at the shelter twice a month.

Pat and Gene's decision to volunteer was also intersubjective. In their case, the communication phase came first. They were already active in their parish but they had no idea that there was a homeless shelter in the church basement until someone asked them if they would volunteer there. This request prompted a decision to volunteer that was based on the exercise of a wide set of norms, including feelings of obligation in response to requests from their neighbors, their desire to give their daughter an appreciation for the bounty in her life, a belief that they should support the programs of the church, Pat's desire to help the homeless, and his relief at being able to do so in an environment in which he felt comfortable. Pat and Gene responded to a request from the congregation to help because it was intrinsically the right thing to do and because it would help the shelter program.[75]

While few debate the fact that Americans volunteer in great numbers, this question of whether or not the decision to volunteer is an act of an unencumbered self or an encumbered self rages. When Alexis de Tocqueville visited America he noted that "when men are no longer bound among themselves in a solid and permanent manner, one cannot get many to act in common except by persuading each of them whose cooperation is necessary that his particular interest obliges him voluntarily to unite his effort with the efforts of all the others."[76] This observation that American individuals are relatively unencumbered and need to be persuaded and recruited into acting cooperatively is one that has been repeated in the works by Robert Bellah and his associates; by Herbert Gans; by Sidney Verba, Kay Lehman Schlozman, and Henry E. Brady; and by a host of others who have analyzed civic action in America. It is also suggested by the Independent Sector survey, which indicated that only 22.3 percent of volunteers volunteered without being asked. While many of the volunteers I interviewed spoke about their behavior in a way that would make it seem to be the classically self-oriented, unencumbered actions of the volunteer, upon further reflection it became apparent that to see their behavior this way was to miss a lot of what they were expressing.

To get the mass numbers of volunteers necessary to operate an enterprise of this scope an intense recruitment effort from the churches is necessary. This is what separates the successful shelters from the unsuccessful ones. At Sacred Heart, Jim Jones and Virginia Brown have been there from the beginning persuading people to volunteer at their shelter. At Fifth Avenue Presbyterian, Peter Saghir and then Kathleen McGuffin began doing the same thing after the shelter nearly closed down because for years no one had been effectively recruiting. It was the lack of effective recruitment that led to the closure of the Riverside Church shelter. Through persuasion, the successful volunteer coordinators have been able to build their shelters into what Tocqueville referred to as civil associations that have a public life.[77] Because these shelters have a public purpose, and because those who run the shelters expend effort to recruit the volunteers into them, they become the sort of places in which the volunteers can become integrated into a group effort. Once the volunteers are integrated into this group effort, they can then learn to perform other functions, such as mediation, socialization, education, and moral development. The church shelters don't actually perform these functions; they simply present the volunteers with an opportunity to learn how to perform these functions for themselves, and by presenting the volunteers with this opportunity, the church shelters take the first step toward becoming sites for the generation of the American Ethic. They also lay the groundwork for the generation of community in a particularly American way.

4

The Mediating Role of the Church Shelters

When I asked Jim and Virginia what effect the homeless shelter had had on their parish, Virginia immediately said, "I think it brought a lot of them close together, and it also brought out people that were on the parish rolls but never volunteered for anything." Even in this fairly close-knit parish, a lot of the people who came out to volunteer were people that Virginia had never heard of before, and this seemed to still surprise her so many years later. Jim felt the same way, and he said that the shelter gave the parish a place for people to get to know each other that they hadn't had before. There were people in the parish, he said, who had lived there for 40 years and finally got to know their neighbors "because they all volunteered in the shelter." In addition to this being "a nice thing" in Jim's mind, it also gave the conservative members of the parish and the charismatics a place and an opportunity to talk out their differences. "They would talk at night, according to Jim, "and they made a lot of friendships."[1]

Early on, when they saw this trend developing, one of the decisions that Jim, Harold, and Virginia made was to get the children involved. This, they both agreed, "was a great thing, because we have so many kids, and so many families involved," and because "so many children . . . have kept at it, too, over the years." The fact that so many of the children in the parish have kept volunteering at the shelter over the years is one of rewards of this work for Virginia. She feels that "when you see someone who started in the seventh grade and then comes back as a volunteer as a college person," that gives you the opportunity to you say to yourself, "we must have done something right" and "the message got through to them."[2]

Jim concurred, and he added that involving the young people of the parish in the shelter was "one of the best things we've ever done."[3]

Before the conversation went further I brought them back to Virginia's statement that "the message got through to them" to find out what they thought that message was. Virginia did not hesitate to say that she thought that the message was "to help other people," to "not just think of yourself," to "think how fortunate you are and how helpful to these people you are," to "think when they see the [homeless] people that they are just like you and I, or relatives that you might have that aren't quite as fortunate as you are," and "that they are no different than my relatives that have come on bad times."

Something else that Jim and Virginia mentioned was that their homeless clients "are most grateful for anything you do" and this is something else that they think has had an effect on their parish and on their volunteers. No sooner had they said this, however, than they added that some of the clients are con artists, "but when you know you have a con artist you've just got to constrain yourselves."[4]

When they decided to start volunteering, the volunteers put themselves in a situation in which they would be part of a series of social interactions that they had likely not been part of before. In the context of the shelters they would interact with the other volunteers and with their homeless clients ("guests," as some of the shelters call them). To varying degrees, the volunteers also would interact with people outside of the shelter who would help them to provide services for their homeless clients. Included in this group are the employees of New York City's DHS, the employees of the drop-in centers, the bus drivers who transport the homeless people to and from the shelters, the suppliers of the bed linens and other sundries, and the employees of the Partnership for the Homeless. For most of the volunteers, these interactions opened up whole new worlds within their city that they had no knowledge of or access to before. It put them in new social situations and in contact with people who run other institutions across the city. This gives them an opportunity to learn and to broaden their horizons, and it was through providing this access and the opportunity for these interactions that the church shelters began to mediate.

The Mediating Role of the Church Shelters

To mediate is to literally be in the middle between two extremes. In this case the extremes are the private lives of the volunteers and the public roles of what have been referred to by Peter Berger and Richard John Neuhaus as the *megastructures* of modern life. Included on Berger and Neuhaus's list of megastructures are "the large economic conglomerates of capitalist enterprise, big labor, and the growing bureaucracies that administer wide sectors of the society such as education and the organized professions."[5] In a city the size of New York, the megastructures are many, they are large and they are powerful. Included among their number are those that administer the social services, a sector of society that Berger and Neuhaus did not mention in their definition.

Berger and Neuhaus explain the reason that this mediation is necessary in the following manner:

> For the individual in modern society, life is an ongoing migration between these two spheres, public and private. The megastructures are typically alienating; that is, they are typically not helpful in proving meaning and identity for individual existence. Meaning, fulfillment, and personal identity are to be realized in the private sphere. While the two spheres interact in many ways, in private life the individual is left very much to his own devices, and thus is uncertain and anxious. Where modern society is "hard," as in the megastructures, it is personally unsatisfactory; where it is "soft," as in the private life, it cannot be relied upon.[6]

While the megastructures provide many benefits for all of us, essential elements of life such as meaning, fulfillment, and identity are not among them. These elements have to be found by people in their private interactions with each other. But in today's modern life the private sphere has been relegated to a smaller role in our daily lives, as the megastructures administer wide sections of society and fulfill crucial functions. With this smaller role for the private sphere, people have fewer opportunities for the sort of interaction that would allow them to find meaning, fulfillment, and identity.

For Berger and Neuhaus the decline of the private sphere, and the usurpation of its role by the public sphere, has precipitated what amounts to a double crisis of modernity. It is a double crisis because it is at once a crisis of the individual and a crisis of the society. For the individual, the crisis is the isolation from others, from the larger public realm, and increasingly from traditions. Fulfillment of important social functions, such as the production of one's economic livelihood, the education of one's children, and the care of loved ones, is no longer a function of private life as it was in the past. Increasingly, therefore, private life is given over to consumption or clientelism. In this situation, individuals are isolated from the production of much of what is important in their own lives as the formerly productive aspect of private life is almost entirely done away with. Private life thus loses many of its sources of meaning and fulfillment. This condition has been described by classical social theorists as *alienation*.[7] For some, this reduction of the scope of their private lives goes further, to the point where their lives are isolated from the lives of others. This condition has been described as *disaffiliation*. Interestingly, before the term *homelessness* was devised in the late 1970s, disaffiliation was the term used in sociological literature to describe what we now call homelessness.[8] While the homeless might be the most visible and startling example of disaffiliation, they are not the only ones suffering from this affliction. Furthermore, people's isolation from traditions has left them questioning their identity in a state that Max Weber described as one of *disenchantment*.[9] These conditions—alienation, disaffiliation, and disenchantment—are the crises of the modern individual.

For modern society, the crises of modernity are political, cultural, and moral. The political crisis is precipitated by transformations that take place in the relationship between the megastructures and modern individuals. As Weber explained, the megastructures may have initially been set up to perform a social function, but over time their prime objective has been transformed from the performance of the intended function to their own self-perpetuation. As people become aware of this transference of objectives, and when the megastructures do not perform their originally intended functions adequately, people lose faith in them and they are delegitimized. The result of this, according to Berger and Neuhaus, is that "the megastructures, notably the state, come to be seen as devoid of personal meaning and are therefore viewed as unreal or even malignant."[10] People are then unwilling to pay taxes to support these institutions, and some begin to call for their reorganization or abolition. This precipitates the political crisis. Furthermore, when the social functions that these structures are intended

98   to perform go undone, those who were depending on them suffer accordingly, and individual crises deepen.

As individuals lose faith in the social institutions of their society, people seek other means to ensure that the services that they and their family require are provided. Because it is usually only the wealthier members of society who can do this, a two-tier society begins to emerge. For societies in which the social order is based on the assumption of equality, such a development amounts to the beginnings of a cultural crisis.[11] As the society's ideology and its social reality fall out of step with each other, and as more people begin to suffer from the fact that the megastructures are not performing the functions that they were set up to do, a moral crisis ensues.[12]

What makes Berger and Neuhaus's analysis of this double crisis interesting for this study is not their analysis itself but their trenchant observation that these crises aren't experienced in the same way and with the same intensity by all of us. Some people do not suffer these crises as intensely as others, they note, and those who are coping with modernity better are those who "have access to institutions that mediate between the two spheres."[13] Berger and Neuhaus call these institutions *mediating structures,* but I will call them *mediating institutions.* They are "those institutions standing between the individual and his private life and the large institutions of public life."[14] The mediating institutions in American society today include the neighborhood, the family, religious institutions, and voluntary associations. This is not a complete list, but these are the ones that are common, that Americans are most familiar with, and that play a significant role in American life. When they function properly, these mediating institutions are thought to be able to alleviate the crises of modernity. By connecting people to each other, mediating institutions can alleviate alienation and disaffiliation. By connecting people to sources of meaning, they can alleviate disenchantment. By connecting people to the megastructures in such a way that the beliefs and values of the people are transmitted to the megastructures, and in such a way that they are reflected in the actions of the megastructures so that the megastructures can be held accountable to individuals, the mediating institutions may alleviate the political, cultural, and moral social crises.

Of course, no one mediating institution can do all of these things by itself. Certainly the church and synagogue shelters that the Partnership for the Homeless runs cannot do these things by themselves. In theory, however, if there is a sufficiently large group of mediating institutions, if they have a large role to play in providing important social functions, and if enough people participate in them and help them to provide these functions, then as a group mediating institutions should be able to do all of these things.

In this chapter I again use statements from the volunteers to explain the mediating role of the Sacred Heart shelter and the Fifth Avenue Presbyterian Church shelter. Churches have long played an important mediating role in America. J. Philip Wogaman, the pastor of the Foundry Methodist Church in Washington, D.C., has elaborated on this role of the church in modern America in a way that helps explain the impact of the work that the church shelters have on the volunteers and on the homeless clients.[15] According to Wogaman, churches can mediate in three ways: by linking people with one another, by linking people with power centers, and by linking people with sources of meaning.[16] These two shelters mediate by connecting their volunteers to each other, connecting them to sources of meaning, and connecting them to some sources of power (the megastructures) in New York City. Neither of these shelters is perfect in its ability to mediate, but they perform this function better than almost all of the others. Even so, there are challenges that these two churches, and almost any other mediating institution in America today, just are not able to overcome.

How Mediation Happens

I didn't ask any of the volunteers how much they were suffering from the crises of modernity, but alienation, anomie, and disaffiliation could be inferred from many of their conversations and responses to my questions. When Joe Pace commented that though he felt empathy for the homeless man that he saw in Brooklyn Heights every day he felt powerless as an individual to do anything about it, and when Jim Jones said that he avoided working with the Community Board when they were opening the Sacred Heart shelter because it would have made the whole thing political, both of them were expressing aspects of the double crisis of modernity. Joe felt powerless to help a fellow man and Jim was distrustful of an institution of his own city government. They weren't the only ones. Anne Walker, another volunteer, said that she began volunteering as a way of "lighting a very small candle instead of being depressed and overwhelmed by the darkness."[17] Steven Romeo said that he began volunteering in order "to assist people in recovering their dignity and to become a functioning, contributing part of society."[18]

Linking People with One Another

The first and primary step in mediation is linking people to each other, as without this linkage, none of the others could take place There are human as well as intellectual implications of this type of link, as the face-to-face link with others is the place where "the individual and social aspects of human nature are most fully joined," and it is at this level that human life, which is both personal and social, is fully realized.[19]

While it was no surprise to me that the volunteers in Manhattan needed to be linked to each other, I was surprised that even in a place like Glendale, in which some of the volunteers and their families had lived for decades, this primary level of mediation was needed. I thought that though the people in Glendale might be distrustful of megastructures, they would at least be connected to each other. This apparently was not the case, as evidenced by Jim and Virginia's observation that many of the people who volunteered in the shelter were people who lived in the neighborhood but whom they had never met. The supreme, unintended irony of these shelters is that the relatively disaffiliated volunteers get linked to each other because of their efforts to help the truly disaffiliated, the homeless people. It was through providing for people who were worse off than themselves that the volunteers were able to improve their lives and the lives of their homeless guests. The linkage to other people that happened in the shelters was both among the volunteers and between the volunteers and the homeless, with the former type of linkage being more prevalent at Sacred Heart and the latter type more common at Fifth Avenue Presbyterian. While linkages developed among the homeless

Recruiting and Retaining a Volunteer Corps

Before the mediation process could begin at any of the churches, first people had to volunteer. At both Fifth Avenue Presbyterian and Sacred Heart, the first active step that the shelter programs took to link people to each other was recruitment. Jim Jones, Virginia Brown, and Peter Saghir subscribed to the philosophy of "the more volunteers the better," and they all became experts at pitching their programs and the open volunteer positions to a wide array of potential volunteers. In both cases there were barriers to be overcome in order for recruitment to be effective in a widespread manner. At Sacred Heart, one of the first barriers that had to be overcome was the fear of homeless people. This was especially the case in the early years when the shelter was a new concept in the neighborhood and when the homeless clients that the shelter received were mentally ill and thus more intimidating. In this situation there was a genuine fear for the safety of the volunteers. As the volunteers got to know the homeless people and as they saw that the homeless weren't harmful if dealt with properly, this fear that the volunteers had for their safety began to dissipate. The dissipation of fear meant that the volunteers were likely to volunteer more often and for longer periods of time. As the volunteers' fear dissipated, so did the fear among the rest of the congregation, which had the effect of broadening the pool of potential future shelter volunteers.

At Fifth Avenue Presbyterian, fear of the homeless people was not as much of a problem. After all, it is a big urban church with a large congregation that has a long history of voluntary involvement in social services. That is not to say that there weren't people in the congregation who were afraid of homeless people or anxious about the notion of spending the night with them, but as Margaret Shafer explained, with such a large congregation, they could afford to let this be a "self-correcting problem." They just left those who were afraid alone and recruited those who weren't afraid. Once the volunteers started volunteering, their safety was not considered to be much of a problem either. This was because the homeless guests at this church are all senior citizens, and the volunteers are mainly young adults. This contrasts with the Sacred Heart situation, in which a lot of the volunteers are senior citizens themselves, or they are junior high or high school students, and it is the homeless clients who are young adults. Though the Sacred Heart shelter no longer accepts mentally ill clients, the legacy of the period when they did is a continued heightened sense of caution and concern over the safety of their volunteers. At Fifth Avenue Presbyterian, meanwhile, there is little reason that a volunteer might find him- or herself in an unmanageable situation. If such a situation were to develop, Fifth Avenue Presbyterian has a security guard on duty throughout the night, and the volunteer is in constant walkie-talkie contact with the guard. While Sacred Heart has had instances in which there were conflicts between the clients and the volunteers and Jim and Virginia had to calm the situation down, Fifth Avenue Presbyterian doesn't seem to have had these situations.

What the Fifth Avenue Presbyterian shelter did grapple with was the competition that they were getting for the attention of the potential volunteers. This is an active congregation and with an estimated 800 volunteers in numerous social service programs, the shelter program had to struggle to make itself seem more attractive than the others. For a long time they did a poor job of this, and in Peter Saghir's estimation the failing was that volunteering to help the homeless was being portrayed as a "very serious and heavy thing," and that wasn't appealing to many people. While Peter noted that volunteering to help the homeless is indeed a serious thing, at the same time he found a way to convey to the volunteers that it also could be enjoyable: "Just lighten up and let's have fun with it."[20] The tactic that Peter developed was to emphasize that the men were interesting and that it was fun hanging out with them. Unlike at Sacred Heart, the congregation at Fifth Avenue had a plethora of singles looking for friendships and Peter was able to sell the shelter as a safe place in which to develop these friendships.

With the dissipation of the fear factor at Sacred Heart and the generation of the fun factor at Fifth Avenue Presbyterian, the shelters were able to recruit people into their volunteer corps and then take subsequent steps to link the volunteers to each other. At both places

the next task was to increase the volunteers' competence in dealing
with homeless people. Both sets of volunteer coordinators believed
that if the volunteers had more knowledge and greater skill they
would be capable of interacting in a manner that would assist the
shelter in performing its tasks more effectively. At Sacred Heart they
had to obtain assistance to do this, so with the help of the Partnership,
the shelter brought in outreach workers from Columbia University
Community Services. These outreach workers taught the volunteers
about mental illnesses and how to recognize when someone was not
taking their medications, and they taught the volunteers how to avoid
the spread of communicable diseases such as tuberculosis and HIV/
AIDS that the homeless people were likely to be carrying. Also, every
year the Sacred Heart shelter rented a bus to take volunteers into
Manhattan to the Action Day that the Partnership ran. Action Day
was a source of more training, as it had workshops put on by social
service professionals on various aspects of working with the homeless
and these were all ways that the volunteers got better educated about
their task. Because a lot of the older volunteers would never have gone
into New York by themselves, this bus rental strategy was critical to
getting these volunteers to Action Day, which also provided an opportunity for volunteers from various churches and synagogues to
meet each other and share their experiences.

At Fifth Avenue Presbyterian training could be done partially in-
house, as they have their own social worker on staff. Emily Dunlap,
their social worker, gives periodic training to the new volunteers, and
the Fifth Avenue Presbyterian volunteers also participate in Action
Day. Because the clients at Fifth Avenue are old, this training involves
learning how to recognize and respond to the symptoms of potentially serious medical conditions. On occasion the volunteers have
had to call an ambulance, and for that they use their walkie-talkie to
contact the building's security guard, who then calls the ambulance. A
lot of the homeless clients from this shelter have had to be hospital-
ized, so a subset of the volunteer corps has been organized into a hospital visiting team. Some of the clients have also had to be admitted to
nursing homes and the shelter volunteers have learned how to manage this situation was well. The constant vigilance that is required of

the Fifth Avenue church volunteers because of the frail health of the men has bonded them to their clients in a way not common at many of the shelters. Furthermore, this has emerged as a shared concern that has bonded the volunteers to each other.

As people became more effective volunteers, the next challenge at both shelters was to retain them. All of the volunteer coordinators said that the key to volunteer retention was proper utilization and management. Proper utilization would get the volunteers to come back over the medium term and proper management would get them to come back over the long term. In both cases, significant effort has gone into building an organizational structure that aids in this effort; however, the organizational structures that have developed at the two shelters are radically different. At Sacred Heart the volunteer coordinators are themselves volunteers, and they have devised an organization that disperses responsibility and has a transparency and a hierarchy that makes it in the self-interest of the volunteers to perform their duties. This organizational structure has been intact for 19 years and has shown itself to be successful over that time. It is heavily dependent, however, on the executive efforts of Virginia Brown and Jim Jones, and there is no evidence yet whether it would survive a leadership transition. At Fifth Avenue Presbyterian Church, on the other hand, years of struggle and a near failure, combined with a volunteer coordinator who is paid, have led to the creation of a much more centralized organization, which has yet to pass the test of time or transition.

The Importance of Finding the Right Job and of Never Turning a Potential Volunteer Away

Jim Jones and Virginia Brown both believe that the first step in utilizing volunteers correctly is finding the right job for them and matching them with the correct partner. Those who are too timid to interact with homeless people, for example, would be given a job that did not require interacting with the guests. Some like to stay up late and watch television and play games and others like to go to bed early. Matching people of different temperaments in an overnight shift can cause friction, so Jim and Virginia and the daily coordinators are always working to find good pairings. The volunteers also help sort this out themselves by making friends with each other. In a lot of the cases, especially for the overnight shifts, couples volunteer together, thereby taking care of the compatibility issue.

Jim and Virginia make a point of never turning a potential volunteer away. Never saying no to a potential volunteer was critically important for the longevity of the shelter's volunteer program. A rejected would-be volunteer could easily go away and spread the word that the shelter didn't need help, and that could cause fatal damage. In order to never say no, Jim and Virginia sometimes had to go to significant lengths to find something for a potential volunteer to do. While it was a fact, according to Virginia, that there was always something to be done at the shelter, whether it was working the dinner shift, staying overnight, peeling onions, or cooking, some people were unsuited for some of the tasks, so creativity was required to fit them in, and both Virginia and Jim have been very inventive in creating new roles for new volunteers. Virginia particularly has been creative in figuring out how to use the 15 seventh- and eight-grade children in the church's confirmation classes and the high schoolers who have to satisfy community service requirements. She has put the children from the confirmation classes on the setup crew to fold the laundry and put away the sundries that have been delivered, and she has incorporated a dozen high schoolers into the 9:30 P.M. to midnight shift on Fridays and Saturdays. While a regular shift interacting with homeless people is too much for a seventh- or eighth-grade child to handle, Virginia figures that no high school student is going to bed before midnight on Friday or Saturday nights, so they might as well be down at the shelter keeping out of trouble and doing something useful. Because the high school students are required to volunteer for a lot of hours each year, many of them come twice a month. In working with the youngsters, Virginia noted, she needs to be patient, flexible, and have a sense of humor. These are characteristics that she needs in her dealings with all of the volunteers, however, and they are vital aspects of proper volunteer utilization.[21]

Effective volunteer utilization is the key to medium term retention at Fifth Avenue Presbyterian as well. Because of the differences in their congregation and because it is open every night of the year, Fifth

Avenue Presbyterian faces some different utilization challenges than Sacred Heart. To begin with, some of the volunteers at Fifth Avenue Presbyterian were reluctant to volunteer in pairs. As Margaret Shafer explained, a lot of the volunteers are single and live alone, and "they really don't like sharing a room with somebody else."[22] While the initial desire was for them to stay in pairs, as is the general rule at all of the church shelters, rather than force every volunteer to do this, a decision was made to let them stay alone. Another factor that contributed to the decision to let volunteers stay by themselves was the fact that the shelter is open every night of the year. This places great demands on the volunteers, especially the overnight volunteers, who do not get a summer break to reflect and recharge for another season. With so many slots to fill, Fifth Avenue Presbyterian needs to stretch their volunteer corps out. Once the decision to allow volunteers to stay by themselves was made, the next discussion about people staying singly or in pairs was about whether or not to permit unmarried people of different sexes to stay together. As Margaret tells it, "We decided that we weren't going to worry about that one way or the other," because "you see, it is a little microcosm of the real world here."[23] While the decision to allow volunteers to stay alone made the volunteers more content, it robbed the shelter volunteers of the first link that most of their colleagues at the other shelters make, and it made mediation more challenging for Fifth Avenue Presbyterian.

This challenge is compounded by both the demographics of the volunteer corps and by their residential patterns. Shafer describes their volunteer corps at Fifth Avenue Presbyterian as being mostly "the 35 and under crowd," virtually all of whom are single. "It is sort of an urban church phenomenon, I think," she said, and in Manhattan, a lot of the under-35 crowd are people who have moved there for work reasons. This makes it a very mobile volunteer corps. Furthermore, the volunteers at Fifth Avenue Presbyterian live throughout Manhattan, Queens, and Brooklyn, and getting to the church takes time.

Peter Saghir's strategy in face of this was one of imaginative job creation and emotional appeals. Because he only was paid for 15 hours a week, however, he couldn't do everything that has to be done to run the shelter so even he needed help with the workload. For this

Fifth Avenue Presbyterian has set up a shelter committee. This committee was initially set up to provide oversight, and when Peter first attempted to parcel some of the work out to them, they resisted, saying "why couldn't [he] just do that" and that this is what they were paying him for. In the face of this resistance, Peter noted that he could do it himself, but that wasn't the point. So he appealed to Margaret and said that they needed a shelter committee that was really going to be involved in the shelter, a committee that had time and energy. So with Margaret's help, he replaced the old committee members with new members and began delegating tasks to them. The members of the shelter committee are either volunteers in the shelter or they are past guests who have found housing and joined the church. His rationale for doing this was that "you have to give them tasks, keep them involved."[24] To further sell the idea to the shelter committee of the need for greater involvement on their part, Peter noted the intensiveness of the operation. He explained that this is the only volunteer program in the church that is open each night of the year, it is the only one with people sleeping in the building, and it requires a greater number of volunteers and attention than the other programs in the church. This was more than one person could reasonably be expected to do successfully, and he claimed that it would therefore be a good idea for the committee to share some of the workload. The new committee agreed, and Peter started them off small by delegating the responsibility for maintaining the first aid kit. Over time, he has gotten them more involved and duties are more widely dispersed among them. There is now someone on the shelter committee who is in charge of organizing the birthday parties and making sure that there are materials for the guests and volunteers to set up the parties. Another member of the shelter committee is in charge of hospital care; whenever a shelter resident gets admitted to the hospital, this person is responsible for finding out what hospital he is in and what his condition is and passing on the details to Peter so that he can notify the rest of the volunteers in one of his emails. Another shelter committee member is responsible for movie night and another for bingo night.

Another approach they take at Fifth Avenue Presbyterian is to involve the homeless men in the running of the shelter and spin-off programs. This is possible due to the very different dynamic that exists between the volunteers and the homeless men at Fifth Avenue Presbyterian, one that has resulted in more friendships developing between the volunteers and the guests. Margaret remarked on this and explained it in the following manner:

> I think that there is some . . . generational need for love and care, which I don't think . . . is universal, but it is, I think, a significant factor. . . . Trying to develop social relationships . . . is an exhausting process. But when you go down to the shelter and somebody just wants to be your friend and love you, there is sort of a no-strings-attached kind of thing. It works, and it is quite wonderful to behold.[25]

Peter explained the close relations between the volunteers and the guests at Fifth Avenue in the following way:

> Something that we are just very fortunate with is that the group of guys that we have, they are a great group of guys. . . . They were kind of like . . . 10 grandfathers, . . . and I think that the volunteers really respond to that, just the warmth and the kindness of the guys. I think they sort of feed off of each other. I mean the volunteers really gave back to the guys, which enabled the guys to let down their guard and really open up and relax.[26]

With the frequent hospitalizations, hospital-visiting teams developed. The volunteers at the shelter have also pulled together to get two of the men admitted into a nursing home, and a group of them visit the one who is still in the nursing home. This, Peter noted, "has been sort of a bonding thing for a lot of the people in the shelter."[27] The volunteers have bonded amongst themselves and they have bonded with the homeless men. As well, the homeless men are actively involved in the Homeless on the Steps program and they help set up and clean up the shelter on a nightly basis and before and after events.

Managing the Shelter

On the heels of proper volunteer utilization comes proper volunteer management. Proper management requires, among other things, making sure that the volunteers have an important task to do, that they don't take on too much too soon, that people keep their commitments, and that the work of running the shelter doesn't gradually fall into a few hands. Doing this requires the creation of an efficient organizational structure and what Virginia calls dividing up the pie: making sure everyone has something meaningful to do, that there are no free riders, and that no one person carries too big a load. Avoiding burnout is crucial, and at Sacred Heart, the summer break helps achieve this goal. Another way to achieve this is to rein in those who may be a little too eager. As Jim and Virginia note, these are constant problems. Every year they get new people who, as Jim puts it, are eager to "jump in with both feet and start right away doing the hardest thing," and he and Virginia have found that it is important to tell those people no. As a good volunteer coordinator you have to give someone the opportunity to learn the ropes, Virginia said, and the way to do this is to have the new volunteer start slowly and work as part of a team with a veteran volunteer.[28]

The main tool that Jim and Virginia use to prevent volunteer burnout, to divide up the pie, to give everyone something meaningful to do, and to prevent free riding is astute scheduling. The monthly schedule divides up all of the shelter duties, ensures that all have a clear sense of their responsibilities, creates a way for people to find backup if they need it, and keeps track of the number of times that people volunteer. Jim credits Harold Brown, a no-nonsense ex-marine, with setting up the system in which everyone had some responsibility and everybody had somebody to report to. Jim began with the following hypothetical situation in explaining the hierarchy to me.

> Say we open for five nights a week for the month of November. She [the Tuesday coordinator, for example] would be in charge of all of the Tuesday nights in November. It would be her responsibility . . . to get the crews there, [to] call them up the day ahead to remind them that they [were] on this night. And she had to be down there every Tuesday of the month.[29]

This way, as Jim explained it, everyone knew who was in charge that day, and everyone knew who to blame if things went wrong. At the same time "they would have somebody that they could look to if something happened . . . if they had a problem, they could look to her and say, well, that's my boss, I don't have to worry about it. Then," as Jim continued, "we would have somebody who was in charge of the whole month" so that she [the Tuesday coordinator] would have someone to pass on concerns to and look to for leadership. This way, "everybody would have that feeling that somebody was going to help them if things really went wrong."

The Mediating Role of the Church Shelters

Virginia said that she looked at the totality of the work at the shelter as if "it was like a pie, and if you had enough pieces, with you doing this and you doing that, the pie would come all together." In her mind "if you tried to do the whole pie [by yourself] it would not work" and "you wouldn't get any pie, [because] you'd be conked out."

This is a lesson that Jim and Harold have tried to pass on to all of the other churches that they have gone to help set up. In each case Jim remembers that there has always been one person who says that he or she is going to run the shelter, and in each case Jim has advised the person that he or she would be burned out in a month. "You have to spread it around," Jim says. "You can't have that one person to be the overall chief, because they will just kill themselves."[30]

Even with the work spread around, however, there has to be a final authority, and at Sacred Heart it was Jim, Harold, and Virginia. If something went wrong, they were the ones who would go down to the shelter and play good cop and bad cop and calm everybody down. All disciplinary issues were their responsibility, in part because they did not want to put any of the volunteers in the position of having to chasten their colleagues. In effect this meant that most seasons they found that at least one of them was in the shelter every night.

At Sacred Heart there is an organizational committee meeting during the third week of every month to plan the schedule for the next month. Once the tentative schedule is set, it is sent that week to the volunteers. This committee meeting relies on the postcards that the volunteers fill out during the summer that specify the times that they would like to volunteer, so this committee meeting usually produces a schedule that is close to final. There are always changes that have to be made, however, and by having the meeting a bit before the next month begins, the organizational committee gives themselves, and the volunteers, time to make those changes. Once the schedule is set, the shifts belong to the people whose names are in the slots. If they can't fulfill their commitment, then they have to get a substitute. All of the volunteers have a directory of all of the other volunteers' telephone numbers that also lists the days and times that the others are available, so that the volunteers can find a substitute for their shift if they need one. If they can't find a substitute, the first person that

they call is their daily coordinator. From there, the next person to call 111
is the monthly coordinator, and from there Jim and Virginia. While
Virginia gets so many calls that she has had a special telephone line
put in her house for the shelter volunteers (which she doesn't answer
until after 6 P.M.), she rarely gets calls about someone needing to find
a substitute to fill in his or her slot. Over the years, the volunteers at
Sacred Heart have developed an ownership of the program, and Virginia rarely has to do last-minute scrambling to fill slots.

With this hierarchy, each shift, in a sense, is the property of the
volunteer, and the success or failure of a particular piece of the shelter
program depends on and reflects upon him or her. And any failure is
very visible in this neighborhood. If the setup or early evening volunteers don't show up, then the homeless people will be left standing out
on the street. In Glendale, homeless people standing out on the street
would stick out and would be the cause of much indignant discussion. Because a volunteer would be upsetting his or her friends and
neighbors by shirking responsibility (imagine the icy glares in the
aisles of the supermarket or the cold shoulders at church the next
week), it becomes in the volunteer's self-interest not to do so. Without
realizing the theoretical label for what they were doing, Jim, Virginia,
and Harold, in setting up this system, were appealing to the principle
of self-interest rightly understood that I mentioned in the last chapter. The appeal to self-interest rightly understood is, in effect, Sacred
Heart's ultimate tool of volunteer retention.

This principle, in Tocqueville's words, "is not a high and lofty one,
but it is clear and true."[31] It is clear and true because "it lies within the
reach of all capacities, everyone can without difficulty learn and retain it."[32] It lies within the reach of all because it is based on the assumption that we will act in our own self-interest or, in Peter Saghir's
words, that the volunteers will most likely do what is convenient. What
makes this principle different than mere self-interest, however, is that it
"checks one personal interest by another, and uses, to direct the pas-
sions, the very same instrument that excites them."[33] Essentially, an
organization that is set up to appeal to and develop the self-interest
rightly understood of the members is one that relies on mutually off-
setting selfishness to ensure that its work gets done. Tocqueville

112 assumed that selfishness exists, but his observations led him to conclude that the scope of an individual's selfishness can be enlarged, if the individuals find themselves properly organized in the right circumstance. Sacred Heart Glendale's shelter is a striking example of what proper organization in proper circumstances looks like. The shelter is set up so that it is in the self-interest of the volunteers to carry through on their commitments, because failure to do so will have repercussions that are not in their interest. An organization that is structured to appeal to the self-interest rightly understood of the volunteer is one in which, to paraphrase Tocqueville, it is in the private interest to do good. It is because of its reciprocal nature that this approach has a strong effect on the volunteer's continued participation in the shelter, an effect that is central to the ability of the shelters to mediate.

Another important function of the schedule is that it helps Jim, Virginia, and the other coordinators see how often people are volunteering, so that they can make sure that some aren't volunteering too often. "We tried to make a rule," Virginia noted, "that you only had to do it once a month." The rationale for this rule is that if a volunteer is asked to do another shift to cover for another volunteer, then he or she is only being asked to do two shifts that month, which Jim and Virginia feel is reasonable, and not three shifts or more, which would be unreasonable. If "you did one [shift]," she said, "you are more likely to do two." If, however, "I already scheduled you for two in a month, you are not likely to do the third, are you?" Jim went on to note that they have some people who "want to do every single Thursday or Friday, whatever night." To such people with such requests they always say no because they want to make sure that everyone gets on the schedule. As they approach the end of the year, according to Jim, "we look [at the schedule for the past year] and find out who hasn't done it in a while and we sort of put them on, so everybody gets a shot at being a volunteer. We don't just say," he went on, "well, you were on in November; we don't need you until April. We don't do that. We just, you know, like to keep everybody current and fresh. We are all contributing." This way, he noted, "everyone feels needed."[34]

Not only does everyone feel needed but at Sacred Heart, everyone
feels at home. This is one of the reasons why so many of the volunteers
come down to the shelter to socialize when they are not volunteering.
Socializing at the shelter is another way that people in Glendale get
linked to each other. A lot of the socializing happens informally; it has
become both a boon and a problem for the Sacred Heart shelter. The
main socializing time at Sacred Heart is 7:30 P.M. to 9:30 P.M. This has
become the time that people from throughout the neighborhood who
either don't volunteer or who do volunteer but are not scheduled drop
by to say hello. Virginia put it most succinctly when she said that the
shelter "was the place to be, to meet and greet people."

People would "go by and bring cake, bring cookies and drinks,"
Virginia added, and "they would visit with the guests, sit down and
have cake with them." "It was a social atmosphere," said Jim. "The Girl
Scouts would come down and bring cookies" and "the priest would
come down and have a coffee, and he would talk to the people. I
would go down, Harold and I would go, and it was every single night."
This happened, according to Virginia, because "there is no [other]
place to go" in the parish and because the neighbors "know the shelter
is open five nights a week." So popular is this time period that on
some nights there are more visitors than guests.[35]

While this socializing helped knit the volunteers together, it could
get out of hand, however, and this too needed management, sometimes policing. For the setup and dinner shifts the problem was that
the socializing sometimes distracted the volunteers on duty from
their jobs, like washing the dishes. This meant that sometimes dirty
dishes were left for the overnight crew to do. Not only was this not fair
but because there were always more volunteers on the setup and dinner shift than on the early evening shift, this made life for the volunteers on the early evening shift difficult. Virginia and Jim knew that
unless they did something about this, they would be in danger of losing volunteers on the early evening shift. So, as Jim noted, "we had to
restrict them a little bit and say don't come down unless you really
have something to do."[36] To their surprise they have also had to try
and clamp down on socializing on the midnight shift. One of the

things that they had to clamp down on was a card game among a few of the volunteers that would often run until 2:00 in the morning. This was in the late 1980s, and on the nights when two certain volunteers were on duty, they and some of the homeless men had a running poker game going. One night Virginia happened to go down to the shelter after midnight, and she found them out.

> I don't think they expected me, and there they were, sitting at the table, with all the lights on, playing cards. And I said, "What's going on?" And they said, "Well, we are having our usual game." And I said, "What do you mean our usual game?" And they said, "We play cards." And I said, "Not down here you don't play cards."[37]

The problem with this late night game was that it was keeping the rest of the homeless people awake, and it was keeping the overnight volunteers awake. The volunteers who were playing cards were not the overnight volunteers but rather the setup people who had never gone home. Virginia had to shut down the game or risk losing the volunteers who were trying to sleep. "If we don't have volunteers" she noted, "we don't have a shelter. We have to save our volunteer base. . . . the volunteers we need. We never run out of guests, but we need the volunteers to keep the guests."[38]

These restrictions tend to work for a time and then wear off; therefore, they need constant enforcement. Jim plays a larger role in this, as Virginia keeps away from the shelter as much as possible because she doesn't like being the bad guy. Jim's method of oversight is very casual. He likes to go down to the shelter and make Jell-O for everybody or just sit in a chair and read. This works for day-to-day oversight. For longer-term oversight, they have an end-of-year prayer service that helps the volunteers keep their focus on why they are volunteering. Jim, Virginia, and Harold decided early on that this was important for them to do. They hold this service after the shelter has shut down for the summer, and at this time all of the volunteers gather in the church to reflect on the past shelter season and on what they did or didn't accomplish. Jim said that he thinks that the prayer service is a good thing because it "refocuse[s] everybody's attention as to why the hell they [are] doing this." They are doing this, in his mind, because "this is actually what you are supposed to be doing."[39] Virginia added that

because of the prayer service, "they [the volunteers] all came together
and it wasn't cliquish [because] you couldn't save seats and you had to
sit at long tables." This way, as Jim noted,

> all the groups, all the crews that we had could meet each other. Because if you're
> on one crew, you'll never meet the overnighters or the early morning, you'll
> never see who they are. And this brought them all together and we could talk to
> each other about [our] experience and they could reminisce about stories.[40]

Links to Other Church Shelters

The Sacred Heart homeless shelter has also developed links to other
church shelters and their volunteers. These links began when two of
the original Sacred Heart volunteers left to begin a shelter at their
own church, nearby Ascension Lutheran. The links expanded when
Jim and Harold began what they called their "traveling road shows" to
other churches to educate them on how to open and operate shelters.
Some of the other shelters they helped open include Faith Lutheran
on Union Turnpike, which they share volunteers with, as well as Sacred Heart in Bayside, Grace Lutheran, Resurrection Ascension, St.
Matthias, St. Andrew Avalino, and St. Kevin's. Ascension Lutheran and
Sacred Heart operate as "sister churches," with Ascension Lutheran
opening on the nights that Sacred Heart is closed, and the two
churches shelter the same clients.

Creating the Opportunity for Face-to-Face Links
at Fifth Avenue Presbyterian

After the near death experience of the Fifth Avenue Presbyterian
Church shelter, which in Margaret Shafer's estimation was caused in
part by the fact that too few volunteers were doing too much of the
work, she made a rule limiting the time that the volunteer coordinator could stay at the shelter to a couple of times a month: "If the coordinator gets lazy about bringing other people in and just stays [him-
or herself], then you lose your pool really quick."[41] This was the situation that Peter Saghir was presented with when he began his tenure
as volunteer coordinator. Given the shelter's near death experience,
Peter, Margaret, and the church deacons are all concerned about making sure there are enough volunteers and that all of the volunteer slots

116 get filled. This concern, their primary one, coupled with the greater burdens placed on the volunteer coordinators at Fifth Avenue Presbyterian, have led the church to turn the volunteer coordinator position into a paid one. With the volunteer coordinator being paid, the expectations of this person are raised and the dynamics among the coordinator, the volunteers, and the shelter committee change. The most significant impact of this, from a volunteer management standpoint, is that the volunteers at Fifth Avenue Presbyterian are more like participants and less like co-owners of the shelter program.

In the face of the greater expectations, Peter decided that the scheduling process should be his responsibility alone, and that he couldn't share it with day coordinators. This meant that he would have to resort to different tactics to transmit information among people and to keep people honoring their commitments. As at Sacred Heart, the schedule is the means of dividing up the pie, seeing to it that everyone has something meaningful to do, guarding against free riders, and avoiding burnout. As Peter explained,

> I pretty much . . . wanted to maintain control of the phone numbers and the emails myself. I just felt that it needed to be centralized. This was "so people would know who to contact and speak to if they wanted to volunteer in the shelter, . . . so that they would . . . have a real point person, and know who to go to.[42]

So at the Fifth Avenue Presbyterian shelter, if somebody had to cancel, they would email or call Peter and he would find somebody else. At the same time he would sign the canceller up for another slot later that month or the next month. If he couldn't find somebody to fill the slot, then he would go in and volunteer himself. With the scheduling centralized, the hierarchy that Sacred Heart uses to convey a sense of ownership and to compel performance is not in place at Fifth Avenue Presbyterian. To compensate for this, and to make it in the interest of the volunteers to fulfill their commitments, Peter did a number of other things. The first was to keep the volunteers informed about the latest shelter developments, which he did through his newsy emails. Most of the news was of the men in the shelter—in a paragraph or two Peter gave an update on each of the guys, such as "Kenneth [one of the homeless men] is still playing the piano, and he en-

tertained us the other night."[43] Kenneth was known by all of the volunteers as an excellent piano player, so Peter would regularly high-
light his piano playing. Because of their age, the men at this shelter get
sick regularly and they have to go into the hospital, so Peter always
kept the volunteers updated on the status and the health of the men
in his news columns. The point of this was to build a sense of belonging among the volunteers. Peter also relied heavily on appeals to con-
science from Rev. Tewell in his sermons. Rev. Tewell is a strong be-
liever that Christian actions are an essential complement to Christian
faith and in his sermons he continuously reinforces the importance
of volunteering to the health of the Christian lives of the volunteers.
This builds a sense of obligation and it appeals to the self-interest that
the volunteers presumably have in their own salvation. What was perhaps Peter's most effective volunteer management strategy, however,
was to foster the relationships that develop between the volunteers and
their homeless clients in the Fifth Avenue Presbyterian Church shelter.

Margaret Shafer explained to me that among the volunteers at
Fifth Avenue Presbyterian there "is a real eagerness for friendships."[44]
This comes from the fact that the volunteers don't live in the neighborhood, that they are more mobile, and that they are more likely to
volunteer by themselves. All of these facts, and the rarity of spontane-
ous gatherings at the shelter in the evenings, makes it less likely that
the volunteers will bond with each other. Peter helped to foster this
natural tendency of relationships between the volunteers and the clients by planning events at the shelter. Hence the movie nights, bingo
nights, birthday parties, and trips to baseball games. As at Sacred
Heart, socializing seems the best way to build links among the people
in the shelter; the difference here, however, is that the socializing has
to be planned and the links run through rather than around the
homeless men. With this effort, relationships are developing and the
Fifth Avenue Presbyterian Church shelter is again doing the job of
linking people to each other. Through effective volunteer recruitment, retention by proper volunteer utilization and management,
making volunteering attractive, knitting the volunteers and homeless
clients together through social occasions, and giving people tasks so

that they feel ownership of the program, Peter and his successor have been able to rebuild the volunteer corps at the Fifth Avenue Presbyterian shelter, where other similar large Manhattan churches have had to shut theirs down. The size of the volunteer corps has grown to the point where Fifth Avenue Presbyterian is now lending volunteers to the shelter at nearby Rutgers Presbyterian so that they can open for another night. Furthermore, they are planning to lend volunteers to help Astoria Presbyterian, in Queens, open its shelter in the near future. Despite the success, however, the relationships are newer than at Sacred Heart, and they remain more tenuous as volunteers and the homeless men come and go.

Though this level of mediation, linking people with each other, is largely the domain of the church shelters, the Partnership for the Homeless plays a crucial coordination role. In the next section I will speak more about the role of the Partnership in linking people to power centers. Without the employees of the Partnership coordinating the massive transportation and supply schedules, training the volunteers, and overseeing the drop-in centers in their screening referral efforts, very few of the church shelters would be able to function.

Linking People to Centers of Power

The next step in the mediation process that the church shelters perform is that of linking people to centers of power. Without being linked to power centers, volunteering in these shelters would be, in J. Philip Wogaman's estimation, a purely sentimental exercise, one that would not effectively combat any of the crises of modernity. Wogaman explains the importance of the link to power centers as follows:

> When people feel alienated from social power, they may find some spiritual relief in group life, but it is the kind of relief that Marx was referring to when he called religion the opiate of the masses. Links between or among individuals cannot assuage the alienation that comes from being subjected to power one cannot affect. One may have a very fine neighborhood government or local community organization, but one feels alienated nevertheless when that government or organization is continually overwhelmed by outside powers over which it has no control, such as city hall, the feds, large corporations, or other large collectives.[45]

This is the aspect of mediation that gives it political importance, and it is perhaps the most difficult of the three types of linkage for the church shelters to accomplish. The difficulty lies in attracting the attention of the power centers and compelling them to be responsive. Some of the ways that mediating institutions have been able to attract the attention and responsiveness of power centers is through building up a large membership and through providing a support base for their leaders, the volunteer coordinators, so that they can build relationships with people in power.

In the case of the church shelters, the main centers of power that they can link to are the New York City DHS, the New York Police Department, the Fire Department, and the other city agencies that occasionally get involved in providing homeless services or deciding the fate of a shelter. Like linking people to each other, this is a multifaceted process, the elements of which include bringing enough voices together so that they become large enough to be heard by the city agencies; learning who the power brokers are and how to deal with them; getting the power brokers to listen and respond; and, if necessary, being able to go around obstacles to accomplish the task. In this aspect of the mediation process, the staff of the Partnership for the Homeless plays a significant role.

What has enabled the Partnership to effectively link its volunteers to centers of power in New York is the apolitical approach that it has taken to homeless service provision. While the nonprofit status of the agency by law precludes it from endorsing or campaigning for specific candidates, it could, if it wished, have an explicitly political and activist agenda in its work. By opting not to take this approach and to be apolitical, the Partnership has reaped two specific benefits. One is that the Partnership has been able to build a cooperative and collaborative relationship with the DHS, and the other is that the Partnership has been able to remove the church shelters from both neighborhood land use politics and from citywide social service advocacy politics.

By building the relationship with DHS, the Partnership and its volunteers have been able to collaborate with a big city agency to provide a social service. This is rare. In its effort to develop this collaborative relationship with people in power, the Partnership for the Homeless started with a major advantage, namely Peter Smith's wealth of connections. As Virginia Brown put it, "when Peter was still alive, he was very active, he was the Partnership. . . . Peter was the stone that built this thing—I don't care what anybody says."[46] Peter brought influential members of the city's business, religious, political, and charitable communities onto the board of directors of the Partnership to give the agency access and clout. With some hard work and salesmanship, Peter and the employees of the Partnership built a citywide operation that has had as many as 150 shelters operating at a time and has more than 500 churches and synagogues participating. The reason for this discrepancy is that there are instances in which a number of churches combine to support a single shelter. The Brooklyn Heights Interfaith shelter alone incorporates volunteers from six churches and synagogues in Brooklyn Heights. Many of the churches that joined the Partnership's network were influential in their own right. Churches with great wealth, history, prestige, and legacy such as St. Paul's, Fifth Avenue Presbyterian, St. John the Divine, and Marble Collegiate lent their already sizeable voices to that of the Partnership.

To make sure that the mayor and the heads of the city agencies noticed their size, Peter made a point of inviting the mayor and the heads of relevant agencies to Action Day every year so that they could see for themselves. With such a draw, hundreds and hundreds of volunteers always turned out. Making the Partnership large enough for the folks downtown to notice was one thing; affecting their actions was another. In the field of homeless services in New York, the Coalition for the Homeless set a precedent of confrontation with city hall as a means of affecting the city's actions. The Partnership took another tack, pursuing mutually beneficial cooperation. With up to 1,600 shelter beds open each night, the Partnership has been a major contributor in getting homeless people off the street. The DHS and the drop-in centers depend on the beds that the church shelters provide, so while the city agencies are the more powerful partner in these relationships, the church shelters have leverage because of their numbers and the importance of the service that they provide. Furthermore, their small, safe, and friendly shelters provide an alternative to the city shelters that the drop-in centers use as an incentive to prod homeless people into treatment. All this helped make Mayor Koch

and his successors and their administrations look good, it engendered
support, and it led to access.

The Partnership has avoided local land use politics by busing in carefully screened homeless people at night to stay in the basements of churches that have been in the neighborhoods for a long time and that have not been visibly altered. By doing this, the Partnership for the Homeless has been able to open shelters where others have not. This is especially so in some of the more conservative neighborhoods outside of Manhattan. Furthermore, because this is an apolitical service project carried out in a friendly and familiar environment, the Partnership and the churches have been able to involve large numbers of people who would not otherwise have considered working with homeless people. In this sort of operation, the volunteer's politics doesn't matter; all that is necessary is that they put in the time to do the job. The result, at Sacred Heart at least, is that they got volunteers "who were very conservative Christians and some that were charismatic, and they would talk out their differences; they would talk at night."[47] Starting from this advantageous, apolitical position, the volunteers in the church shelters have been able to devote their energy to their work with their homeless clients and have not had to worry about fighting community resistance or trying to build community support. Because they were not trying to subvert or change the patterns of relations in their community, they have also in some cases been able to function as rallying points around which their communities could be developed and strengthened.

While being apolitical, the Partnership for the Homeless has also purposefully maintained an independence from the city agencies that it works with. The most telling indicator of this independence is the fact that despite the city contracts it receives for outreach work and other programs, the agency works hard to make sure that the majority of its budget still comes from foundations and individuals. This independence is crucial for the agency to be able to stand in the middle—that is, to meditate. The wrong linkage at the wrong time can rob the institution of its ability to mediate. Prime examples of ostensible mediating institutions that don't actually mediate are the

community boards, one of which Jim and Harold declined to involve
in the formation of the Sacred Heart shelter.

The Mediating Role of the Drop-In Centers

A crucial component of mediation is the nine drop-in centers. Though they don't actually mediate themselves, their professional social service support enables the church shelters to operate. St. Paul's Chapel, as part of Trinity parish, has its own drop-in center, the John Heuss House, so it could operate on its own, but all of the other church shelters depend on separate drop-in centers to screen out inappropriate clients, keep clients who are using drugs and alcohol from coming to spend the night, refer clients to social services, and find housing for the clients who are in the shelters. The drop-in centers also feed the homeless people during the day, and their staffs work to support the volunteers in their efforts to help the homeless people keep on the track toward leaving homelessness. So important are these roles that the drop-in center that wasn't performing them adequately, the Moravian Coffee Pot, was shut down, largely due to complaints from the shelters.

The relationship between the shelters and DHS develops out of the interaction that running the shelters requires. This interaction starts once the shelter has passed inspection and opens. When a shelter opens, DHS sends out an introduction kit. At Sacred Heart, as at the other shelters, this kit contained 20 bed sheets, 20 pillow cases, towels, a few razors, and other sundries. While the volunteers donate many of the supplies, the beds, bedding, and towels are all provided by the city and they are laundered. Every week fresh bed linens are dropped off and the dirty ones are picked up and it is over such simple things as whether or not the shelter submits the correct numbers of bed sheets for laundering that complications can arise. Virginia portrayed one such complication for me.

In the early 1990s there was an incident in which someone at DHS had complained about how Sacred Heart was handling its bed linen laundry submissions. DHS was extremely precise about its laundry bagging rules. As Virginia stated, "You are only allowed to put 20 sheets into a bag, 25 pillow cases, and 20 towels. And it has to be

double bagged with your name on it [the name of the shelter]." Rather
than doing this, whoever had been bagging the dirty linen at Sacred
Heart was putting 25 dirty sheets in the bags instead of 20 and this,
she said, "messed up the tracking system that DHS used and made the
bags too heavy to lift." Furthermore, sometimes the bags accumulated
for a while before they got picked up from the shelter. It was after one
pickup following a time when the bags had accumulated for a while
that Beverly Koster, then an employee at DHS in charge of coordinating deliveries to the church shelters, called to say that the people who
picked up the sheets to bring them to the laundry had complained and
that someone from the shelter would have to start counting the linen
and getting the number correct or DHS would cut off service. Because
many of the homeless people who came to the shelter rarely showered,
neither Virginia nor the volunteers wanted to take the dirty bed linens
out of the bags and check how many there were and Virginia refused,
quite vociferously. "I said oh no, no, not me. I am not putting my hands
in those bags. I don't care what they say. I'll throw it out in the garbage
before I'll count those things," was her exact comment, and to Virginia's
surprise Beverly said, "Well, I'll have to come over and do it myself."
And that is exactly what Beverly did—she came to Sacred Heart and
sat on a chair in the basement and counted dirty bed linens.[48]

The frequent interactions between DHS and the church shelters,
though often without incident, serve to familiarize the volunteers
with city agencies and put a face on what would otherwise seem to be
a monolithic bureaucracy. These relationships also familiarize the
employees of the city agencies with the citizens of their constituents.
Because the relationships that develop are strong, when there are incidents, the individual shelters are usually capable of mediating the
situation themselves. When there are minor problems that can be re-
solved, they are actually not problems as much as they are relation-
ship-building opportunities. Sometimes the shelters need help from
the Partnership, however, if they are not able to get DHS to alter its
ways. This usually occurs when DHS decides to try new approaches to
supplying the shelters as a way, from their perspective, to simplify
things. Often the perspective from the shelters is different and inter-
cession from the Partnership is needed for DHS to understand this.

Virginia recounted a situation for me in which Laura, who replaced Beverly, called and asked Virginia what supplies she needed. After Virginia told her what the shelter needed, Laura replied that DHS was trying to cut down on the amount that they spent on delivery so they were going to send supplies for three months, rather than continuing to send them on an as-needed basis as they had been doing. This sounded fine to Virginia, until the first shipment arrived at the church: "I went over and these guys kept bringing in big cases. . . . She sent me a box of bar soap that we don't use. Two hundred bars of soap in it. Five hundred razor blades that I could have gone to New York to a flea market with. . . . Two cartons of toilet tissue. Everything was in bulk."[49] When Virginia saw all of these supplies she thought they had made a mistake and she called Laura to tell her that cases of supplies had been delivered in error. This was when Laura let Virginia know that this was not an error and that DHS was now sending supplies for three months at a time.

This, of course, was much more than a three-month supply for Sacred Heart, and they had nowhere to put everything. Moreover, DHS had sent some of the wrong things. For example, they sent bars of soap instead of liquid soap, and Virginia's explanation that in a situation in which you were sharing a shower with people that you knew, bar soap was fine, but in a situation in which you were sharing soap with total strangers, it was better to go with liquid soap. In any case, Virginia's complaints fell on deaf ears. The response from DHS was that the people at Sacred Heart should give whatever supplies they didn't want to others who could use them, and that they should just use the bars of soap.[50]

To help get Laura to understand why the soap bars were inappropriate, Virginia appealed to Bill Appel and Brenda Griffin at the Partnership for the Homeless. Their job is to mediate between the churches and DHS when the volunteer coordinators can't manage the mediation themselves. Bill and Brenda manage all of the paperwork that the volunteers would never have time to do and wouldn't be willing to do and they try to stop small frictions from becoming large ones. They can also explain to city employees why requirements that might make sense from the city agency's perspective are nonsensical to the volunteers in the church shelters. There are two employees at DHS whose job is to work with the church shelters and they are Bill and Brenda's contacts. Beverly Koster used to be one of them, but after working at DHS for a few years, she left and went to work for the Partnership. Now Laura is one of the two whose job it is to work with the Partnership and the shelters. Part of Brenda and Bill's job is to be the voice for the shelters on miscommunication, and where they can they get the city to change its operations so that the shelters can work more effectively.

Despite the difficulties that arise out of working with DHS, especially filling out the reports that have been deemed necessary for tracking the whereabouts and the situation of all of the homeless clients, at least DHS and the church shelters are trying to accomplish the same thing. Therefore, they have an interest in collaborating, and both sides are usually willing to change in order to make the relationship work better. This makes the mediation a relatively conflict-free process. That, and seeing city policy get changed and the actions of city agencies altered, even over such mundane and seemingly trivial matters as bars of soap versus pumps, makes the impersonal bureaucracies of the city more human and less alienating to the volunteers. Thus a crucial aspect of mediation takes place. The shelter volunteers interact from time to time with other city agencies that are less willing to change. In these occasionally antagonistic relationships, the challenge is to take on the city agency and compel change in a manner that does not jeopardize the good working relationships with DHS and does not hurt the program. For doing this, there are great advantages conferred by being under the umbrella of the Partnership. One example of such mediation was the time that Peter Smith took care of a problem that Sacred Heart was having with the Fire Department.

The incident began, Virginia suspected, because "somebody must have turned us in that didn't want the shelter there."[51] One night Virginia got a call at home from the priest, who said to her, "The Fire Department is down in the basement, and he said, you better get down here, and I told him, I said why am I getting down there, it's your church basement."[52] Because the shelter was the only group using the basement at the time, the priest wanted Virginia to go deal with the firemen. In the intervening years the shelter volunteers have cleaned up the basement, they have painted the walls, they have gotten the local chapter of the Kiwanis Club to get one of their members to replace the old termite-ridden floors with new cement floors, and the church basement has become a hive of activity. Before all of this, however, there was only the shelter down there, and in the priest's mind, the shelter volunteers were the ones responsible for the basement. Because he insisted, Virginia eventually had no choice but to go down to the basement to talk to the firemen. When she got there a fireman looked at her and said,

> Oh, lady, this is bad. And I said, what are you telling me for? Tell the pastor, it's not my business. And he said, well, you have a shelter down here for homeless people. And I said yeah [and they said] how many people do you have? Do they sleep here? And I said yeah. [And they said] Oh, no, you've got problems lady. And the main things [were] that we didn't have emergency lighting, we didn't have the signs for the exit, all the things like in a movie house. . . . He said you are going to have to go to court, and I said I'm not going to court. I said just give me that [the citation] and I gave it to the pastor, and he said you are going to court, and I said like hell I am going to court. . . . Because I said it is your basement and you are supposed to have emergency lighting. And they said, well, we will shut the shelter down, and I said I don't care what you are going to do, I am not going to court.[53]

The next morning Virginia called Peter Smith and told him about the incident. She told him what the firemen said and that she was being ordered by the Fire Department to go to court. Peter asked her why she was the one being ordered to court, and she told him that it was because the pastor had told the firemen that she was the one in charge. She finished off by declaring to Peter that she wasn't going to court and asking him to see if he could do anything. Peter did a lot. First, he spoke with the pastor, and he got him to agree to go to court, in his vestments. And as Virginia recounted,

> the pastor went [to court], and he got in front of the judge and the judge read the papers, or whatever it was, the citations that the Fire Department gave us, and he said this is nonsense, case dismissed. So Peter had to have gotten in touch with the judge and he made sure.[54]

Without Peter's mediation on her behalf, Virginia, like any other citizen, would have had to go in front of the judge, where in all likelihood she would have had a rough ride for violating fire codes, and

A month later a man from the branch of the Kiwanis Club that met at Sacred Heart heard about the problem that the shelter had with the Fire Department. He called Virginia and told her that there was a very active member of the club who was an electrician. This man came out to the church and put emergency lighting in the basement. He also said to Virginia, "You women shouldn't be walking in that dark place between the rectory and the church," so he lit the outdoors. Virginia continued, "Every time I say where is the bill he says I will send it to you, and he never sent it."[55]

In both of these instances the individual church shelter and the Partnership for the Homeless were functioning as mediating institutions, as both of them were working together to connect the people, in this case the volunteers who would have lost their shelter and the homeless people who would have been out on the streets, to sources of power. It is difficult to overemphasize the importance of the service delivery approach that the Partnership adopted for its ability to connect people to sources of power. This service delivery approach is a very different approach to attacking homelessness than advocacy work, which is the type of work that many of the high-profile homeless organizations in New York City do. Advocacy work is inherently divisive. The advocacy counterexample to the Partnership for the Homeless is the Coalition for the Homeless, which is the organization that Bob Hayes founded following his successful lawsuits against the city in the early 1980s. The focus of this organization is suing the city and, to the extent that they use volunteers, they use them to monitor city services rather than to provide their own. While they have won many suits, their ability to function as a mediating institution is doubtful.

By decoupling the provision of homeless services from the divisive politics of homelessness, the Partnership for the Homeless and the church shelters have built organizations that promote sociability, develop personal integrity, and socialize people into community norms. They have been able to do this among both the volunteers and the homeless men while providing a service for men and women

128 whose very presence, if left unattended, would indicate a failure of the social and political system. Because the volunteers have channeled their work through familiar institutions, they have taken feelings and emotions that might otherwise have developed into an antagonistic protest movement and instead focused them in such a way as to hold existing institutions accountable and strengthen the ability of existing institutions to perform the functions that they were created to do.

While the Partnership and DHS have managed to maintain a collaborative relationship, conflict has cropped up between other parts of the city bureaucracy and individual shelters. I already mentioned the difficulty that Sacred Heart had with the Fire Department and they are not the only church shelter that has run afoul of the FDNY. Aside from the estimated 80 to 100 churches that would like to open shelters but don't meet the fire code and can't afford the renovations, others that are in operation have been forced to shut down or move their shelters. For example, St. Bartholomew's had to move its shelter from the church's beautiful narthex to two nondescript rooms in the basement. Though everyone preferred the narthex, with its vaulted ceilings and detailed ceramics, it only had one means of egress—that is, only one way in or out—and the Fire Department insisted on two. Fortunately, St. Bart's is a big church with a lot of room, and they were able to use another room for the shelter, albeit one without much charm. A more serious conflict, however, has been the one between Fifth Avenue Presbyterian and the city over the church's Homeless on the Steps program.

The Conflict over the Homeless on the Steps Program

To save the Homeless on the Steps program, Fifth Avenue Presbyterian Church joined with the New York Civil Liberties Union to sue New York City in order to get the New York Police Department to stop harassing the homeless people who slept on their steps. The church suspects that the problems began when a few neighbors complained to the city about this program.[56] After the church allowed homeless people to sleep on its steps for two years, the city of New York, shortly after Thanksgiving Day 2001, informed the church that it would have to discontinue this ministry. Over the two years that this program had been in existence, as Margaret noted the church had developed good relations with the local precinct and with the beat cops. This policy switch was not the decision of the police, however, and as Bob Herbert noted in the *New York Times,* "a couple of the cops I spoke with at the church this week made it clear that harassing the homeless was not their idea of appropriate police work."[57] "The orders came from on high," said one officer whom Herbert spoke with, and this officer, when asked to explain the crackdown, "pointed toward the Fifth Avenue street sign [and said] 'They think it's bad for the area's image.'"[58]

Following the December 4, 2001, raid, Rev. Tewell sent a letter to the police commissioner and asked for a meeting the resolve the situation. Such a meeting did not take place, but at a subsequent meeting with representatives of the city "the church agreed to move the nightly arrival time of the homeless people to 9 P.M. from 8 P.M., to increase the services the church provided to get the people off the street and to try to find programs to feed the people at other locations."[59] Despite this progress, which the church hoped would allow the program to continue, there were three subsequent raids in December.

The city's opposition to the church's street outreach program, as stated by Daniel Connolly, the city's special counsel, is that Fifth Avenue Presbyterian is "in effect operating an illegal shelter by allowing the people to sleep outside in the cold and rain" with no heat or beds.[60] "They are basically running the world's worst homeless shelter," Connolly said.[61] "They provide absolutely nothing but permission to be there." This sort of program was not necessary, according to Connolly, because "The city's shelter system is not at capacity. There are beds with clean sheets available. . . . We can do better. It's not rounding up these people for arrest. It's providing meaningful social services."[62] "What the Police Department is doing," Connolly noted, "is enforcing those laws. Imagine the worst kind of landlord in a slum neighborhood providing this type of service."[63]

Fifth Avenue Presbyterian Church disagreed. Rev. Tewell opined, "I think we provide a wonderful resource for homeless people," and he noted that "A lot of people are afraid to go to city shelters because they are beaten up, harassed and abused. They know they are not going to be harassed or abused or approached sexually here."[64] In response to these raids, Fifth Avenue Presbyterian, along with the New York Civil Liberties Union, in a move never before undertaken by any of the Partnership's church shelters, sued the city in December 2001, asking for an emergency order to protect the people who sleep on its front steps from further police harassment. The church's lawsuit alleges that the city is violating its First Amendment rights, and those of the homeless people, "by depriving them of freedoms of association, religious expression and the 'freedom to be left alone.'"[65] The suit also accused the city of trespassing and of doing irreparable harm to the trust that the volunteers had built up with the homeless.[66]

Despite efforts by Rev. Tewell to reach an out-of-court settlement, the city would not budge and the suit went forward, with the Partnership for the Homeless signing an amicus brief. This incident illustrated that despite efforts to promote sociability, develop personal integrity, socialize people into community norms, focus and channel the attitudes of the volunteers in such a way as to hold existing institutions accountable, and strengthen the ability of existing institutions to perform the functions that they were created to do, sometimes confrontation is inevitable. The hope in this instance is that in the future, Fifth Avenue Presbyterian, its neighbors, and the city can rebuild a collaborative relationship that involves the requisite give and take and willingness to change.

Linking People to Sources of Meaning

Church shelters also link people to sources of meaning. Again, Wogaman outlines the importance of this specific linkage by noting that

> Human fulfillment in small associations is not enough, and a sense of historical accomplishment is not enough, if people cannot believe that their lives have enduring purpose and that the values by which they live have some ontological status. . . . Here again the mediating structure is very important.[67]

In Wogaman's estimation, the church, "when it is true to its nature, is the quintessential mediating structure in society."[68] This is especially the case for this third aspect of mediation because "religious groups are by definition the bearers of human tradition concerning

ultimate meaning and value; and by common practice they are organized in local, face-to-face, associational form."[69] From what I have
seen and from what I have heard from the volunteers, there are two
elements to this type of linkage. One is linking people to meaningful
pursuits; the other is linking people to meaning in an ethical or moral
sense. Church-based homeless shelters are good places for linking
people to meaningful pursuits, and sheltering the homeless is but one
of the many types of meaningful pursuits that Sacred Heart and Fifth
Avenue Presbyterian are engaged in. They aren't necessarily better at
this aspect of linking people to sources of meaning than other organizations, however. Instead, they excel in the second element, linking
people to meaning in a moral sense, and the church shelters are excellent at this linkage for three reasons. The first is that these shelters are
set in churches and churches are places in which people expect to be
confronted with the question of the enduring purpose of their lives.
People, therefore, come to church prepared to deliberate the issue of
meaning. Some even come prepared to do meaningful things. The
second reason is that by presenting such people with a task like working with the homeless, the church shelters confront them with a concrete situation that moves their deliberation from the abstract to the
real. Furthermore, and this is the third reason, the smallness of the
church shelters personalizes this concrete situation in a way that dis-
pels old myths and forges new ones. In the rest of this chapter I will
focus on these three aspects of the linkage to meaning.

This tendency of large numbers of Americans coming to churches
to find meaning is not new. Alexis de Tocqueville noted this in 1840
when he observed that

> there is no country in the world where the Christian religion retains a greater
> influence over the souls of men than in America. . . . In the United States religion
> exercises but little influence upon the laws and upon the details of public opin-
> ion; but it directs the customs of the community, and, by regulating domestic
> life, it regulates the state.[70]

For years, observers have been anticipating the decline in the central
social role of the church in American life, but so far this has not happened. On this subject, Seymour Martin Lipset noted in 1973 that statistics attest to "a continuous 'boom' in American religious adherence

and belief."[71] In the same vein Garry Wills notes that over the course of American history the presence of "religion does not shift or waver; [only] the attention of its observers does."[72] To make his case he cites the following figures and statements:

> Nine Americans in ten say they have never doubted the existence of God. Eight Americans in ten say they believe they will be called before God on Judgement Day to answer for their sins. Eight Americans in ten believe God still works miracles. Seven Americans in ten believe in life after death.[73]

Wills and Lipset, following Tocqueville, are not alone in acknowledging the widespread role of religion in contemporary American life, nor are they arriving at their conclusions because of any biases. As Wills notes, when the Social Science Research Council assigned Andrew M. Greeley the research task that would result in the publication of Greeley's *Religious Change in America* (1989), their assumption was that a study of religious indicators over the last 50 years would document the secularization of American life. Wills notes that Greeley demonstrated that no fair reading of the data could lead to that conclusion. Indeed, in a typical week 40 percent of the American population go to church and 90 percent say some form of prayer. When asked to rate the importance of God in their lives on a 10-point scale, in an international comparison only the Maltese outrank Americans with an average rating of 9.58 out of 10, to Americans' 8.21 out of 10.[74] Because of the moral authority that they possess, and because of the faith that Americans clearly have in them, religious (or faith-based) institutions are places in which Americans feel disposed to contemplate issues that they might not otherwise. While I have no empirical data for the volunteers in the church shelters, logic suggests that if they differ from the rest of the American population, the difference is in the direction of being more likely to go to church, praying more often, having more faith, and being more likely to feel that God is important in their lives. In short, if anything, the volunteers are more likely to go to church looking for meaning than other Americans, who themselves are already very likely to go to church to look for meaning.

For the people who attend churches with homeless shelters, willingness to contemplate meaning moves from abstraction to reality because of the presence of these shelters. For at least a few of the vol-

unteers the fact that a church was engaged in activities like sheltering
the homeless made the church more attractive to them. This is why
Peter Saghir became a member of Fifth Avenue Presbyterian. For others who were already members of their churches, like Jim Jones and
Virginia Brown, the homeless shelter represented an opportunity to
finally do something meaningful at their church. For years, as Virginia and Jim both noted, Jim and Harold had been members of the
Parish Council, and they had accomplished nothing. The homeless
shelter was their big chance to change that.

For many, the reality of the engagement with homeless people was
an opportunity to become a better Christian, a pursuit that constituted the enduring purpose of their lives. Gene Durant explained her
voluntary effort at the shelter by saying, "my family and I have common ground and a goal and we like to share with others who are not
as fortunate. It makes us appreciate what we have [and it] helps us
[to] be better Christians."[75] This desire to be a better Christian was a
very common one, and the following sample of citations gives a flavor
of this sentiment.

> Because I believe [that] the work of the shelter is an important part of the effort
> to deal with the homeless problem that we have in NYC and it is an important
> part of my religion.[76]

> I want to be a better person and Christian through giving of my time and attention to these men. I get as much out of this as the men do.[77]

> 1. Trying to see God in every volunteer and guest [that] I meet and to then serve
> God by serving those various manifestations of him. 2. Trying to have some of
> my spirituality rub off on others and vice versa. 3. Trying to perform a practical
> function of providing food and shelter to guests. 4. Performing work which is
> [a] good accompaniment to developing spiritually.[78]

For others, the homeless shelters gave them the chance to help
solve a social problem, which is itself a source of meaning. Ginger
More said that she volunteers because "I want to be part of the solution rather than a part of the problem of homelessness. I get a sense of
satisfaction by being of help. Besides, there is a kind of familial connection so I get a great deal out of it more than I give."[79] It may not
seem obvious to outside observers what she could mean when she
said that she gets a great deal out of it more than she gives. To her,
being part of the solution, developing a sense of satisfaction from

helping, and the building of a familial connection to the homeless people and to the other volunteers are all the benefits that she accrues because of her voluntary involvement and these all mean a lot to her.

For still others, the opportunity to alleviate human suffering and to be compassionate has had the most meaning for them. Steven Black noted that he wanted to "in a very small sense, help alleviate the burden of homelessness, and through a direct sense, have some compassion for these people with their problems."[80] Una Burden felt that her efforts were helping "those less fortunate live with some dignity."[81] Timothy Gold said that he was trying to "provide a sense of warmth and caring atmosphere for others less fortunate than myself. I truthfully enjoy providing community service for others in this world. We are all the same in the eyes of Jesus. I believe that on earth whether homeless or not, we need to support and care for each other. We need a greater sense of peace among all people, something which is on the decline."[82] Kenneth Rong simply said that he was volunteering because he felt "empathy for the plight of the homeless."[83] Dan Marina, on the other hand, was a bit more expansive in expressing a similar motivation when he said that he was "just trying to allow some women to have a nice safe and peaceful environment to get a good night's rest," that "letting them know that someone cares about them is important to me," and that "it's nice to have a connection with other New Yorkers who are not your immediate friends or family."[84] Dan also indicated that he felt an obligation to help the church by saying, "if I don't volunteer maybe no one else will and places such as this may have to close."[85] I will pick up this strand later, when I talk about feelings that the churches engendered in the volunteers.

There were a few volunteers for whom the opportunity to help homeless people in these shelters had an even more personal meaning. Kathy Rich said that she was volunteering "to give hope to homeless people" in part because "I have a fear that I may become homeless."[86] Frank Short felt similarly and he said, "I am trying to help those who need a hand to get back to a position where they can live an independent life. It is important to me to help because it is clear that everyone could be in the shoes of our guests if circumstances change."[87] The personal meaning of the work, for some others, didn't come simply out of fear of the potential for circumstances to change. They had actually been the beneficiaries of the work of the volunteers in the church shelters and they came back to volunteer themselves so that others could benefit in the way that they did. Elmer Jang said, "Volunteering at St. Paul's is helping me with my own personal gratitude." He continued by adding, "I am a recovering alcoholic (sober 13 years) and I find that many of the residents seem to identify with me and I with them. I don't advertise that I'm a recovering alcoholic but also I don't hide it from other recovering people."[88] Lloyd Green said, "I personally experienced the helpfulness of the program and [I] know it can work when properly utilized."[89] Brenda Lane "felt a need to lend a hand for this very worthwhile cause." This sort of work was important to Brenda because it "makes me feel good to be helping others."[90] Susan Mayhew "just want[s] to help those in need."[91] Bertha Rankin explained that she was volunteering because "I'm fulfilling a need to be helpful and [I] hope those unfortunate enough to be homeless will realize that there are others who really care about them."[92] Although Bertha, a 73-year-old widow and lifelong resident of Glendale, had not been into "the city" (as Manhattan is often referred to in New York's outer boroughs) in 25 years and although she told me that she did not want to have anything to do with what went on in the city, she didn't look at homelessness as one of the things in the city that she didn't want to have anything to do with. Instead she looked at the homeless shelter as a place where she could go and care for unfortunate people who needed her help. For her, this was a meaning of the church shelter: it gave her the opportunity to help the unfortunate and to convey a message to them.

As the volunteers settle in to their positions in these shelters, homelessness becomes something personal for them. In these small and safe little shelters, volunteers get to know people who they might find intimidating or frightening in another setting. Pat Collins, for one, noted that he had long thought about helping homeless people but he knew there was no way that he could have just found someone at a subway station and brought them home. He could, however, volunteer to help that person, or someone very similar, in the Sacred Heart shelter. For him, the meaning of this personalization was that the way in which he regarded homeless people began to change. I will talk about the meaning of this change at length in the next chapter, but here I will say that for Pat, volunteering in the shelter changed the homeless people from faceless, dangerous people to people who have problems and who, with his help, were trying to solve them. The people hadn't changed, but Pat's perception had.

Daily, face-to-face confrontation with a group of destitute people on whose lives one is having a positive and visible effect will have a powerful effect on even the least reflective person. The particular poignancy of this homeless crisis is that it so literally illustrates the double crisis of modernity that Berger and Neuhaus refer to. Because of the social and individual choices that have been made, a compound crisis exists in which poor, disaffiliated individuals find themselves living a horrible existence on the streets of the major cities of a wealthy country. The homeless people suffer an individual crisis of modernity in a way more severe than the rest of us, as their dislocation and disaffiliation is complete. At the same time, the other inhabitants of the cities in which there are significant homeless populations and who are compelled to interact daily with these destitute individuals are confronted by a political crisis. In face of this destitution and powerlessness, most of the residents of these cities see no way that their actions can improve the desperate lives that they are confronted with. In this situation many people become disenchanted and alienated from the governing institutions of the city, which themselves seem incapable of solving homelessness. That is, except for the church shelter volunteers. Antionette Canelli reflected on the meaning of this personalization of homelessness to her as follows:

> I feel that if we can give hope and responsibilities to the homeless, then they would change. Most people have given up hope when they are in that situation. They need help and guidance on what to do next to help themselves. Then they need encouragement that they have what it takes and can get themselves out of the situation. While at the shelter they should be given odd jobs to make them feel important, to help them believe that they have what it takes to make it in this world. God didn't have time to make a nobody, only a somebody. When we can help another believe that about themselves by giving them responsibility and encouraging them by also helping them with faith then we can develop people to have pride and move on. I also believe that they would want to help others.[93]

Earlier in the chapter I identified the double crisis of modernity as both an individual and a social crisis. The individuals are susceptible to alienation, disaffiliation, and disenchantment, and society faces political, cultural, and moral crises. Despite their failure to solve homelessness, so far the work that these shelters are doing is an antidote to these crises. To explain why I make this claim, an exploration of the scope and roots of this crisis is in order so that the work of the shelters can be put in a meta-historical context. To start, consider Robert Nisbet's 1953 outline of the scope of the problem. Nisbet notes that in modern societies there are many people who have experienced what he calls a dislocation from the functions of "the extended family, neighborhood, apprenticeship, social class and parish." Historically, he notes, the relationships that existed in these settings were both deep and inclusive because they had functional significance. What he meant by this was that even if informally, the family, the neighborhood, the parish, and the other social settings that he mentioned had authority, and they performed important social functions. He explained the part about authority in the following way:

> By authority I do not mean power. Power, I conceive of as something external and based upon force. Authority, on the other hand, is rooted in the statuses, functions, and allegiances which are the components of any association. Authority is indeed indistinguishable from organization, and perhaps the chief means by which organization, and a sense of organization, becomes a part of the human personality. Authority, like power, is a form of constraint, but, unlike power, it is based ultimately upon the consent of those under it; that is, it is conditional. Power arises only when authority breaks down.[94]

Because the social settings had authority and because they performed important social functions, they had meaning in the lives of individuals. Having function, they could create a sense of individual function, which is one of the two prime requirements of community.

To Nisbet, the separation of the individual from the traditional functions of community and the status and allegiances that come from membership in a functional association are the root cause of the crisis of modernity. The roots of this dislocation, and the nature of the traditional functions of community that were usurped, were most famously outlined by Ferdinand Tonnies in 1887 when he put forward his famous distinction between gemeinschaft and gesell-schaft.[95] Surveying the changes that industrialization and urbanization were bringing to his native Germany, Tonnies developed these two ideal types to categorize the way German society was and the way that it was becoming.

Gemeinschaft is the term to describe the old ways of preindustrial German society. To Tonnies gemeinschaft developed out of preindustrial villages where the residents were kin. Social relations in these villages were intimate, enduring, face-to-face, and multistranded.[96] People were dependent on each other for virtually all of their daily needs. If a house needed to be built, if a sick family member needed to be taken care of, if children needed to be educated, if bandits needed to be repelled, if the crops needed to be harvested, it was the people in the village who performed these essential social functions. The villages were ruled by solicitous, paternal authority, people were secure and rooted in the permanence of place, and their work revolved around their crafts and their folk art. They produced what they needed and hopefully a bit extra for any hard times to come. Invariably your spouse would have been from the village, as would your children's spouses. The line demarcating public life from private life, if it existed at all, was a thin one. The concept that Tonnies used to characterize the ethical basis of this sort of society was natural will. The will, which was the will of the people in the village, developed organically and authentically out of the daily interaction of the people in the village. Part instinctual and part rational, this will was the moral basis of village life and of the community, and it was embedded in the local traditions, customs, and symbols. Tonnies believed that the community, the gemeinschaft, was a means to an end, with the end being survival and hopefully prosperity.

Gesellschaft, on the other hand, was the future. This was the descriptive term for the social relations that were developing in the new urban settings. Social relations in these settings were turning out to be impersonal, fleeting, and unidimensional. People that you worked with were not necessarily the same people who lived near you, and they were not even necessarily your friends. Your private life was now separate from your public life. If you got sick, you could now go to the hospital, hopefully, and there were now a whole host of other institutions, often state run in Germany, that were created to perform the social functions that the people of the village used to perform informally for each other. Sometimes as well, in the big city, these same functions, especially for the poor, just went unperformed. The ethical basis of this social order was what Tonnies called *rational will*. This will was contractual and it was amoral. Rules and procedures that were developed by courts and by large institutions increasingly governed your daily life and it was very unlikely that you had played any role in developing these rules.[97] Science had displaced craft and traditions; symbols and customs were being overturned. Where community was enduring and personal, association was temporary and impersonal. The metaphor that Max Weber soon developed to describe this world was the *Iron Cage.*[98]

Despite protestations to the contrary, in which he recognized the limitations and the tyranny of village life, Tonnies's dislike for the modern industrial world was evident, as was his nostalgia for the past. In his conception, the shift from the village to the city brought about by industrialization had demolished communities, substituted the artificial for the organic, and torn people away from what had always been the foundation of their social lives. Tonnies saw little hope for an emotionally satisfying life for modern man with this arrangement. Critics were quick to point out Tonnies's naive idealization of the old ways—and an enduring portrayal used to counter Tonnies was Karl Marx's characterization of the idiocy of village life in 1848 in *The Communist Manifesto*. People in the villages, according to Marx, were enslaved by a feudal system that exploited them, and by their own parochial world views that prevented them from understanding that they were being exploited and that they should and could work to do something about it. Where Tonnies saw virtue in the old ways, Marx saw backwardness. Where Tonnies saw natural will, Marx saw serfdom. As Tonnies became the best-known first skeptic of modernity, Marx became the best-known first optimist. While Marx's optimism was based on his vision of the potential of the future and the reality of the past, Tonnies's pessimism was based on his vision of the reality of the present and the potential of the past.

As time has gone on, many urban sociologists have tempered both the pessimism of Tonnies and the optimism of Marx. This is especially the case in America, where we have neither the centuries of village-based tradition nor the historic unity of Germany, such that we are the most future oriented of societies. American urban sociologists began pointing out that communities, albeit different ones than the kin-based communities that Tonnies was familiar with, could be formed in cities, and that people could develop methods of living happy lives there. These sociologists also felt that there was no way to attain the ideal world of Marxism. Worse than that, the attempts that had been made to attain this ideal world ended up creating new problems that were as bad as or worse than the ones that they set out to replace. Of course critics and optimists remain, but most urban sociologists have tempered their visions in relation to these starting points. On the question of the potential for community in urban settings, for example, writers such as Jane Jacobs and Herbert Gans have argued that, over time, city neighborhoods can indeed become sources of community and emotional sustenance.[99] To drive home his point, Gans, in a nod to Tonnies, described such places as *urban villages.*[100] Despite their resurrection of the term *community* in a modern urban context, however, urban sociologists continue to be virtually united in the view that modern life is dislocating and that this constitutes a crisis to which we must find a solution.

Exactly why this crisis of modernity is upon us, and how severe it is, is a matter of debate. There are, of course, die hard individualists who deny that this crisis exists at all, but putting them aside, there are many different theories as to why people in America today feel alienated, disaffiliated, and disenchanted. Some blame America's remarkable mobility and say that we relocate too often for any real roots to take hold.[101] Others argue that dislocation is the result of the demise of the nuclear family and the attachments that come from having children in the local school and a stay-at-home mother who could carry the burden of community maintenance.[102] Some note that entertainment-related technological developments absorb more of our free time, thereby leaving us less time for social pursuits in public spaces.[103] Even household architecture has been blamed for the demise of socializing by architecture critics who point to the lack of front porches in modern houses and to so-called "snout houses" in which the street face of the house is dominated by the garage.[104] Others note that the fact that working people spend more time commuting to and from work and are increasingly likely to work somewhere other than where they live leaves them little time to do things in their neighborhood and leaves them less inclined to know their neighbors anyhow.[105] Still others, more controversially, argue that with the increased role of state social service provision in areas that used to be the realm of the family, relatives, and community organizations, people have less reason to get involved in the place where they live, so they don't.[106] What may have started out as state benevolence, according to this argument, ends up as state usurpation. The public sector eases the private realm out of some of its formerly primary roles, with the end result being alienation and dislocation of individuals who find that the megastructures are not a replacement for the personal touch. Whatever the reason, Berger and Neuhaus, Wogaman, and others see mediating institutions as part of the solution.

Conclusion: Do the Shelters Meet These Challenges?

The quick answer is that it depends on which challenge you look at. What the church shelters do very well is connect people to each other and to sources of meaning. They connect the volunteers to other volunteers and they connect them to their homeless clients. What the church shelters do moderately well is re-affiliate the disaffiliated. In association with the drop-in centers and the Partnership, homes are found for many of the homeless people. What the shelters do least well is to connect people to sources of power in a way that they can have an influence on those in power.

While the shelter program of the Partnership does connect volunteers to people in power, it is usually only the more active volunteers like Jim and Virginia and Peter who form relationships with power brokers. These relationships do enable the volunteers to do things like get DHS to change its bed sheet pickup policy, but as the case of the Homeless on the Steps Program at Fifth Avenue Presbyterian Church illustrates, they have a harder time getting those in the higher reaches of the city administration to substantively change their policies or approaches. Even a wealthy church like Fifth Avenue Presbyterian was not able to engage in a discourse with the mayor that resulted in a mutually acceptable outcome. The result of this was the lawsuit, which the Partnership joined in by submitting an amicus brief.

Of all of the mediating activities, the one that is least fair to judge the shelters by is how successful they are at finding homes for the homeless. In the system that the Partnership for the Homeless has set up, this is not their responsibility. Instead, it is the job of various employees of the Partnership and of the drop-in centers. Nonetheless, some of the volunteers do judge their shelters this way, and when they don't see progress, they get frustrated. Margaret Pender, for example, said that she began volunteering because of a desire to be part of the solution, but that she was feeling frustrated by the length of time that it was taking for the shelters to reach this solution. As she noted, "I am actually at this time disenchanted with the shelter program because it seems self-perpetuating. Guests are entrenched. I've seen the same men year after year. [There is] no movement, no improvement in their lives."[107]

Because of this, the shelters are forced to react, and different shelters react to this potential problem in different ways. In their efforts to try to keep up the spirits of the volunteers, most of the shelters imposed a time limit on how long guests can stay. For some the time limit is official and for others it is unofficial, but generally it is from six months to a year. The places that have the shorter time limits are usually those that get homeless people whose lives are in better order, like St. Paul's, and those that have the longer limits are the shelters that get the more difficult clients. Of course, supporting the motivation of the volunteers is not the only reason for the time limit. The limit is also important because it helps keep pressure on the homeless guests to make necessary changes in their lives in order to move into an apartment and become self-supporting. This is something that I will talk about more in the next chapter.

At St. Paul's, as Joe Pace informed me, they initiated their six-month time limit after they had been operating for a few years and noticed that some of their clients were becoming a bit too comfortable in their new home. The point of this time limit, in his eyes, was to "encourage the men to view their stay as a temporary one, and to encourage them, as much as possible, to find either jobs or housing." Joe thought that it made sense to start out from the premise that the shelter is transitional, "because as often is the case with human nature you can get into a situation where you are comfortable, and it becomes a routine, and it becomes a disincentive for you to pick up the pieces and get on with your normal life." Without making a rule that the shelters were transitional, Joe noted that there were people he had seen for whom the shelter "really became their normal life." While this was so, Joe also acknowledged that there had to be exceptions, such as in "situations where if the person is making a diligent effort to find housing or work, or both, particularly housing because that is the important thing, and they have been unsuccessful in doing so." In such situations, you "have to treat each person on an individual basis." And St. Paul's did make exceptions, as was the case with one older man who couldn't make it on his own in the outside world and who ended up living at the shelter for a couple of years and then he died there.[108]

The effect of the time limit at St. Paul's was that there was turnover, and this was good for the volunteers to see. Sacred Heart imposed a time limit as well, and at one point they also switched their affiliation to a different drop-in center in hopes of getting guests who were more capable of making progress in their lives. Jim and Virginia said that they switched affiliations because they found that the volunteers "were getting stale because we were getting [clients] from Moravian and we were getting older people." These clients had little energy and because of this, the volunteers "weren't seeing any movement . . . they weren't seeing anybody getting anywhere. They were seeing the same people from year to year." With the switch to the Neighborhood Coalition for Shelter, on Manhattan's Upper East Side, Sacred Heart got a younger clientele and the volunteers were now able to see that "there's movement, that somebody is getting an apartment, that somebody is getting out of the system." This, Jim figured, "helped the volunteers a lot to refocus their attention; yes, we are doing something good because somebody is not coming back."[109]

Imposing time limits and switching affiliations to a different drop-in center is not the ultimate solution to the problem that Margaret is identifying, but shelters use these tactics to put pressure on the drop-in centers, the Partnership, and the homeless men and women to find housing. They also use these tactics to make sure that the homeless people do not treat the shelters as if they were a permanent housing option. The irony of this is that meeting the needs of the homeless people, which is the core task of the volunteers, is only a means to the end of connecting the volunteers to each other and to sources of meaning. Time limits, as it turns out, are a good tactic to use to prevent the volunteers from becoming dispirited. Preventing the volunteers from becoming dispirited is a key part in getting them to continue volunteering and this creates the opportunity for the shelters to perform the tasks that they do well.

The volunteers attest to the fact that in the shelters they get connected to others and they find the sort of emotional sustenance and meaning that is otherwise missing in their lives. While the relationships and communities that they form in these shelters are not those of a gemeinschaft, at least not in a manner that Tonnies would recognize, they are intimate, they are enduring, they are face-to-face, and they are multistranded. The volunteers in the shelters may not be each other's kin, but over time, and through shared effort, they develop close attachments with each other. The volunteers themselves do not find homes for their homeless clients, but they play an important part in a program that does. While the Fifth Avenue Presbyterian Church might be struggling in its attempt at linkage with and influence on the mayor, the church shelters are very able to link people to each other, they are able to link them to sources of power, and they are very successful in linking them to sources of meaning. Importantly, the shelters help the volunteers make these linkages in a manner that does not require them to be heroes or go too far out of the orbits of their daily lives.

The shelters have also proven themselves to be quite capable of connecting their homeless clients to other people and to sources of meaning. In evaluating the work that the Fifth Avenue Presbyterian shelter did in meeting the needs of its clients, Peter Saghir said that in his opinion, they were meeting the most important needs, which he saw as being to "give the guys this environment, this community." With their movie nights and their birthday parties, because the volunteers know all of their client's names, because the homeless guys come in every night and see a familiar face from a consistent volunteer, because the volunteers show up at the hospital to visit clients when they are sick, Fifth Avenue Presbyterian is able to give their clients a "surrogate family feeling" and a "sense of community." This is what Saghir thinks they are able to do the best at their shelter.[110]

While these crises of modernity, as described by Tonnies, Nisbet, and Berger and Neuhaus, seem to be massive problems that small volunteer programs like these are ill suited to address, Peter's comments in effect inform us that the exact opposite is true. By doing a good job at the task of providing the homeless clients with love, support and a surrogate family, the volunteers end up providing the same things for themselves. Moreover, through their efforts in these settings, the volunteers have regenerated the productive capacity of their private lives, and in so doing they address the political, cultural, and moral social crises of modernity that I spoke about at the beginning of the chapter.

There is a tendency, Tocqueville noted, that comes along with democracy and equality, which leads people to think that they "owe nothing to anyone" and to "willingly fancy that their whole destiny was in their hands."[111] Because of this tendency, "not only does democracy make each man forget his ancestors but it hides his descendants from him and separates him from his contemporaries; it constantly leads him back toward himself alone and threatens finally to confine him wholly to the solitude of his own heart."[112] With people thus isolated in their own individualist views, their private lives would be isolated from any public function, and people would lose the capacity to act in concert to solve social problems as they arose. Without the ability to solve their problems, citizens would be independent but weak. While aristocracies could count on a few great people to do great things when needed, in democracies there was no such fallback position. Rather, democracies were faced with one of two choices. There was what Tocqueville thought was the natural inclination of abandoning the care of common affairs to the state, or there was the option of developing the habits of cooperation among the citizens by having them work to administer their common affairs themselves. He was disturbed by the fact that in America he saw the former beginning to happen as he observed governments stepping in and usurping the productive role of associations.

In his travels in the United States Alexis de Tocqueville saw that through participation in the civil associations that were still involved in public life, citizens could be "drawn from the midst of their individual interests, and from time to time, torn away from sight of themselves."[113] He wasn't claiming that the grand affairs of state should be turned over to the citizens but rather that "by charging citizens with the administration of small affairs, much more than by leaving the government of great ones to them, one interests them in the public good and makes them see the need they constantly have for one another in order to produce it."[114]

This then is one of the great social benefits of mediating institutions. While they may not have solved the homeless problem, and while they may not always work collaboratively with the city, the Partnership shelters do draw people out of their isolation, they do develop the productive capacities of their private lives, and they do teach their participants to look beyond themselves and to attend to public affairs. For New York, the result of the efforts of these shelters is that more citizens are capable of playing an important public role. For the individual volunteers, the result of their effort is that they are less isolated, better informed, and more capable of taking action to improve their own city. This change undoubtedly has many effects on them, with perhaps the most important being that it develops their sense of morality.

5

The Moral Effects of the Volunteer Experience

We tell ourselves stories in order to live. . . . We look for the sermon in the
suicide, for the social or moral lesson in the murder of five. We interpret
what we see, select the most workable of the multiple choices. We live
entirely, especially if we are writers, by the imposition of a narrative line
upon disparate images, by the "ideas" with which we have learned to freeze
the shifting phantasmagoria which is our actual experience.[1]
It is a good idea to get someone rehabilitated. It's a moral duty; everyone
has to help.[2]

As the volunteers learn to dispel abstractions about homelessness and,
to borrow Karl Barth's phrase, as they develop the ability to see the
man in humanity and the humanity in man, they begin to search for a
moral lesson in homelessness.[3] This is a search that develops the volunteers' sense of morality and their sense of moral duty.

I use *morality* here in the manner that T. M. Scanlon does, which is
that morality is the conception that we each hold within us about
what we owe to each other as fellow members of the same society.[4]
Robert Wuthnow defines morality similarly as being a set of codes
that "define the nature of commitment to a particular course of action."[5] These codes are "the whole set of principles that govern, or
should govern, an individual's relations with the other people within
a community."[6] Our conception of what we owe to each other and
these principles that govern our relationships with each other are
what I mean by morality.[7]

Building on this definition, Wuthnow notes that these moral codes
are socially constructed, at least in part. By this he means that although every society has some notion of what its members owe to
each other, the particular details of what constitutes a fair deal vary. It
is these details that are constructed through social interaction. So, for

example, while Canadians and Americans would both likely agree that as members of their respective societies they owe something to their fellow citizens, what the Canadian thinks he owes to his fellow citizens is likely to be different than what the American thinks he owes to his fellow citizens. The interactions that happen in the church shelters develop the volunteer's moral senses by affecting their conceptions of what they owe to their homeless clients, and it is this development that I am going to examine in this chapter.

The Stages of Moral Development in the Shelters

Like most social processes, the process of moral development among the volunteers in the shelters has noticeable stages. These include learning to see the humanity in the homeless people; learning about the importance of the development of a moral order in the shelter; learning more about why people become homeless; developing a sense of unsentimental compassion; and, finally, forming opinions about what needs to be done in order for someone to cease being homeless.

Seeing the Homeless as People

For the shelter volunteers, this stage in their moral development begins with encountering homeless people in a situation in which they have never encountered them before. In the safe, small, and domestic confines of the church shelters the volunteers and the homeless people get to know each other and the volunteers learn to see "the homeless" as "homeless people." Before they begin volunteering, the volunteers are likely to have had some version of the combination of feelings about the homeless that Joe Pace had—revulsion, some degree of fear, and an element of compassion. Apprehension also factors into the feelings that a lot of the volunteers have when they begin volunteering. This is certainly what I felt before spending my first night at St. Paul's. Jim Jones and Harold Brown had a great deal of apprehension going into the first night of operation at Sacred Heart, some of which, as the already mentioned story from Jim illustrates, was caused by misinformation.

> The first night that we had the shelter open, it was terrible. There is a couple in
> the parish who have a son who is a priest, and he dealt with homeless families, . . .

so Harold and I felt that he could teach us some things and tell us what was going to happen. So Harold and I went to talk to him and he said, "Well, who is going to search them for guns and knives and take their drugs away?" And Harold and I turned to each other and said, "What, what guns, what knives?" So we were very shaken up.[8]

On that first night, the fear of the volunteers was compounded by the fact that they were about to host women who were mentally ill. They weren't severely mentally ill, but they nonetheless had problems that the people in the Sacred Heart parish were not accustomed to working with. What helped the volunteers to begin overcoming that fear was familiarization in a safe setting.

Exposure over time changed the perceptions of the volunteers, however, and Pat and Gene Durant, from Sacred Heart, spoke eloquently about the perceptual change that Pat had as a result of working with homeless people in the Sacred Heart shelter. Pat remarked to me, as I recounted in chapter 3, that for years he had seen homeless people in the subway and at work, and that he had always wanted to do something about it but felt powerless. That is, until he and his wife Gene found out about the Sacred Heart shelter and began volunteering there. Once they began working at the shelter, the following change took place in their outlook:

> Pat: When you see them in the street they are kind of like faceless people, but when they come down here, take off their coat, jump in the shower, sit down and eat. . . .
>
> Gene: They've got needs, they've got wants, they've got names. You know, they hurt, they're cold, you're making them warm, you're helping them get clean, you know it's not like the box people that you see in Manhattan that you just pass by and you go eewh!
>
> Pat: Although those are the same people. But when you get to see them on this level, they are not all junkies, thieves, and murderers. They are people that have problems, whatever they are, and they are lucky enough to be here.[9]

For Pat and Gene, homeless people were transposed from being faceless junkies, thieves, and murderers to being people with problems. They were the same people, which Pat realized, but he looked at them differently now. Pat implicitly and explicitly recognized that there were a number of factors that affected why he came to look at the homeless people in the shelter differently. To begin with, there was the change in perception from the abstract group level of "faceless people," "the box people that you see in Manhattan that you just pass by," who seem like "junkies, thieves, and murderers," to the personal individual level of "people that have problems, whatever they are."[10] The homeless people themselves were still homeless, but he now knew them better. The change in setting enabled a change in relationship, one in which Pat went from perceiving "the homeless" in the third person plural to seeing homeless people in the first person singular.

Jim and Virginia shared a similar story when they explained how time, exposure, and familiarity reduced the fear that they, and others in the neighborhood, had of the homeless people in their shelter. On the first night that Sacred Heart was open, Jim and Harold, scared by the priest who mentioned that they would have to take knives, guns, and drugs away from their homeless guests, took extra precautions. These precautions led to a series of comical misadventures, which I have already mentioned but which are worth repeating as they are integral to the beginning of the process of developing an understanding of the homeless people in their shelter.

On the night that Sacred Heart opened it was raining outside and Christine De Angelo and Irene Apple were the overnighters. Harold and Jim, who had been so frightened by what the priest told them, went down to the church basement and took all of the knives out of the kitchen. They then put a big carving knife under Irene Apple's pillow, without telling her, and they turned down the lights in the basement to make it feel homier. No sooner had they done this than, as Jim recounted, "who should walk in but five Black ladies, in this lily-white neighborhood, and we looked at these ladies walking across the church basement and thought, 'What the hell have we done?'" Jim and Harold were so nervous that they called the shelter every half hour until 11:00 to make sure that everything was all right.

Because of the rain, one of the female guests that night was wet and she asked if she could dry her clothes. Irene Apple said she would help her. As she got up out of bed, she felt the knife under her pillow and she took it out. Because the shelter had no dryer, Irene turned on the oven and hung the woman's clothes in the kitchen, near the oven, to dry. This set off the smoke alarm, which woke up the other volunteer and the rest of the clients. As they were all running around trying to get the alarm to go off, including the one naked woman whose clothes were hanging in the kitchen, the pastor dropped by to pay a visit. In all of the excitement, Irene forgot that she had a knife in her hand. The scene that greeted the pastor as he arrived in his church basement was one of smoke, the smoke alarm, a woman running around stark naked, and one of his parishioners with a knife in her hand.

Virginia tried to put some of this in context by telling me "you have to realize that when we started in 1983 we were getting people that came out of the [mental] hospital, so these people had very big troubles." Mental hospitals or not, that was quite an extreme first night, and Jim observed, "We said if we can get over that night, we can get over any night." And get over it they did. It helped, both Jim and Virginia thought, that they had prepared people for the fact that they were getting psychiatric patients, and it helped that in the beginning they usually had three overnight volunteers per shift. This meant that there was always at least one person awake.[11]

In addition to always having one person awake, Jim and Virginia decided that they didn't want any of the volunteers to be in the position where they would be responsible for calling the police or an ambulance, so they made a rule that if any of the volunteers were having a problem that was getting out of hand, no matter what time it was, they could call Jim, Harold, or Virginia and one of them would come down to the shelter and manage the situation. This was something that both Virginia and Jim said they have only had to do once or twice, but they both think that it was an important decision for taking pressure off the volunteers.[12]

After the first month, the volunteers saw that they could handle this job, and by word of mouth it spread through the neighborhood that volunteering at the shelter wasn't so bad. As Jim put it, "when they saw that they weren't going to be knifed, that they weren't going to be killed, and that the ladies, even though they were psychotic, they were funny," people were much more eager to volunteer.[13]

After this hilarious near disaster, which would have made the Marx Brothers proud, Jim, Harold, Virginia, and the volunteers began to lose their fear of the homeless. This was in part because they saw that the homeless weren't as fearsome as they had initially thought, as least not the homeless who were being sent to their shelter. In the safe setting of their church basement the volunteers were able to start understanding this.

Creating Order and Respect in the Shelters

In addition to learning to see the homeless as people, the volunteers also learned how to handle themselves around their clients through experience and training. The volunteers also started to feel more comfortable because each shelter devised rules to minimize the risks to the volunteers and to provide a safe and supportive temporary environment for the homeless guests. The rules were critical, because with them the church shelters were able to create an atmosphere in which the volunteers and the homeless people could become comfortable with each other.

Pat Durant explained to me how his change in perception was not just the result of a simple change in venue, but that it was also a result of the slow day-to-day process of rapport building and the setting and reinforcing of rules and modes of behavior. At Sacred Heart, he observed, there was the constant potential for the volunteers and the clients to rub each other the wrong way, and there were clients who continually tried to push boundaries of acceptable behavior to see what they could get away with. "I think probably the biggest problem, as far as the rapport goes," Pat said "is [that] being from the street, they [the homeless clients] will see how much they can get away with." In face of this, the volunteer had to learn how to enforce behavioral boundaries. This is a skill that he noted many people did not have and had a hard time developing. Those sorts were not suitable to be shelter volunteers because, in his mind, rules and respect combined to create the homelike atmosphere and environment of the Sacred Heart shelter. This is an atmosphere that he felt the homeless people responded to very well and it was one that they learned to appreciate and welcome.[14]

Maintaining the rules and behaviors needed for a homelike atmosphere was a never-ending process, Pat noted. "If somebody gets out of line," he said, "it's addressed." Furthermore, "if these people start disrespecting one another they are asked not to come back." Of course

people do disrespect each other and get out of line and the volunteers
have to reprimand them, and the following pattern was typical:

> After an episode happens, they [the homeless people] walk on eggshells. . . . They
> are going to see what they can get away with, and [when] you put a stop to it,
> they know that, hey, this is as far as we are going to get with this guy, and that is
> as far as they'll go. And then there'll be a period of, you know where they're very
> quite, they're in bed early, they don't challenge anything. And then it will open
> up again and you'll have the interaction again. The longer they are here the more
> they feel like this is their home. But there are still rules.[15]

This dance of reprimanding people who get out of line and maintaining order is critical for relationship building in the shelters, which
in turn made it critical for the development of community in the
shelters. This is one of the main and most difficult roles that the shelter volunteers have to play. Learning to play this role takes time, as
volunteers have to learn how to do this dance, and this is one of the
reasons why maintaining continuity in the volunteer corps is critical
for the well-being of the shelter and for community generation.[16] All
of the participants needed to feel comfortable in a situation that they
could predict, and disrespect and disorder were antithetical to relationships.

Peter Saghir described the atmosphere at Fifth Avenue Presbyterian shelter in a somewhat different manner.

> You have to pay attention to security and stuff like that. . . . The guys are not
> children, . . . they are grown men, and . . . if we are going to expect them to be
> human beings—I am not trying to be all philosophical, this is obviously basic . . .
> we have to treat them like human beings, and give the same kind of respect.[17]

Despite the different approaches, with the parent-child relationships at Sacred Heart and the grandchild-grandparent relationships
at Fifth Avenue Presbyterian, both shelters could aptly be described as
households, and well-disciplined households at that. At Fifth Avenue
Presbyterian, the homeless men are old and less likely to get into any
trouble. At other churches this is not the case, and like recovery programs, these shelters need structure. Otherwise the clients will be trying to "get over" on the volunteers and anarchy could develop. After
volunteers have been on the job for a while, they become accustomed
to the fact that some of their guests may see what they can get away
with, so part of their on-the-job learning is to become more adept at

containing and disciplining such behavior. Modifying the behavior of the guests is a major part of the volunteer's job, and it is a major element in the job of creating what I call the moral order of the shelter.

Creating Moral Order in the Shelters

The moral order of the shelter is the set of rules and the codes of behavior that are acceptable in that environment. It is, in effect, the social contract for the shelter. The volunteers and the homeless people all play a role in forming this moral order, and they all have to comply with these rules and codes. This moral order is important for at least two reasons. One reason is simply to maintain order in the shelter. This is why there are rules. Most of the shelters forbid smoking, for example, and they all have curfews. Once the guests are on the premises, they are generally not allowed to leave until the next morning. There is no drinking allowed, nor is foul language tolerated. Everyone has to keep his or her bed and sleep area clean. Because most of the shelters have foldaway cots and most are one of many programs in their church utilizing the same multipurpose space, they don't allow the homeless people to keep any possessions at the church. The shelters that do have a dedicated space may have lockers for the homeless guests, and these shelters require the guests to keep their lockers clean and uncluttered.

Usually if the guests do something that is egregiously wrong, especially if the wrongdoing involves drugs or alcohol, they are supposed to be caught by the drop-in centers and removed from the shelter program. Sometimes the drop-in center misses some of these cases and the shelter screens these wrongdoers out. This is a double screen, and the volunteers learn that screening must happen or the whole enterprise may be jeopardized. Likewise, the volunteers learn that they must deliver on their commitments and that certain types of behavior are out of bounds for them as well. If the volunteers do something wrong, the wrongdoing is supposed to be caught by the volunteer coordinator and the volunteers are supposed to be reprimanded. As necessary as rules are, they aren't universally appreciated, as Joe Pace notes.

> A lot of turnover is based on . . . men who either don't like the program or get tired of the structure of the program, because it is very structured. There is also turnover because sometimes people move away; some of the men will get kicked

out of the program because they are not following the rules of the program. But there was a fairly stable, core group. The intention of course, at least in my understanding, is that this is a temporary measure so that if someone is down on their luck and having hard times, that they are there and it's structured, and it gives them an opportunity to have a roof over their heads while they get back on their feet and find either a job, or housing, or both.[18]

In this statement, Joe alludes to the second reason why the moral order is important, which is that the shelters are supposed to be therapeutic. This is why codes of behavior need to be developed. Within the structure of the rules, the volunteers and the guests develop relationships and ways of interacting with each other that are supposed to help rid the homeless guests of the sort of street behavior that Pat was referring to and instead train them in behaviors that they will need to maintain a job and an apartment. Developing codes of behavior is a learning process in which the volunteers and the guests struggle through trial and error to achieve the right mix of constraints and liberties. A significant component of this is the volunteers and the guests learning how personal they can get with each other. Some personal relations are necessary for such a confined operation to work, but if the relations get too close the therapeutic potential of the shelter will be jeopardized. Setting the tone for the nature of the relationships in the shelter is the job of the volunteer coordinator and, by extension, of the veteran volunteers. They are the ones who have been through this struggle in the past and they are supposed to socialize the new volunteers into the culture of the shelter and what is and isn't considered appropriate behavior.

Occasionally there are examples of relationships that are obviously inappropriate. There was, for example, the case of one female volunteer in a shelter at a large Manhattan church who began a sexual relationship with a homeless man from her shelter and moved him into her apartment. The volunteer coordinator at that shelter found out about this activity, and with the assistance of some of the staff of the Partnership for the Homeless, she fired the volunteer and found another placement for the boyfriend.

Such incidents are the easy ones to handle, as right and wrong are obvious to all. Usually, however, the relationship problems are subtler than that because they arise in the minute interactions that occur between the shelter volunteers and clients. These are harder to handle, as the wrongdoing is more amorphous, negative reactions are unanticipated, right and wrong are not as clear, and the learning for the future is not so obvious. Sacred Heart had one of those incidents when the volunteers tried and failed to throw an Easter party for their clients. In describing the incident to me Jim mistakenly began by saying that it was a Christmas party in which the shelter got presents and a Santa Claus and the clients didn't show up, but Virginia corrected him and said that it was Easter. I include this aside because this incident clearly continued to loom large enough in Jim's mind for him to mistakenly think that it had happened on a more major holiday than Easter. So instead of a Santa Claus and a tree and presents, the shelter volunteers had actually made Easter baskets and filled them with candy and painted eggs and they were going to surprise the guests with them when they arrived. But on that night, which was a regularly scheduled night for them to be open, nobody showed up, and the excited volunteers were left by themselves. "God punished us," Virginia said, recalling the letdown that they all felt. Jim and Virginia first described how the volunteers had made Easter baskets with eggs and candy and placed one on each bed to await their clients' arrival, and when no one showed up they got concerned that something had happened. To allay that concern, Jim remembered that "somebody called up Moravian," he doesn't remember who exactly, and the official at the Moravian center told the caller that they had been told that Sacred Heart was closed for the night. With concern put out of their mind, disappointment took over.

When I asked if they know who had called, both Jim and Virginia emphatically stated that it wasn't anyone from Sacred Heart. They later found out that it wasn't anyone from the Partnership either, so they were left to conclude that it had to be one of the homeless guests. When I asked why a client would sabotage a party that was being thrown for him or her, Jim said that he thought that it was because the homeless people felt that "we were getting too close to them" and that probably "they didn't want this emotional time of Easter. Maybe it brought back bad memories." Virginia agreed with this, and she explained to her daughter, Virginia, who was with us, that "it was very hard for them, Virginia. . . . They [the guests] must have seen them [the volunteers] making up these baskets and the whole bit and they just could not take it." So they brought the Easter baskets into the Moravian church and left them there, where the homeless people could get them anyhow, and Sacred Heart never planned an Easter party again.[19]

From this situation, the Sacred Heart volunteers decided that the meaning of this party gone awry was that "you can't get that involved . . . you can be friendly, but don't delve into their lives." The volunteers also came to believe that "they [the homeless guests] are on the street for a reason" and that as a result of being on the street they have erected barriers around themselves. *Barriers* was the word that the volunteers used, and Virginia said that they learned that "the only time we break through [a barrier] is when they [the clients] break through it." What this meant practically was, as Jim said, the volunteers only had real conversations with the clients when the clients wanted to talk and that the volunteers were instructed not to pry into their clients' lives. As Virginia, said, we "just leave them alone. When they get to know you well enough they will start to tell you what their problem is. And that's it." Any more, the volunteers feel, is none of their business.[20]

It was through accumulating experiences from situations like this that the Sacred Heart volunteers learned where the boundaries of their relationships with their homeless clients should be. By keeping a friendly, yet approachable distance, in which special events were the result of cooperative planning, the volunteers developed a workable moral order in their shelter. That their learning has been incremental is partially because they have been lucky and partially because they run their shelter well.

Other shelters have not been as fortunate in being able to learn incrementally, as they have had major incidents that forced quick learning. One such incident occurred at the shelter at Madison Avenue Baptist one cold night early in 1993. Because Madison Avenue Baptist Church was so close to the drop-in center that its clients come from, the Moravian Church center in this case, and because its clients were old and sedate and unlikely to get into any trouble, they were allowed to walk over to the shelter every night rather than take the bus. The first client who left the drop-in center brought the roster of those who were supposed to be spending the night at the shelter, and each guest was to initial the roster when he or she arrived. The roster functioned as the certificate from the drop-in center for the volunteers on duty to signify that the guests had all been screened and that they were all supposed to spend the night at Madison Avenue Baptist. This process, as it had been set up, constituted a double screen. A similar system was in place at all of the other shelters, and it worked well for many years, with all respecting the rules. That was until a new administration took over at the Moravian drop-in center and they started getting lax. One result was that they began occasionally sending out clients to the churches who were not sober. In a system of this size, occasionally there will be a problem of sobriety among the guests. This is especially so if the guests can walk over to the shelter themselves. But at the Moravian Church, sobriety problems were starting to become more frequent than at the other drop-in centers, and churches began complaining about it. This is one of the reasons why this drop-in center was shut down. Still, with the double screen, the volunteers should have done their part and rejected any client who was high or drunk. Usually this system works just fine, and it is not at all unusual for a guest to be rejected from a shelter by one of the volunteers because of his or her condition or behavior. This happens all the time. One cold night, however, the new volunteer coordinator at Madison Avenue Baptist, being unsure of how to exercise his new authority, while trying to be compassionate and hoping to avert a conflict, let an obviously drunk guest come in to the shelter so that he could spend the night. The other guests, some of whom had walked over with this man and knew that he was drunk, were outraged by this and they all marched out and headed straight back to the drop-in center.

When the volunteer coordinator failed to punish a clear rules infraction, he became a participant in a flagrant violation of the moral order of the shelter. Right and wrong in this situation was so clear-cut, and the course of action that needed to be followed was so obvious, that by doing the wrong thing the volunteer coordinator violated the social contract underlying the moral order of the shelter.

Earlier I likened the moral order of the shelter to a social contract so that I could convey the sense that the moral order is both created in social interaction and that it is a contract. While political theorists typically use the notion of a social contract as a heuristic device for conceptualizing and describing the bundle of explicit and implicit mutual understandings and agreements that go into the development and the functioning of the collective mind-set that a social group needs for internal cohesion, in the shelters this is no heuristic. Generally, a social contract is thought of as being a shared moral vision of how a social group ought to function and how decisions ought to be made. This vision needs to be so internalized within the individual members of the community that they will act on it subconsciously. In democratic societies, for the social contract to be seen as valid it has to have arisen, at some point, in response to the requirements of daily social interaction.

For most of us and in most social situations, we are far enough removed from the creation of the social contract that it appears as a given. We don't know why the customs were developed or how. We just know that they were and that they seem to make sense, so we follow them. Pierre Bourdieu calls this *genesis amnesia,* which literally means the forgetting of the conditions of and the reasons for the origin of a cultural practice.[21] Through genesis amnesia, according to Bourdieu, "history [is] turned into nature."[22] What was obvious at Madison Avenue Church that night, however, was that the sober guests were not far enough removed from the making of the social contract to suffer from—or maybe benefit from—genesis amnesia. Rather, they were very conscious, often painfully so for those of them who were in withdrawal, of the moral commitment they made and struggled with on a daily basis. The admission of the drunken client to the shelter, seen by the volunteer as a charitable bending of the rules, was to the guests an egregious and personal affront to their hard-earned morality. They saw no charity in the volunteer coordinator's act, only a slap in their faces. So seriously did they take this issue that they exercised the only means of protest that they had; they all got up and left. The violation of the social contract at Sacred Heart was less obvious, but it was still felt and reacted to by the guests. The Sacred

Heart volunteers put forth a good deal of effort to put together an event that they were looking forward to. The problem was that they failed to consult the homeless guests to find out how they felt. Clearly at least some of the homeless guests felt that this party wasn't for them as much as it was for the volunteers. They protested by calling in a false report that the shelter was closed.

Through daily interactions, and through trial and error, the volunteers learned how to better run homeless shelters, ones in which there are reasonable and mutually acceptable rules and regulations for everyone to follow and in which the relationships are not any closer than the homeless people want them to be. With this greater knowledge the volunteers were free to relax and just be folks. The homeless people could also relax and just be folks as well. Soon they were getting to know each other, even becoming friendly. With this change the volunteers began to differentiate and distinguish characteristics, actions, needs, and capabilities among the homeless people in their shelters. With this greater ability to differentiate, the volunteers started to see their homeless clients as people, and they began to relate to them more as people and less as vessels of a certain condition. Abstractions were replaced by personal realities.

At this level, as Pat Durant said later, they were not just statistics. Instead they were people. With the development of the ability to see their homeless clients as homeless people, rather than as simply the homeless, the volunteers began to see a larger range of human capacity in them.

Learning about the Causes of Homelessness

For some of the volunteers, this change to seeing the homeless as homeless people made them feel that if not for the luck of the draw, they too could be in the same position. For the majority, however, as they got to know the homeless people as people, they began to see that there were differences between themselves and their homeless clients. The volunteers got to know these differences through the same daily interactions that the moral orders developed out of. Again, the learning was often indirect, and again it was often the moments of friction that became learning moments.

One such learning moment for the volunteers at Sacred Heart began at 5 A.M. one winter day in the late 1980s when Virginia Brown Jr.
and one of her friends had been the overnight volunteers, and one of
the clients began screaming at Virginia Jr. As the rules dictated, Virginia called her mother and told her that she had to get down to the
shelter immediately. It is no more than a two-minute walk from the
Browns' house to the shelter, and Virginia Sr. was at the shelter immediately. When she got there she asked what the problem was and as
she remembers it, the man who had been yelling pointed at her
daughter and said that she was the problem. At this point Virginia Sr.
asked her daughter what she had done to the man and Virginia Jr.
replied that she hadn't done anything other than ask him if he wanted
an omelet. This is what started the whole incident.

The man who was yelling at Virginia Jr. was a young Black man
about her age, and he had been staying at Sacred Heart for a few weeks
without incident. Virginia Jr. recalled the incident as follows:

> He went out of control. He was screaming in my face this close and he wouldn't
> back up. I would back away from him, and he followed me and he was like, I
> don't want any of this. And all I did was say, "Can I make you an omelet?" That
> was what started the whole thing.[23]

Looking back on the incident, Virginia Jr. said "he hated me." To this,
her mother replied,

> He didn't hate you.... I think the idea that two young girls, his own age, ... were
> baby-sitting him while he was sleeping—and then when he got up in the morn-
> ing, to know that he really didn't have anything to look forward to and these two
> young girls were feeding them and saying get on the bus. And then the explosion
> happened. But . . . it was just him in his situation. You [her daughter] just hap-
> pened to be there for it to crystallize around. And that was it.[24]

The bus to take the clients back to the drop-in center in Manhattan arrived soon after Virginia Sr. did, and her initial attempts to get
the man to settle down and get on the bus were to no avail. This just
got him angrier and when the bus driver, who was also a young Black
man, came into the shelter and heard what was going on he started
yelling at Virginia as well, telling her that she couldn't treat clients like
that. In the midst of all of this, the angry homeless man told Virginia
that "you're nothing but a honky racist." At this point Virginia said to
him, "why don't you just shut your mouth, and I'll shut my mouth,"

162   which she thought would calm things down. Rather than make things better, this prompted the man to call Virginia Sr. a four-letter word and then to explode. The situation got so bad that Virginia threatened to call the police if the man didn't get on the bus, and this eventually got him out of the shelter.[25]

Reflecting on that morning, Virginia Sr. said "if you were down there [talking to Jim] or if I was there, I don't think it would have bothered him, but I think it was just his ego going out." He had nothing to look forward to, she figured, and the thought of being baby-sat by these two girls, who were his age, was too much for him to tolerate.[26]

While this situation would not tell anyone anything directly about what causes homelessness, it does indicate to the volunteers that the homeless people grapple with issues that they, the volunteers, do not. As the incidents pile up, the volunteers come to the inescapable realization that the homeless, their humanity and all, are in different circumstances in their lives. This realization invariably leads to the question of why the person is homeless in the first place. This is a question that the volunteers are trained not to ask the homeless people, but as they get to know the homeless people it is one that they will usually discover the answer to. And as volunteers get more experienced and get to know their homeless clients better they answer the question, "Why do you think people become homeless?" very differently than those who have just begun volunteering do.[27]

When I asked them this question, the veterans gave the following answers.

People become homeless for a variety of reasons.[28]

Everybody is different.[29]

Lack of support from their families. Drugs and mental problems.[30]

Variety of reasons—some (few) simply because of hardship, a bad break—most [because of] addictions-recovering—lost in society.[31]

Emotional abuse, substance abuse issues, and inadequate family support.[32]

Most [became homeless] through substance abuse, and some through personal or medical difficulties. These render them unable to cope with the responsibilities of daily life.[33]

Breakdown of family structure, drugs and alcohol.[34]

I think a lot of people have difficulty in maintaining a job and assuming responsibility. Many have unrealistic expectations.[35]

Drug and alcohol abuse problems primarily; mental illness, although none of
the men I've met are mentally ill; health or money problems—losing their jobs,
illegal aliens without papers. Some stay homeless because they lack resources
(money-friends), some seem like loners, some lack initiative.[36]

By contrast, the following responses were typical of the new volunteers:

Unfortunate circumstances.[37]

The government, which doesn't do much for their people, like they do in Nor-
way.[38]

Moronic individualism since Reagan.[39]

It could happen to anyone.[40]

Circumstances out of their control.[41]

As a group, the new volunteers were twice as likely to blame reasons such as "circumstances beyond their control" for people being
homeless.[42] The veterans, on the other hand, had dispensed with such
explanations and replaced them with multidimensional ones in which
the homeless people were not seen as passive, incapable victims of society but as actors, or at least as potential actors, just like the rest of us.
They were actors who had stumbled over obstacles in life and had
ended up living on the streets. In order to get off the streets, these obstacles would have to be overcome, but the veteran volunteers believed
that they could be overcome. Moreover, the veteran volunteers believed
that these obstacles could not be overcome *for* the homeless people—
rather, they now thought that the homeless people had to overcome
the obstacles themselves (with volunteer help, of course).

While some of the veteran volunteers undoubtedly brought this
view with them to their work, I believe that the large difference in
thinking between the veteran volunteers and the new volunteers
about the causes of homelessness suggests that most of them developed these views on the job. This development is what I term the *development of unsentimental compassion.*

Developing an Unsentimental Compassion

Distinguishing between sentimental compassion and unsentimental compassion and focusing on the latter was a critical aspect of the

volunteers' moral development. Unsentimental compassion is described by Gertrude Himmelfarb in the following manner:

> In its sentimental mode, compassion is an exercise in moral indignation, in feeling good rather than doing good; this mode recognizes no principle of proportion, because feeling, unlike reason, knows no proportion, no limit, no respect for the constraints of policy or prudence. In its unsentimental mode, compassion seeks above all to do good, and this requires a stern sense of proportion, of reason and self-control. . . . it is sometimes necessary to feel bad in order to do good—to curb their own compassion and restrain their benevolent impulses in the best interest of those that they are trying to serve.[43]

Very rarely is the importance of the moral order of their shelter community, and its basis in a sense of unsentimental compassion, brought home to the volunteers as starkly as it was to the volunteers at Madison Avenue Church that cold night. It usually happens in much more subtle ways than that, like the incident at Sacred Heart. What the volunteers at Madison Avenue Baptist Church learned that night—and at subsequent meetings about what had gone wrong—and what the Sacred Heart volunteers learned, as well, is that in the long run, in these shelters, the benefits of unsentimental compassion outweigh the benefits of sentimental compassion. They learn that despite the fact that the volunteers are in charge in the shelters, it is the homeless people who make the true sacrifices in the development and maintenance of the moral order, and they learn that for the benefit of the homeless people they need to be unstinting in honoring and upholding the social contract.

Thinking Differently about the Solutions to Homelessness

As the volunteers learned to see the humanity in the homeless people, as they struggled to create and uphold a moral order in the shelter, as they learned more about why people become homeless, and as they developed a sense of unsentimental compassion, the last stage of their moral development started to take place; they began to think differently about solutions to homelessness. These solutions were grounded in their new visions of what causes homelessness, such as the following one expressed by volunteer Susan Monk:

> Today I think that people who are homeless are those who have no family foundation to turn to for help, so they turn to the streets. I see what I do at the shelter as a replacement for what was once done by the family.[44]

In effect, Susan Monk and the other volunteers who thought like her learned to reframe homelessness as disaffiliation, and with this reframing, they saw the clear solution as reaffiliation. To different volunteers, reaffiliation meant different things and the following give-and-take with Peter Saghir, who had been an experienced volunteer with the homeless before he became shelter coordinator and who continued to volunteer after quitting the coordinator position, illustrates some of the complexity of this notion.

I began by asking Peter what his conception was of what caused people to become homeless and if he could reflect on how volunteering affected that. In his reply Peter reminded me that before he began volunteering he "had known enough about homelessness [not to] really buy into any of the general stereotypes." I asked him what these stereotypes were, and he replied that "all homeless people are alcoholics or all homeless people are drug addicts." After explaining what he perceived the stereotypes to be he then added that while "there are a significant portion [who are alcoholics] . . . one thing that volunteering did for me . . . is [to teach me that] you cannot fairly group homeless people, because there are a million different reasons. The other thing that I learned . . . was that it is really about resources. . . . Resources [are] the biggest thing that separates people who are homeless from not being homeless."[45] I pressed him on this point for a further explanation and he gave me two examples. This was the first:

> If you have somebody who works for IBM, . . . and they are an alcoholic, the company, a lot of the time, will say, "Hey, why don't you go check yourself into a rehab, come back, and your job will be here for you. Furthermore, we will pay for the rehab." As opposed to a guy who is driving a truck, [if] he is an alcoholic, he gets fired, they sure as hell are not going to send him to some rehab.[46]

The second example that he used was about the mentally ill. Peter noted that the difference between mentally ill people who are homeless and those who aren't is often whether or not they have a family to care for them.

So Susan Monk saw affiliation as connection to a family foundation, and Peter Saghir saw affiliation as connection to people who had the resources to help someone in need. In his mind, these people could be your family, the company that you work for, or the volunteers in the shelter. Through reaffiliation, the homeless people would be able to have access to what Peter called *resources* and what others call *social capital*. Social capital is defined by Pierre Bourdieu as "the aggregate of the actual or potential resources which are linked to possession of a durable network of more or less institutionalized relationships of mutual acquaintance and recognition."[47] The volunteers, who understood how important their own social capital was in their own lives, saw that this is what the homeless people were missing. Unfortunately, affiliations are difficult to provide.

At Fifth Avenue Presbyterian, when their client Grandpa was dying, Peter and a few of the other volunteers tried to prod him to let them get in touch with his family, but as Peter's recounting of the event shows, that did not work. Grandpa had told Rick (the social worker at the church) and a number of the volunteers that he had a wife and a daughter, and they were all eager to get him back in touch with his family before he died. No matter how hard they tried to get the names and addresses from Grandpa, however, and no matter how much they asked him to give them permission to get in contact with his wife and daughter, he refused adamantly. This upset the volunteers and Peter said that he and the others reconciled the emotions that they felt about the incident by reflecting that they didn't know what the circumstances were with Grandpa and his family.[48] Like the volunteers at Sacred Heart, they had to learn to leave some things alone.

Grandpa must have had a reason for being so adamant that his family should not be contacted, and Peter did not push too hard. Though Grandpa ended up dying and being buried in the church's cemetery plot, at Woodlawn in the Bronx, without his family finding out what had become of him, in place of his actual family he had his surrogate shelter family with him to the end. While Grandpa never did get a home, thanks to his shelter family he did avoid the ignominy of Potter's Field.

As Grandpa's example shows, the task of reaffiliating homeless people is difficult, especially because the volunteers do not know the details of these people's pasts, details that explain why the people are disaffiliated in the first place. However difficult this task is, it is a different task than what homeless advocates see as the solution. In New York, as elsewhere, advocates for the homeless have long said that the solution to homelessness is obvious: it is housing. This seems only logical. To the volunteers, who are disinterested in the politics of homeless advocacy and sheltered from the political implications of their views of the causes of homelessness, housing, though necessary, is not the solution. This is because the volunteers have, in effect, learned that homelessness itself is not the problem that their clients face, but rather it is the symptom of another problem. With this learning, the volunteers have, in effect, reconceptualized homelessness as a residual concept.

The notion of seeing homelessness as a residual concept was first expressed to me by Joel Sesser, who became president of the Partnership following Peter Smith's death. When I interviewed him, Joel described for me his version of the development of the concept of homelessness. When he first came to New York to work in the social service field with the Bowery Resource Center (BRC) in 1981 or 1982, he wasn't sure exactly which, he noted that "the word [homeless] was not the first word that we used." Instead, when he was interviewing for the BRC, "they talked to me about people who were disaffiliated, and I didn't know what they were talking about." According to Joel, the word *homeless* became popular later because "it is a common denominator that explained the outcome of all of these different things that were converging" and because "the word doesn't blame the people who were the clients like some other clinical terms do."[49] In addition, Joel noted, this term *homeless* was understandable to the general public as a problem and it was one that suggested a straightforward solution. "Set up as a problem/solution pair, the word *homelessness* implies the solution as being homes," he observed. With homelessness as the new label, the solution became, in the phrase popularized by the Coalition for the Homeless, housing, housing, housing. So, as Joel noted, the solution to the problems that left these people on the streets was no longer seen to be drug treatment, or alcoholism counseling, or education, or welfare reform, and, he added, "people preferred to not focus on the root causes of people being homeless. . . . That they had lost their housing for reasons that would interfere with them being rehoused was not the first thing to worry about. That's when homelessness took on some political usefulness as a concept."[50]

As Joel noted, as have many others, there have always been homeless people in New York, and a Lexis/Nexis search of major newspapers in the United States supports his contention that it was only in the early 1980s that they started to be called homeless. There were only two instances of use of the term *homelessness* in 1975, and both were in articles in the *New York Times*. One was about Arab refugees, and in the other Jesse Jackson used the word *homelessness* to describe the threat that faced hundreds of public housing tenants who were faced with foreclosure of their subsidized housing by HUD. From this one domestic reference in 1975, the number sank to 0 in 1976 and rose to 25 in 1977 (all of which were about Americans). In 1978 there were 40 references in major American newspapers to homelessness, but only 29 were about the sort of people that Joel Sesser was talking about. There were 10 about refugees and migrants in other countries and there was 1 about the lack of a permanent home for a collection of decorative arts. In 1979 the number rose slightly to 45 and in 1980 to 102, with 71 about domestic homelessness and 31 about those in other countries who were victims of earthquakes—as in Italy that year—typhoons, dam bursts, and other disasters. In 1981 there were 176 stories that mentioned homelessness, and from there the numbers increased dramatically. In 1982 there were 302; in 1983, 454; in 1984 there were 710; and in 1985 there were 1,143. While this sort of a search leaves many sources uncovered, by looking at the major newspapers in the country it is a good indicator of the use of the term in the popular parlance.

While the term may have spread because of all of the reasons that Joel Sesser described, another reason for its spread was its emotional appeal—which is perhaps what made it so useful politically. The term *homelessness* has struck an emotional chord in our national consciousness because so many of us find it confusing, appalling even, that so many people should be without a home in a wealthy nation with one of the highest rates of home ownership in the world. Because it did not blame the victim, the term *homelessness* shifted the focus of the search for causes and solutions away from the people who were suffering and onto the society that was causing them to suffer. For that the advocates were rightly thankful, and it represented an ideological shift in that this is one of the few instances in American history in which the dominant conception of a group of poor people cast blame on society rather than on the individuals. This ideological shift provided both advocacy and service organizations with political opportunities that enabled them to raise funds and build organizations. It is doubtful, for example, that the creation of an organization like the Partnership for the Homeless would have been possible without the use of this compassion-invoking term, and it is equally doubtful that advocates for the homeless would have been able to bring enough political pressure on New York City to create a $500 million a year DHS without this term.

In hindsight, the ethical neutrality of the term needs to be called into question, however, as one of its major accomplishments has been to elicit sentimental compassion for this unfortunate group of people. The compassion that the term *homelessness* elicited was sentimental because, to follow Himmelfarb, it enabled "an exercise in moral indignation, in feeling good rather than doing good."[51] I say this because the ability of the term *homelessness* to aid in doing good was compromised by its analytical and descriptive uselessness. Descriptively it is useless because, to follow Aristotle's logic, "groups that are defined by the absence of a characteristic are very confusing, and are not real groups."[52] Analytically it was useless because it obscured the reasons why this diverse group of people were living in the conditions that they were. It does not get at the root causes because, as Joel Sesser noted, those who created the term preferred not to focus on root causes because to do so would, in their conception, blame the victim. Because the term hampers accurate description and analysis of the conditions that it purports to describe, it has slowed the search for a solution. The people at the Bowery Resource Center who used the term *disaffiliated* in the early 1980s seemed to have it right, only to throw it away for political purposes.

At this point, it is worth restating the fact that these shelters do not exist for the benefit of the moral development of the volunteers.

Rather, they exist to perform tasks and those tasks are to provide shelter and a supportive atmosphere for homeless people. And that is what they do. At Fifth Avenue Presbyterian, in addition to settling guests into housing and nursing homes, they have welcomed six former guests as members of the congregation. Two of these men are now on the church's shelter committee. At Sacred Heart, when their clients get apartments, as Jim notes, "we've given them a nice little stake in life to start—dishes, money, a television, whatever."[53] This is one of the ways they reaffiliate their homeless guests.

Peter Saghir described the feeling of the Fifth Avenue Presbyterian shelter as "a community center as opposed to just this bare necessities provider." Drawing on the example of how the shelter volunteers responded when Grandpa and others got sick and had to go to the hospital, and citing how the shelter clients had come to trust him and the other volunteers to the point where they would seek the volunteers' counsel when they were trying to decide on their options, Peter said that at the Fifth Avenue Presbyterian shelter they have created "the sort of community where everybody is looking out for each other, and the guys look out for each other and the volunteers are always just very supportive." What they have done at Sacred Heart, and what they seem to be doing at Fifth Avenue Presbyterian (although time will be the true judge), is generate a community. This has happened despite the fact that both places only set out to shelter homeless people for a short while. In order to shelter the homeless people, however, the volunteers had to develop associations to run their shelter, and these associations have proven to be capable of generating communities.

6

The Church Shelters as
Community-Generating Institutions

Over the course of its existence, the Sacred Heart Church homeless shelter in Glendale, Queens, has become a community-generating institution. The founders of the shelter didn't set out to create a community-generating institution; they just set out to create a well-run, volunteer-staffed homeless shelter in their church basement. They have succeeded admirably in this task, and since its founding the shelter has maintained a volunteer corps that averages over 200 people each year. There have been times when so many people wanted to volunteer that the shelter has had to stop people from volunteering in consecutive years so that others can have a chance.

Initially the founders of the shelter at Fifth Avenue Presbyterian Church didn't set out to create a community-generating institution either. As at Sacred Heart, all they wanted was a well-run, volunteer-staffed homeless shelter in their church basement. Since the shelter opened in 1986, however, there have been long periods in which there were barely enough volunteers to keep the shelter open. In 1999 the volunteer corps had shrunk to six, and the only reason that the shelter was able to stay open was that the shelter coordinator spent three to four nights a week there as the sole volunteer. This wasn't what the church session had in mind and they ordered a reorganization of the shelter or a shutdown. Since reorganization the volunteer corps has grown to approximately 160, and the Fifth Avenue Presbyterian shelter now seems to have developed into a community-generating institution as well.

These two churches and their volunteers have little in common except for the fact that they are in the same city and that they both shelter the homeless. For a long time, the way in which they operated their homeless shelters was also very different, but since the Fifth Avenue Presbyterian reorganization in 1999 the organization and operation of the two shelters are similar. It is on the basis of these similar characteristics that I will draw out lessons on how to build community-generating institutions.

Contending Conceptions of Community

Before our current era, no one doubted that communities were firmly rooted in particular places. Place was an essential element of Ferdinand Tonnies's archetypal village-based gemeinschaft, which many still hold today as the idealized form of pre-urban community. Even well into the twentieth century, when more and more people were living in cities, pioneering urban sociologists such as Robert Park and Ernest Burgess saw place, in this case in the form of the neighborhood, as the locus of community. This conception of community as place based is still visible in much of the theorizing of community that goes on today and it is integral to many of the deliberate attempts at community formation that take place.[1]

In recent decades, however, many theorists have come to believe that to insist that the only true communities are those rooted in a place is to miss a fundamental social shift that modern communications and transportations technologies have enabled. In our era, so this argument goes, people live their lives in many spheres that may be exclusive of one another, and they are not necessarily bound to the people in any one place. Although proponents of this view acknowledge that this means that the old neighborhoods aren't as cohesive as they used to be, they argue that people haven't stopped forming communities; it is just that people who analyze our society with outdated concepts cannot recognize the new forms that communities have taken. In this new camp are found authors such as Benedict Anderson, who writes about imagined communities that can be comprised of isolated newspaper readers who feel some sort of belonging to the group of others who read the same newspaper; Melvin Webber, who writes about communities without propinquity; Manuel Castells, who writes about information technology that has created a "vast array of virtual communities"; and

Robert Booth Fowler, who claims that there are actually now three
types of communities: of ideas, of memory, and of crisis.[2]

As if these disagreeing definitions weren't enough of a complication, there is a tendency in many definitions of community to conflate descriptions with preconceptions and prescriptions and to conflate social units with social relationships.[3] It is for this reason that *community* qualifies as a contested term, one that is seen to have a "high level of use but a low level of meaning."[4] This is unfortunate because communities are essential for fruitful human existence and disagreement over definition and use has led many to dismiss community as a topic of investigation. For a usable conception of community, one that will distinguish a community from its impostors and that will guide attempts at community generation, an operationalizable definition is necessary. What thwarts the creation of such a definition, however, is a seemingly fatal problem that communities in America face today: the exit option.

At the root of these definitional disagreements is a dispute over the question of the nature of the relationship between choice and community. Those who insist on place-based definitions of communities see placeless communities as impostors, largely because the ostensible members of the community can opt to exit too easily, thereby undermining the bonds and limitations that come with mutual norms and mutual obligations. "As individual choice expands," argues William Galston, "the bonds linking us to others tend to weaken."[5] This is a point of view that Andersen, Webber, Castells, and many others would consider out of date or maybe even beside the point. Choice is here, they would argue, and our need for community hasn't diminished. The result is that we still have communities; it is just that more of them are voluntary.

The problem with this point of view is that voluntary communities, in which the members can leave too easily, run the risk of being incapable of acting as communities and mislabeling them as such. But is this necessarily the case for all voluntary communities? Not if Robert Bellah and his co-authors are to be believed:

> We found many people . . . for whom private fulfillment and public involvement are not antithetical. The people evince an individualism that is not empty but is full of content drawn from active identification with communities and traditions.[6]

As they examine the various strains of American individualism, Robert Bellah and his co-authors acknowledge that "perhaps the notion that private life and public life are at odds is incorrect." While many people in America have become detached from a public existence, many others have not. For some of those who have not become detached, Bellah explains how their attachments have not come at the expense of their individualism, but rather that their attachments and individualism are "so deeply involved with each other that the impoverishment of one entails the impoverishment of the other." This American characteristic of committed individuals who are deeply involved in community is on display at Sacred Heart and at Fifth Avenue Presbyterian, which are structured in a way that allows them to incorporate individuals into a group in a characteristically American manner. While these are communities that the members have the choice to opt in or out of, they are communities that the volunteers choose to stay in because of what they provide for them. Through their success in playing important functions in the lives of their volunteers, the church shelters have created a situation in which the public and private lives of their volunteers "work together dialectically, helping to create and nurture one another."[7]

Two conceptions of community that help to bound such an operationalized vision are Michael Taylor's and Thomas Bender's. Taylor defines a community as "shared values and beliefs, direct and many sided relations, and the practice of reciprocity," while Bender defines it as "a limited number of people in a somewhat restricted social space or network held together by shared understandings and a sense of obligation." He goes on to say that in a community, "relationships are close, often intimate, and usually face-to-face. Individuals are bound together by affective or emotional ties rather than by a perception of individual self-interest. There is a "we-ness" in a community; one is a *member*.[8]

In an effort to be less dismissive of other types of communities, others such as Etienne Wenger have characterized such communities as communities of practice. [9] Following Taylor's definition, associations whose operations lead to the development of these direct and many-sided relations and reciprocity can become communities. From

this perspective, most pretenders to the title "community" are elimi-
nated. There is no such thing as a community of scholars, for example,
because it is too narrowly confined to one area of life to be direct and
many sided. Also ruled out are groups in which relations between the
ostensible members are mediated by "representatives, leaders, bureaucrats, institutions such as those of the state, or by codes abstractions
or reifications, because there is no reciprocity."[10] These characteristics
that Taylor identifies are important and useful for devising an operational conception of community because, for a group to possess them,
the members of that group need to be the ones to produce them.

What makes these characteristics important is that groups that
possess them in sufficient depth are able to perform important functions in the lives of their members. This is what makes a community,
according to Robert Nisbet, and the failure of groups to perform important functions can lead to community decline.[11] Therefore, opera-
tionally, community can be defined in terms of the functions that it
can perform, and this sort of operational definition can be used to
create an institution that will produce the characteristics of a community. This was Nisbet's insight, and it is an insight that corresponds
with my own observations of how the church shelters generate communities. I call this approach to understanding community a *functional approach,* and I call the types of communities that are developed out of these shelters *functional communities.*

In Wenger's analysis, communities of practice are those that are
formed through joint enterprise, mutual engagement, and the development of a shared repertoire. Such communities need not be comprised of members who live in a particular place, although the members do need to come together within a common institutional setting.
These relationship dimensions accurately represent the types of relationships that have developed at Sacred Heart and at Fifth Avenue
Presbyterian. It is through this sort of interaction that people "sustain
dense relations of mutual engagement organized around what they
do."[12] This is the essence of a community of practice, the fact that the
members develop their functional capacity. From my reading of the
relevant literature and my observations of the relations in the shelters, I
have judged these functions to be integration, mediation, socialization

and education, and moral development.[13] Using this approach, a community is a group of people who, through their membership in an association and through their practice in this association, develop the ability to perform these functions for themselves and for others.

As Wenger notes, "what it takes for a community of practice to cohere enough to function can be very subtle and delicate" and "the kind of coherence that transforms mutual engagement into community of practice requires work."[14] For the rest of this chapter I will explain how the shelters have created and sustained their communities of practice. I follow this up in the next chapter with a discussion on how to build the sorts of institutions that can create communities of practice.

How Institutions Generate Communities

The two homeless shelters that are the focus of this book possess the characteristics that Michael Taylor identifies as those of community. I believe that they possess these characteristics because they both perform the functions that I have identified in the lives of their volunteers and because through the process of performing these functions the volunteers have turned the shelters into communities. Despite the fact that these are homeless shelters, sheltering the homeless is not one of their community-generating functions. Sheltering the homeless is simply the task, what Tocqueville would call the small affair that gives these shelters a reason to exist. Because they need to perform this task, however, the shelters must integrate the volunteers into a group, socialize them, and educate them about the task that they have volunteered to perform. As the shelters then mediate in the lives of the volunteers and give their private lives a public purpose, they become places in which the volunteers undergo a process of moral development. One way to generate communities, therefore, is to create institutions that give their members a reason and the ability to perform these functions in their lives. If you do that then you will have created a place in which people can develop the "shared values and beliefs, direct and many sided relations, and the practice of reciprocity" that Taylor deemed essential to community.[15]

Going beyond the discussion of functions, it is important to keep in mind that a community is, above all, a social environment, and for any institution to succeed in generating a community its environment must be attractive to people so that they will join it, socialize in it, and stay with it. This is especially so in an individualistic country in which people have many demands on their time and many options for how to spend their time. Creating these sorts of environments is not alchemy. Rather, as Seymour Mandelbaum notes, it is a classically conservative act, one that "appears to be engaged more with daily life than with commanding visions; with routines, social bonds, and the web of interactions (albeit new ones) more than with charisma."[16] Mandelbaum calls the types of communities that can develop in settings like church shelters "open moral communities." They are open because membership is voluntary, and they are moral because they are bound together by an unforced contract and a shared sentiment among the members. Developing and refining daily routines, creating and maintaining social bonds, and interacting are the work of community generation. Furthermore, it is through such daily life that the aforementioned functions of community are performed.

A careful look at the two church shelters shows that the reasons why their "daily life" resulted in community generation was that it was directed by an institutional framework, which was organized and run by effective leaders. As it happened at these two shelters, the process of institutional creation was largely intuitive and ad hoc. At Sacred Heart, a well-organized Harold Brown realized that in order for the shelter to last it would need an efficient organization. All three leaders of this shelter knew that they would need a lot of volunteers, and they also knew that for the volunteers to be effective, they would have to use them wisely, train and discipline them, and keep them happy and interested. At Fifth Avenue Presbyterian, when Peter Saghir came in to take over the struggling shelter, he too realized that he needed to build an efficient organization. From here on I categorize these two ad hoc approaches in order to articulate a pattern that can be followed by others who desire to replicate what these two shelters have done. I am not claiming that this is the only way to generate communities; rather, I am simply describing a successful model of community generation so that others may learn from it.

Throughout this book I have described the functions of community generation. In the next few pages I explain how particular actions fulfill specific community-generating functions. My purpose is to clarify the links between actions and community generation so that these actions can be duplicated by others seeking to generate communities of their own. I begin with a discussion of the importance of finding and creating the right context and then move sequentially through integration, socialization, education, mediation, and moral development. In actuality, the distinctions between the functions of community generation are always sharp, but I believe that discussing them individually makes the points clearer.

Creating the Right Context

In the early years, Peter Smith and the early shelter coordinators developed the model of church shelters linked to drop-in centers that the Partnership for the Homeless has since used so successfully. These shelters were small, their task was well defined and limited, and they were set up as part of a network to give them the necessary outside support to carry out their task. The volunteers in the shelters also were able to influence what this network looked like. Ostensibly, the Partnership for the Homeless was set up as a membership-led corporation: on its organizational chart, the members hold the paramount position, and all of the employees of the corporation answer to the members. Each church can elect one member and all of the members are called together at an annual meeting to vote on the business of the corporation. Like most annual meetings, this is a highly choreographed affair, and the few dozen members who do show up rarely object to the resolutions put before them. This doesn't seem to have a negative effect, however, which is good, because if an organization had to operate in ideal form to generate a community, then there would be even fewer functioning communities than there are.

Peter Smith died shortly after I began working at the Partnership for the Homeless, and I never got to ask him why he decided to open the shelters in church basements; but whatever the logic, these locations conferred numerous advantages. The space was free, and the churches were full of potential volunteers, people who by the very nature of their attendance at church were predisposed to help their fellow man. The churches could also offer support in the form of their good name and their imprimatur. The support of Cardinal Cook and the Catholic Archdiocese, the Episcopal Diocese, and the New York Board of Rabbis served to elevate this proposed organization above politics and make it seem like a genuinely worthy cause. Because churches and synagogues are among the most trusted institutions in America, their neighbors were not suspicious of them. That is not to say that there was no opposition, because there was, and some planned shelters were never able to open. But the opposition was minor in comparison with the scale of the enterprise.

Places that already attract people in large numbers, that are perceived favorably, that have been in the same location for a long time, and that already have members who are involved in an array of programs are likely to be fertile places to try to start community-generating institutions. Churches fit this bill, and in the case of the Partnership for the Homeless, its member churches have provided a congenial context for the shelter leaders throughout the city to go about the day-to-day work of building and running community-generating institutions.

Integrating People into the Organization

Once the congenial context was created, the next step in building a community-generating institution was getting people to join up, to volunteer. Organizations can exist with very few members, but as they found out at Fifth Avenue Presbyterian, the organization likely won't last for very long and it won't generate a community. So the first concern in building a community-generating institution is finding potential members and integrating them into the association. In order to do this the shelter coordinators had to develop their own theories of why people volunteer and implement them. Chapter 3 uses social science literature to evaluate and describe what Jim Jones, Virginia Brown, and Peter Saghir did intuitively. They realized that different people volunteered for various reasons, but that if they wanted a lot of people to volunteer they would have to go out and recruit them.

They made announcements from the pulpit, held shelter open houses, asked their friends to volunteer, had the volunteers ask their friends to volunteer, got local high school teachers and organizers of church classes to make volunteering in the shelter a required activity, and got other church groups to make volunteering at the shelter a group activity. They got wives to ask their husbands, parents to bring their children, and vice versa. When an approach worked, they repeated it, and when an approach didn't work, they tried something else. They constantly sought out new sources of volunteers and thought up new ways to use volunteers. They tried to make the tasks seem attractive and fun, and they created a variety of jobs to be done at the shelter to have something for everybody to do.

Peter Saghir's theory was that if you wanted a lot of volunteers, you had to make the shelter experience fun. Show movies, have birthday parties, play bingo, go to baseball games. He also believed that he had to get them emotionally involved. At Fifth Avenue Presbyterian Church the congregants were scattered all over New York, so there needed to be an emotional hook. Peter used the homeless men, the 10 grandfathers as he called them, their well-being, and their activities as this hook. He wrote newsy emails to all of the volunteers, keeping them abreast of what was going on with the men and what was going on with the other volunteers. This way, the volunteers would get emotionally attached to their clients, and they would want to continue volunteering.

Jim and Virginia thought that the key to getting and keeping volunteers was to provide them with the opportunity to do something meaningful. My interviews with the shelter volunteers supported this view. They welcomed the opportunity to contribute to the solution of a nagging problem in their city. Even more, they welcomed the opportunity to help solve a nagging social problem within the friendly confines of their church, where they knew that the homeless men and women they would help had passed through a screening process. This made volunteering with the homeless less intimidating than it might otherwise have been, which meant that more people came out and volunteered. Even more people volunteered after they saw that their neighbors were doing so and not getting hurt.

Getting people to volunteer is only the first step in integrating them into a community; for them to truly be integrated into a community they have to be active members over a long enough time to develop relationships. Peter, Jim, and Virginia all believed that if you wanted people to become long-term volunteers you had to give them an important job to do. The critical jobs that absolutely had to be done were the shelter host jobs, and in all of the shelters these were the ones that were staffed first. But these jobs were not for everybody; some volunteers were too timid, too young, or too old to be put in that position. Others didn't like the thought of sleeping in a strange bed, and some didn't like the length of the shift. Jim and Virginia and other coordinators in other shelters heard the complaints about the length of time of the overnight shifts early on, and they split this shift in two so as to remove that barrier.

Despite what Jim and Virginia said about never turning away a volunteer, in reality there were criteria for excluding potential volunteers from the shelter and for expelling people who were already volunteering. Safety was paramount, and it was an issue that both of the shelters took seriously. The overnight volunteers were instructed that if any of them were having a problem with one of the guests and they felt that things might get out of hand, they were to call Virginia, Harold, or Jim, regardless of the time. Virginia said, "We never wanted one of the volunteers to be responsible for calling the police or calling ... an ambulance ... because it would end everything." Rather she and Jim made sure the volunteers understood that "the phone was right there and they could call somebody and they would come down and take over, that they didn't have to feel guilty about it."[17]

Beyond safety, there are exclusionary criteria that are essential for the integrative function of a community. In the church shelters, when people were excluded or expelled, it was usually homeless guests, with the most common reason for exclusion and expulsion being refusal to follow the shelter rules and conduct detrimental to the domestic order of the shelter. Potential volunteers could be excluded and volunteers could be expelled, for many of the same reasons.

Virginia Brown told the story of one older woman, a devout Catholic and member of the Blue Army of our Lady of Fatima, an organization of Catholic women devoted to spreading teachings given by the Blessed Virgin Mary. She seemed like an ideal volunteer. But just after her first shift, she told Virginia that she would not "wait on niggers" and so was promptly expelled from the volunteer corps. This woman was not the only expulsion for outlandish behavior. One was expelled for sleeping with a male guest, and many others have been excluded for less outlandish reasons, such as proselytizing, which all of the shelters prohibit. Expulsions and exclusions are necessary to preserve the congenial social climate in the shelter. They are also necessary if a shelter is to have any hope of turning into the sort of place that can develop the aforementioned social order. Without a social order, these shelters have nothing that distinguishes them from the big chaotic city shelters, so they have to be able to develop order to have any worth at all.

Developing and maintaining a social order required decorum, and maintaining decorum was perhaps the most difficult job in the shelter. It was crucial for integration as well as for socialization. This was the job of the shelter host, who needed to be good at recognizing and dealing with someone else's attempt at manipulation. Manipulation is a "skill" that many of the homeless clients have, and for some of them it has been a valuable survival technique in different phases of their lives. In a small environment like church shelters, however, it is an extremely disruptive force. This is one of the reasons why the Partnership for the Homeless suggests certain rules to the shelter coordinators, and this is one of the reasons why the shelter coordinators are supposed to teach these rules to the volunteers. Rules make the volunteers' lives easier. If they know the rules for a situation, they can be more sure that they are doing the right thing and less likely to make an incorrect judgment.

With their jobs in the homeless shelters, the volunteers were now able to do something useful, not just feel useful. (Although doing something useful is the surest way to feel useful, doing something useful is more that just a feeling.) Jim and Virginia provided their volunteers (and also some nonvolunteers) with a reason to bake cakes and pies for their neighbors. They also provided a coffeehouse, a place to work off their required community service hours, and a place to hang

out. People who had lived near each other for years, but hadn't the
faintest idea who each other were, now had a place to go and a reason
to get to know each other. They made friends, and they got more connected to the place they lived in.

Because the volunteers at Sacred Heart lived right around the
church, Jim and Virginia didn't have to go out of their way to create
the attractions that Peter did to get people to congregate at the shelter.
It just sort of happened at Sacred Heart, and that is why it is easier to
create communities from propinquity. Because of the propinquity at
Sacred Heart, however, they haven't had to try innovative tactics, like
including the homeless men more in the shelter operations, that
might make the shelter community more diverse and interesting.

For those who are not up to being a shelter host, there are a multitude of other jobs that have to be done for the shelter to operate.
There is food to buy and cook, provisions to be stored, laundry to be
done and put away, kitchens and bathrooms to be cleaned, dishes to
be done, floors to clean and repair, walls to paint, newsletters to be
written and mailed out, events to be organized, service awards to be
given out, and former clients who have found housing to be kept in
touch with and brought back to the shelter as examples to be followed.
Also, committees that relate to the operations of the shelter need to be
staffed. All of these are potential volunteer jobs, and it is important
that they are performed well for the shelter to function well. At Sacred
Heart, and at the other shelters that do not have paid volunteer coordinators, there is a lot of administrative work for the volunteers to do.

Once a volunteer was slotted into the right job, he or she was on
the way to becoming integrated. To be truly integrated, however, volunteers had to be organized into the structure of the volunteer corps
and become a part of things. At Sacred Heart and at Fifth Avenue
Presbyterian this meant becoming known as a regular at your task
and becoming part of the subset of the volunteers who did what you
did. It also meant filling in when someone else couldn't show up to
volunteer as planned.

At Sacred Heart, Jim, Harold, and Virginia built an organization
to distribute the work, parceled out responsibility and accountability,
and set up a method for finding a backup to ensure that the work was

　done. With these steps people were integrated into the association. At Fifth Avenue Presbyterian, where Barbara was paid for her work as the volunteer coordinator, she was tempted to do all the work herself rather than find others to share the load. Without intervention, this would have proven lethal to the institution, as it has at other shelters.

Socializing People into the Norms of the Organization

The next step after integration is socialization, two functions that are very closely related. Once new volunteers are recruited and start to work, they either learn the rules and the ways of the community and begin to contribute or they become a liability. In the shelters, socialization is both a formal and an informal process that begins with training. Many of the shelters introduce themselves to their new volunteers with a formal packet that includes a description of the Partnership and job descriptions for their shelter. At Fifth Avenue Presbyterian the initial training includes a talk by the shelter's social worker. Other shelters that don't have their own social workers send their volunteers to the Partnership for the Homeless for training sessions. Sometimes they also send them to other social service agencies that do volunteer training.

When I was director of volunteers one of the best training sessions for volunteers who would be working with people with AIDS was at Gay Men's Health Crisis in Chelsea, and many volunteers attended this training. In all of the shelters, the other common way to begin training a new volunteer is to partner them with a veteran volunteer. This partnership will last for at least a few months, and after that the not-so-new volunteer will have the option of finding a new partner, most likely another veteran volunteer. This way the new volunteers learn the subtleties of the job, and they begin to be socialized into the shelter.

How frequently a volunteer worked also played a role in socialization. New volunteers worked at least twice a month for the first few months, so that they could plant their faces in the minds of the homeless men in the shelter. Once they became a known quantity, they could scale back to the typical once per month.

Of course, a good informal way to socialize people is to provide opportunities for them to participate in the many subtle ways of being that make up the social order of the shelter. This is the underlying purpose of the parties and bingo and movie nights at Fifth Avenue Presbyterian and of Sacred Heart's end-of-year prayer meeting. The need to maintain decorum and knowing the rules for different situations applies here as well. Socialization doesn't happen just through the application of rules and regulations, however, as the atmosphere at the shelter needs to be friendly and welcoming to the homeless guests and the volunteers. If it isn't, then community generation will be virtually impossible. But the atmosphere needn't be too friendly or too personal either. Asking people why they became homeless, for example, is taboo, as are other questions of a personal nature. The goal is for the volunteers and the guests to feel comfortable enough to participate in the shelter, but not for the guests to feel so at home that they want to stay. The shelter is transitional, after all, and actions that slow down the transition are counterproductive. The "restrained openness" that the volunteers should have has to be practiced in order to be perfected. One important aspect of socializing is knowing what to expect, and perhaps the most important expectation is consistency. Peter Saghir spoke about the importance of consistency in the shelter at Fifth Avenue Presbyterian. "I think it is better for the guys, because everything else . . . is so unstable in their lives."[18] One small example of this stability was the fact that at Fifth Avenue Presbyterian they always held the group birthday parties on the last Tuesday or Wednesday of the month.

Socialization, like integration, needs structure, and it sometimes needs policing. This is the only way to ensure that the social order that is created in the shelter aids in the goal of transitioning the homeless clients to housing. A simple practice like consistency needs structure when its existence is a product of the behavior of many. Having birthday parties on the same day every month, requiring the guests to clean up their sleeping areas every morning, and always having dinner ready when the homeless people arrive at night are simple acts that are integral to the development and maintenance of a stable social environment. With such consistency the homeless people learn again, or maybe for the first time, how to pattern their lives in an orderly, functional fashion. They also learn that there are people they can trust and things in life to look forward to. As the homeless people learn to trust the volunteers, they also learn that they are expected to respond in kind and behave as promised. This honest reciprocity can be a powerful force for change in their lives and in the lives of the volunteers.

For people to be linked to each other within this associational framework, socialization has to be followed up with discipline. In the shelters this is as necessary for the volunteers as it is for the guests, both new and veteran. Some types of socializing are easily recognizable as being out-of-bounds and damaging to the social order of the shelters. Because they are so obvious, the volunteer coordinators don't have many problems explaining the reasons behind their disciplinary actions to those being punished and to the rest of the shelter community. For the guests, sobriety, smoking, schedules, and sociability are always issues, and the discipline for these sorts of infractions has to be uniform and immediate. Included in the obviously out-of-bounds category of volunteer behavior are the aforementioned late-night poker games, the rare occasions of sexual relations between volunteers and clients, and racially prejudiced comments. An unannounced failure to show up for a volunteer shift is another type of easily recognizable problem. Volunteers who miss their shifts or behave inappropriately need to be disciplined immediately and consistently.

A less obvious disciplinary issue is the need to keep the volunteers focused on their work. This is particularly the case at Sacred Heart in the 7:30 P.M. to 9:30 P.M. period, which is the social gathering time. This is when the Girl Scouts and other neighbors bring cookies and cake and people come down to have dessert and socialize with the guests and the other volunteers. Because there is no place else in the neighborhood to go, people go to the shelter and hang out, the pastor sometimes goes for coffee, and on some nights there are more volunteers and visitors there than homeless guests. This, as Virginia noted, can get out of hand and it can get in the way of the volunteer's ability to do his or her job. To keep an eye on things, Jim often goes down and sits in a chair and reads or makes Jell-O, something that keeps him out of the way but right there in case they have any problems.

Other potential disciplinary problems are harder to recognize and are more subtly damaging. For example, no one at Sacred Heart could

have been expected to realize beforehand that the planned Easter
party was out-of-bounds, and if it hadn't been a surprise, it probably
would have been okay. Likewise, it would have been hard to know
beforehand that having three young women volunteer to, in effect,
baby-sit a group of young homeless men was probably not a good
idea. These types of problems require a sure hand to respond to and
to weed out. Surprises are not generally conducive to the successful
operation of a shelter. Again, consistency is the watchword.

Failures to socialize people and to educate them are also problems,
but they are not usually as serious as the failure to integrate. There are
many ways that the shelters can get around these problems or even
disguise them. A number of the bigger Manhattan churches rely on
their professional staffs and do not require volunteers to be as competent as churches like Sacred Heart do. Similarly, churches that have
transient young urban professional volunteers have been able to make
do for years with a lower degree of socialization than what they have
needed to develop at Sacred Heart. All that such churches require are
for the volunteers to adhere to a few basic rules: showing up on time,
enforcing a curfew, making sure that none of the men are drunk or
high, turning the lights out at a certain time, and making sure that
everyone gets on the bus in the morning. Some of the shelters even go
long periods of time without a volunteer get-together. This sort of
"getting by" attitude will prevent the shelters from developing functional communities, however, and these shelters can usually only last
for just so long with these sorts of failures. Eventually all of the shelters have a day of reckoning when they are compelled to rethink the
way that they operate or shut down.

Educating People about Their Tasks and about Each Other

As people become socialized, they also start to become educated. Theorists have long recognized that socialization and discipline are linked to
education and in the shelters the socialization and disciplining of the
volunteers has been enhanced by creating opportunities for them to
become more competent at performing their tasks.[19] This is a key element in the development of the volunteer's ability to be a contributing
member of the shelter. There is a difference between socialization and

education, however—while the socialization function is about learning the ways of the shelter, the education function is more explicitly focused on learning the skills necessary for fulfilling the task at hand. The Partnership for the Homeless assists in this educative function by holding workshops for the volunteers during the annual Action Day on such issues as recognizing the symptoms of tuberculosis or of various types of mental illness and understanding how to treat them. The Partnership or its consultants also offer these sessions periodically at the various shelters. At Fifth Avenue Presbyterian, where the homeless men are integral members of the community, their socialization and discipline has been aided by the education that they have gained through being members of the church committees.

By education I am referring to both the need for the volunteers to become more competent at running the shelter and to the learning experiences that the volunteers have actually running it. Running a homeless shelter is itself an education for the volunteers. So while volunteer training is partially an aspect of socialization, it is also an important aspect of educating for competence. Running a homeless shelter, even a small one in a church basement, is an exercise in logistics, planning, budgeting, social relations, social work, public administration, and diplomacy, and a well-run shelter needs volunteers who are competent in all of these areas.

The logistical challenges regarding the procurement and usage of supplies and the planning challenges regarding schedules and the movement of people are immense. In each of the shelters there needs to be at least one volunteer (usually more) who figures out ahead of time what supplies will be needed and takes the necessary steps to procure them. In both of these aspects of shelter operation the Partnership for the Homeless and DHS offer support, but interacting with these two agencies is in itself a logistical challenge. For the shelters to procure supplies and financial assistance from the Partnership and DHS they need to develop a means of tracking their expenditures and their usage of supplies and they need to create a means of reporting this information. In a system with so many parts that is responsible for the movement of so many people, and that divides responsibility among so many hands, planning is crucial.

Both DHS and the Partnership have a master schedule of the entire system that is created to ensure that all of the multiple tasks get assigned and completed. Creating this schedule is an enormous task, especially because the each shelter is free to create its own schedule within this system. Some of the shelters are year-round and some are not, some are open every night and many are not, and DHS and the Partnership need to know ahead of time what the individual shelters will do so that they can coordinate the movement of the homeless people with the drop-in centers. Because of the tracking requirements of DHS, which needs to know where the homeless people are, not only do the regular schedules have to be communicated ahead of time, but any changes in the schedules need to be reported as well. While some of the new volunteers already possess such skills from their jobs or from other voluntary activities, many of them develop these skills on the job.

Because developing these skills among the volunteer corps is a particular problem for many shelters, some actively recruit people with administrative skills to help run the shelter more effectively. Often this quick-fix approach works, but many times it doesn't and the shelters have to develop their administrative capacity indigenously. One major obstacle to the quick-fix method of developing capacity within the volunteer corps is that people with particular skills volunteer in order to get away from what they do at work and are unwilling to perform this job for their shelter. I was made aware of this as the director of volunteers at the Partnership when a senior executive of a Wall Street bank that was one of our big financial supporters called me looking for a volunteer opportunity. I tried to place him in a shelter that I knew needed his financial expertise, but he refused that assignment and asked for another, one that had nothing to do with finance. He told me that over the years he and his wife, who was a social worker, had gradually grown apart as their two professional worlds diverged, and that he was volunteering in order to learn more about his wife's world so that the two of them would have something in common again. I referred him to a different shelter that needed overnight volunteers and looked elsewhere for the financial expertise. In addition to occasionally finding administrative volunteers, the Partnership for the

Homeless often helps the shelters to develop their own administrative capacity by giving workshops on a regular basis. The staff of the Partnership is also readily available to help when called.

In almost all of the churches, money is tight and the volunteers need to learn how to operate the shelter as economically as possible. While there is limited financial support to be had from DHS and the Partnership, budgeting is critical to successful long-term shelter operation. Space is also tight in most of the churches and the homeless shelters generally share multiuse spaces with other groups. Relationships among the various users of a space can quickly get strained if they don't learn how to get along with each other and to resolve their differences quickly. Special events that will require some alteration in the transportation need to be reported to the Partnership for the Homeless, which in turn needs to report them to the DHS so that they can alter the bus schedules. Maintaining good relationships with neighbors is crucial if the shelters are going to stay open. This is especially the case in the neighborhood churches outside of Manhattan, where the merest hint of controversy would be enough to close a shelter. Usually problems can be avoided before they happen, and the most effective tactic that people have learned for avoiding problems is to operate incognito. Staying small, avoiding any outward signs that there is a homeless shelter within, having the bus that brings the homeless people arrive after dark, and making sure that the homeless people get inside the church as soon as they arrive and stay inside until they leave are the most effective tactics that people learn for maintaining good neighborly relations in a crowded city. In the rare instance in which the church has open space on its property, like the graveyard at St. Paul's, the homeless people are allowed to go out of the shelter and wander around. Even there, however, the gate is locked at a certain time and it stays locked so that people remain on the church property. St. Bartholomew's, which is across 50th Street from the Waldorf Astoria, uses the 51st Street entry for its homeless guests, so as not to irritate the hotel.

Sometimes the shelter can't hide what it is up to, however, and in these situations diplomacy is required. Such was the case with the Homeless on the Steps program at Fifth Avenue Presbyterian. For two years diplomacy worked, and despite a subsequent lawsuit (won by the church), the church still hasn't given up on diplomacy and would prefer to settle with the city out of court. Such confrontational victories are costly and they generate negative associations that could be detrimental to the long-term health of the overall enterprise of 120 church shelters. Because the goodwill and the active cooperation of city agencies are essential for the operation of the church shelters, suing the city is clearly not something that the shelters want to do too often.

In order to work effectively with the homeless people, all volunteers need to be made competent in recognizing the signs of disease, drug use, and drunkenness, and they all also need to learn to recognize when someone is trying to manipulate them. At St. Paul's and Fifth Avenue Presbyterian the volunteers can call on the expertise of an on-staff social worker when they recognize a situation that is going to require professional help. In others, the volunteers must learn to go it alone to the extent possible, or they learn to call the drop-in center and describe the problem to the social worker there. They then need to be able to follow the directions that the social worker gives them to remedy the situation.

Of course, on many occasions people do not perform these tasks appropriately, and the functioning of the shelter suffers accordingly. In some cases the inability of shelters to develop the capacity to perform important functions is fatal and the shelters shut down. This is especially the case when it is the integrative function that the shelter is failing in. The Riverside Church homeless shelter failed in this function and it closed due to a lack of volunteers. The Fifth Avenue Presbyterian Church shelter nearly shut down for the same reason.

Mediating in People's Lives

Once people begin to get integrated, and as they are socialized and educated, the shelter arrives at a point where it can begin mediating in the volunteers' lives. As I noted in chapter 4, there are three elements to the mediating function: linking people with one another, linking them with power centers, and linking them with sources of meaning.[20] The link between people is usually the first thing that people think of when they speak of a place as having a sense of community. This is the

192   connection that they develop to other people in the neighborhood or at church, people they can say hello to at the grocery store or they might ask to baby-sit or cat-sit when they go out or take a vacation. This connection is indeed part of what makes a community, but to function as a community in the manner that I have stipulated, this link between people is necessary but not sufficient. Through the connections that people make they need to develop the capacity to work together to accomplish something.[21] In the shelters, as people work together and get socialized and educated together, they develop a mutual dependence and become obliged to come to each other's aid to take care of their clients. Out of the process of developing these mutual dependencies and obligations, the volunteers start to develop working relationships.[22] They accomplish things together and some of them become friends. Even conflicts and disagreements can be community generating: people either learn to work through them or they leave. In the larger shelter programs people can avoid those they don't get along with by working a different shift. Those who are enthusiastic about their volunteer jobs come back year after year. The majority of the volunteers at Sacred Heart have been at it for years, and some have been volunteering since the shelter opened. Virginia says that they keep coming back because they are really interested in the people.

This interest in people that a lot of the volunteers have makes them the sort of people who can be more easily connected to like-minded others. In order to continue to provide the volunteers with the tasks that link them to each other, however, the church shelters have to be linked to powerful external organizations that provide the resources that allow them to operate. Furthermore, without this link, a community would not be generated.

This link to what Berger and Neuhaus call the megastructures, which are sources of power in our society, is a two-way link.[23] Support and resources flow from DHS to the drop-in centers, to the Partnership for the Homeless, and to the shelters; so do policy directives and regulatory codes that shape how the shelters operate. At the same time, effort, local knowledge, ability, and influence emanate from the shelters to the Partnership, to the drop-in centers, and to the New

York City DHS. The volunteers as individuals are able to influence the Partnership through their status as members running a membership institution, and cumulatively with the assistance of the staff of the Partnership, the volunteers are able to influence the DHS and the drop-in centers. The relationships between the volunteers and the people who work for the various organizations are the key to the volunteers' ability to influence. They connect the volunteers to sources of power and give them a voice in their big city.[24]

Through their connection to important tasks and to influential and powerful people, the volunteers develop the productive capacities of their private lives. Rather than simply looking helplessly, disgustedly, and piteously at homeless people living on the streets of their city, they have banded together to do something about homelessness in New York. Their activities have transformed them from alienated and disassociated bystanders in their city's life to active creators of that life. At least one megastructure in New York life is no longer alien to them because they know people who work there. The impact of this on an individual life can be powerful and it can amount to reversal of the afflictions that Berger and Neuhaus identified as being typical of modernity.

The volunteers also get connected to sources of meaning that help to combat the disenchantment that characterizes modernity. Max Weber wrote about the potential for the triumphs of bureaucracy and science and the routinization of modern life to disenchant people. What he meant by disenchantment was the demise of spirituality and belief in the transcendental power of the human spirit and a simultaneous rise in the belief that science and bureaucratic administration could explain all questions and solve all problems.[25] While Weber saw efficiency in the development of bureaucratic routines, and while he applauded the ability that science would have to puncture superstitions, overwhelm ignorance, and find answers to vexing human problems, he also realized that dispensing with enchantment and spirituality would make life incomprehensible and unsatisfactory for many people. Weber had little faith in the ability of science and bureaucracy to replace enchantment with something new and better, and he feared that the modern world would become an Iron Cage.

194   Since Weber's time, our faith in scientific and bureaucratic rationalism has waned, but bureaucratic and scientific rationalism has tri-
umphed, and the Iron Cage has become a reality. People attempt to
confront this particular crisis of modernity in many ways; various
forms of escapism and fatalism are two of the most prominent. In
places like the church shelters, however, people find a real enchantment, one that is not based on superstition or escapism. Instead, it is
an enchantment based on bringing real caring, hope, and the promise
of a better future into the lives of people who previously had none.
Being able to bring this hope and promise into the guests' lives makes
the job meaningful for the volunteers, and through this connection to
meaning the volunteers are at least partially released from the Iron
Cage. This partial release is apparent in Margaret Shafer's reflection
that the work at the shelter is bringing her and the other volunteers
"close to the kingdom of God."[26] It is also apparent in Jim's and
Virginia's belief that the reason so many of the children who were
required to serve at the shelter stay with it or come back after finish-
ing college is that "the message got through to them."[27]

Providing a Space for Moral Development

By performing all of these community-generating functions and by
connecting volunteers to meaning, the church shelters become those
rarest of places in our modern world, spaces for moral development.
The volunteers develop a firsthand sense of why the homeless people
are in these circumstances, and they develop an unsentimental sense
of what they owe to each other as members of the same society. This is
a particularly pressing need in America today, because many Americans lack the opportunity to encounter and to get know people of
other races and socioeconomic status. Instead of a clear, unsentimental sense of what we owe to each other as members of the same society, what we have in America today, as placeholders for morality, are
prejudices or amoral open-mindedness. The impulses behind the two
are very different, with one being motivated by fear, loathing, and
hatred and the other motivated by dispassionate attention. The effect
of the two is similar, however, in that the realities of people's lives are
ignored and potential real solutions to their despair are missed.

In the shelters, however, the volunteers gradually learn to put aside prejudices, reject the hands-off attitude of modern amorality, and instead develop an active moral sensibility.[28] This sensibility is based on knowledge and unsentimental compassion rather than on prejudices or uninformed sentiment. The volunteers develop this sensibility not as members of the same society but as members of the same community. By working to foster socialization, discipline, and advancement, sentiments such as duty, obligation, hope, love, and trust become part of their lexicon rather than remaining as abstract ideals. Rather than simply feeling good, the volunteers learn to actually do good for the homeless people who are in their shelters by helping them take necessary steps to improve their lives. They learn these things by interacting with their homeless clients and the other volunteers who themselves interact with the homeless clients.

This learning takes place because the volunteers have developed relationships with each other and the homeless clients that allow discourse to take place. Discourse, which is defined by political theorists as interactions in which all of the communicating parties have a voice, speak up, learn from each other, and are willing to change their opinions in the face of convincing arguments from other, is a critical form of communication for moral development.[29]

In the two shelters the daily face-to-face interactions, the committee meetings, the end-of-year prayer sessions, and the formal and informal social gatherings are all opportunities for discourse to take place. This discourse, what Alexis de Tocqueville referred to as "the reciprocal action of men upon one another," has been recognized by many as the crucial communicative element in community formation. From the reciprocal effect that people can have on each other in a discursive situation, moral development takes place.[30]

The Challenge of Generating Community in America

In recent times it has become commonly assumed that community in American is hard to come by because the values of individualism and community "involve an irreducible tension between agency and responsibility."[31] Tocqueville anticipated this tension when he noted that in a democracy people tend to become isolated and absorbed in

196 their own affairs, a condition that he referred to as *selfishness*. In Tocqueville's analysis, the remedy to selfishness was the delegation of the administration of small affairs to the citizens and to their civil associations. In this way, individuals would work together to solve local problems and thereby develop communal bonds. But Tocqueville wrote 150 years ago and much has changed since then, not the least of which is the complexity of the problems that American society faces. To many, these problems seem too much for civil associations to handle.

Not so, says Herve Varenne. In his book *Americans Together: Structured Diversity in a Midwestern Town,* he illustrates how small voluntary organizations, like the church shelters, still bridge this gulf between community and individual. Where Tocqueville saw selfishness, Varenne saw aimlessness that arose from the American freedom to move and to associate. Aimlessness is a condition of modernity that Tonnies would likely have recognized, and for Varenne, American individualism and aimlessness set up the Tonnies-like question, "How do we go from individualism to community?"[32] Varenne, who set his book in the fictitious Midwestern town of Appleton, created the following visual model of the town's social relationships:

With this diagram, Varenne showed what he considered to be the typical links between individualistic Americans and the larger society: the individuals create small groups "and the smaller groups . . . generate larger groupings or identifications."[33] In Varenne's current-day analysis, as in Tocqueville's, it is only through voluntary association that the linkages and relationships necessary for the generation of community can be made. Moreover, the relations that people develop within these associations are the closest that most people today, especially those not living in small towns, can get to the sort of enduring linkages whose passing Tonnies lamented. The main difference between these groups and the ones considered by Tonnies is that these are voluntary while the ones in Tonnies's conception were primarily ascriptive. While ascriptive associations would likely run into conflict with Americans' individualism, in these voluntary shelters community and individualism are not in conflict. Varenne reflects on this symmetry and notes that, because of the voluntary nature of the groups, "community and individualism are not in conflict; they are intimately integrated into one system of unit-definition and relationship-definition. Each implies the other; each is, in a certain sense, a restatement of the other."[34]

Unlike in Tonnies's archetypal small town, Americans today have the choice to reject the order and the responsibility of community. With voluntarism comes the option of leaving the group, so the would-be builder of a community-generating institution needs to understand what qualities entice people to join and stay as volunteers in these groups. In Varenne's analysis, people stay together in communities because of love, whereas in Tocqueville's analysis it is because of the application of self-interest rightly understood.

From what I have seen in these two New York shelters, it can be a bit of both. Self-interest rightly understood seems to be the binding element at Sacred Heart, whereas love of the grandfatherly clients seems to be the binding element at Fifth Avenue Presbyterian. While conjuring up love may seem like a very tall order for a would-be community generator, applying self-interest rightly understood really isn't. And once one applies self-interest rightly understood to make the institution function smoothly, love and other moral sentiments will follow naturally. This is what Tocqueville anticipated, and this is what I have seen at the shelters.

Even to people who are familiar with Tocqueville's arguments, generating communities in a mobile and individualistic society such as America's is thought to be an impossible task. They point to the fact that there are lots of civil associations in America today, but few of them seem to have the effects that Tocqueville and Varenne claim that they should. This is correct, unfortunately, because many civil associations do not possess this community-generating ability. Fortunately, though, many do, and the distinction between those that can generate community and those that can't is the distinction between community organizations and community-serving organizations. Community organizations, which are rooted in a location and are "'of, for and by' the communities they serve," provide opportunities for their members to participate, and they are locales in which the practices and deliberations that can develop and maintain communities take place.[35] All of the church and synagogue shelters are community organizations, and for an association to become community generating it must first be a community organization. Community-*serving* organizations are valuable in many ways, but they are not capable of generating communities. Simply being a community organization isn't enough to ensure that an association will be community generating, however. If it were, the Fifth Avenue Presbyterian Church shelter would have produced vibrant community years ago. The community-generating association needs to have other characteristics.

7

Social Architecture: The Art of Building Community-Generating Institutions

We need to understand how much of our lives is lived in and through institutions, and how better institutions are essential if we are to live better lives.[1]

The free institutions that the inhabitants of the United States possess and the political rights of which they make so much use recall to each citizen constantly and in a thousand ways that he lives in a society. At every moment they bring his mind back toward the idea that the duty as well as the interest of men is to render themselves useful to those like them; . . . One is occupied with the general interest at first by necessity and then by choice; what was calculation becomes instinct; and by dint of working for the good of one's fellow citizens, one finally picks up the habit and taste of serving them.[2]

In the past decade social scientists have again become interested in studying institutions—including those of the sort that Jim, Virginia, and Peter have built. Among the various approaches to studying institutions that have been developed are new institutionalism, sociological institutionalism, historical institutionalism, and even rational choice institutionalism. While scholars in each camp differ in the types of questions that they try to answer and in the methods that they bring to their examinations of how institutions operate, they are united by their common view that understanding human social action requires understanding the institutions that people interact within.

In the broadest sense institutions are rules that structure social and political behavior.[3] Another way to think about institutions or organizations is to see them as "social designs directed at practice."[4] The types of behavior that the institutions can structure are as varied as the institutions are themselves, and in this chapter I will focus on one specific type of institution, the community-generating institution. This is a subtype of the community association that I spoke about in the second chapter and at the end of the last chapter when I employed Peter Dobkin Hall's label of community organizations. Not all community organizations are community generating, as communities are living things that require constant renewal. The features that distinguish those that do generate community from those that don't are not accidental, however, and experts who are interested in the link between organizations and learning have identified steps that someone interested in community generation can take to create a community-generating organization.

Steps to Creating Community-Generating Institutions

When the shelters are functioning effectively in all of these dimensions, and when there is discourse among the volunteers and between the volunteers and their clients, what happens is, in effect, the development of a voluntary gemeinschaft. For the volunteers who run them, the church shelters are labors of love. This is evident in the way that they speak about their fellow volunteers and about the men and the women whom they shelter. The fact that they love what they are doing is one of the things that keep the volunteers coming back to volunteer month after month, year after year. Love is not the only reason why they come back, however; obligation, fulfillment, and moral duty also play a role in ensuring the continued involvement of the volunteers. While love might seem like a high and unpredictable aim for those who are building institutions, obligation, fulfillment, and moral duty are not, and in my experience situations in which these sentiments are present can breed love. Given a supportive institutional setting, love and other binding emotions that are integral to the development of community can arise as a matter of routine. The key to community generation is the development of these supportive institutional settings. Community associations that have tasks to perform, that have the requisite outside support to be able to perform these tasks effectively for a long time, and that organize people into situations in which they can have reciprocal influences on each other are excellent examples of such settings, and out of such community associations, communities will likely be generated. At least this has happened in the church shelters.

While these community-generating shelters were developed in an informal manner, the craft of building these sorts of community-generating institutions can be undertaken deliberately. It is a craft that Howard Perlmutter has labeled *social architecture,* an apt description of the work of Peter Smith, Jim Jones, Harold and Virginia Brown, Peter Saghir, and those around them who helped develop and run their shelters.[5] While none of these people would have described themselves as social architects, that is exactly what they were. Though their institution-building work might seem to have been idiosyncratic and localized, with reference to Perlmutter's and Etienne Wenger's analyses, I will outline specific steps that can be taken to replicate them.

Elements of Social Architecture

An interdisciplinary literature that is focused on how social learning takes place within an organizational institutional framework is developing and this has great applicability to community generation. Though management literature has some of the most developed analyses of this issue, there are contributions being made by developmental and cognitive psychologists, computer scientists, planning theorists, and education theorists.[6] While many of these authors speak about institutional design, they do it at a conceptual level that is harder to translate into practice. Perlmutter and Wenger are exceptions, however, and it is their work, especially Perlmutter's, that presents the most complete framework for the process of social architecture. Perlmutter was not explicitly focused on building communities; rather, he was focused on building the sort of nonprofit organizations that he referred to as *essential organizations*—that is, organizations that would undertake essential human service work.

Following Edward Bakke and Chris Argyris's template, Perlmutter outlines seven essential organizational areas that need to be attended to for building essential institutions. These are establishing work processes; creating a system of authority; developing a means of evaluation; creating a system of rewards and penalties; developing a system of communication; fostering a group identity; and ensuring the perpetuation of the association.[7] If a social architect focuses on making sure that his or her institution is strong in each of these areas, and if this work is done on the individual, interpersonal, group, intergroup, and organizational levels, then the institution that he or she builds will be one that can be a successful community generator. I say that such an institution can be a successful community generator because this will be the sort of institution that, to restate Wenger's dimensions of a community of practice, can keep people mutually engaged in a joint enterprise out of which they can develop a shared repertoire. It is important to pay attention to all of the work areas because for an association to be able to successfully perform the community-generating functions, it will have to be able to operate well in all of these work areas and on all of these levels.

The advantage of such a schema is that it demystifies the process of association building and of community generation so that city planners, public officials, or the board of deacons of a church can easily conceptualize what their role would be in developing and operating a community-generating association. So, for example, rather than worrying about something that seems unplannable and ephemeral, like creating the space for moral generation, a would-be social architect could instead focus on something more concrete, such as creating an association that operates well in all of the organizational areas and on all levels. By attending to these very concrete pieces of work, however, the social architect would, in effect, be developing a context in which the people who join the association can carry out these more ephemeral tasks in such a way as to give them and their association the potential to develop community-generating functions. At the same time, however, the social architect should be aware that he or she is not the one who generates community, rather it is the members of the association who do. Even good social architecture doesn't guarantee community generation. But if the association that the social architect creates, or takes over, does not generate a community, then he or she should be able to use this framework to analyze why it hasn't and may be able to fix what is wrong.

In the real work of institution building these work processes are entwined. Here I will try to separate them out for pedagogical and presentation purposes as I present examples from the two shelters to show how each work process actually was done and how it is managed so as to have the desired effect. In explaining how this work was done I will follow Perlmutter's suggestion and begin with what he calls the essential question that needs to be answered to make explicit the values of the organization and guide the design of each organizational area.

Social Architecture–Community Generation

Social architecture work areas	Community-generating functions
Establishing work processes	*Integration* *Socialization* *Education*
Creating a system of authority	*Socialization* *Education*
Developing a means of evaluation	*Socialization* *Education*
Creating a system of rewards and penalties	*Socialization* *Education* *Mediation*
Developing a system of communication	*Integration* *Socialization* *Mediation*
Fostering a group of identity with symbols and rituals	*Socialization* *Mediation* *Providing space for moral development*
Ensuring the perpetuation of the association	*Mediation* *Providing space for moral development*

Establish Work Processes

The first step in building community-generating institutions is figuring out what sort of work the institution is going to do and then dividing up the work into tasks that are structured in a simultaneous, successive, and interdependent sequence that will achieve the desired results. The essential questions that institution builders need to answer as they consider the work processes of the prospective organization are the following:

- Should it be individual or group centered?

- If it is going to be group centered, how big should the group be?

- Does the work need to be done at a specific site?

While the answers to these questions should be ones that enable the association to perform its task optimally, when faced with two potentially workable choices, the institution builders should think about who the people are who are going to be doing the work. They should structure the institution in a way that lets the members use and develop their abilities and that finds outside supporters to help the institution do the things that its members are not good at doing. This will enable the institution to maximize its community-generating potential. The steps that need to be taken to establish the work processes are as follows:

- Secure the necessary outside support.

- Find the line between challenging work and intimidating work.

- Get enough volunteers to do the work.

- Break the work down into doable pieces.

- Decide on the ideal workload.

- Organize the volunteers into appropriately sized work groups.

- Decide on the work site.

I will briefly explain what each entails.

Secure the Necessary Outside Support

In the church shelters the work was hard and it was being done by volunteers. Because community-generating associations will invariably be staffed mainly by volunteers, as this is one of the features that distinguished a community organization from a community-serving organization, these are challenges that will be common. To begin with, the substance of the work was a concern and the social architects had to ensure that the work that they were taking on was of the type that volunteers could do, either by themselves or with outside support. In the church shelters this outside support came from the paid staffs of the Partnership, DHS, the drop-in centers, and other partner organizations, and for those who look to create and operate community-generating associations, securing such outside support will likely be crucial to the success of the endeavor.

Find the Line between Challenging Work and Intimidating Work

From what I observed in the shelters, the work needs to be challenging enough to be meaningful, but not so challenging as to be intimidating. Sheltering homeless people is challenging in itself, perhaps too challenging for most, so the shelters relied on outside supporters to direct the cream of the crop to them, thus reducing the challenge of the work. The drop-in centers were created as the sites for the professional social work and as the gatekeepers for the church shelters. The paid staff of the Partnership also took on a gatekeeper role, but their main support task was administrative. They took care of securing grants and public sector contracts to pay for shelter expenses and they made sure that the homeless residents got the services that they were entitled to. The staff of the Partnership also worked with the two members of the DHS, who play crucial support roles, to schedule the buses that picked up and dropped off the men and to make sure that the proper supplies got to the churches when they needed them. Even so, taking care of the cream of the homeless crop was still too challenging for many, as the threshold between meaningful and intimidating differs for each person, so the shelters had to develop a wide variety of tasks that different people of different abilities and tolerances could be assigned to. Many tasks involved no face-to-face contact with homeless people, but these were not "make work" jobs. While the shelter host volunteers were the only ones who had real face-to-face interactions with the homeless people, the supporting volunteers who did not have face-to-face contact were still doing important jobs.

Get Enough Volunteers to Do the Work

With the substance of the work decided, the next concern is the need to get enough volunteers to do the work. Because most volunteers are unlikely to be able to devote their full-time attention to the tasks that they have been given, the builders of the shelters had to recruit a lot of them. This is likely to be the case in most community-generating institutions that have an ongoing human service as their task.

Break the Work Down into Doable Pieces

Because many people will be doing the work, the work must be broken down into small pieces that can be done by people with limited time, and it must be structured so that it can be done sequentially by many different people. Heroic individuals are too few and far between to be a reliable base for an organization and overreliance on such people will diminish the need for the involvement of others, thus depriving a community of its very essence, its membership.

Decide on the Ideal Workload

In the shelters, after some trial and error, the coordinators decided that the ideal workload for an individual volunteer was a shift that lasted for a few hours, and they also decided that there would be a number of shifts each night. Thus a volunteer could do one shift on his or her night, which lasted a few hours, and could come once a month, and with enough volunteers the shelter would function just fine. With this amount of work people who had other commitments that kept them busy most of the time, which is almost everybody, could still find time to volunteer. In the early days at Sacred Heart the longest shift was the overnight shift of nine hours, but Jim and Virginia split this shift into a three-hour early night shift and a six-hour late-night shift after the volunteers complained about the length. Of course there was significant variation in this time commitment as the volunteer coordinator was continually on duty, and the day coordinators at Sacred Heart were on call at all times on their days.

Organize the Volunteers into Appropriately Sized Work Groups

With a small group of homeless people in each shelter, the volunteers were organized to work in pairs, and sometimes in singles. While there were often more than two volunteers at a time at the shelter, it was only two who were working at any one time. The others were invariably there visiting, something that was encouraged but also had to be monitored so that it didn't get in the way of the two volunteers who were on duty. The decision to have two volunteers at a time was initially made for safety reasons, but it soon came to be seen as practical, as no more than two at any one time were really necessary. With the shelters so small and domestic feeling, the two volunteers functioned, in effect, like two parents, and if the workload at a certain time got heavy, for example at dinner time, the shelter residents could easily be pressed into service.

Decide on the Work Site

Almost all of the work that required face-to-face interaction with the homeless people took place in the shelter and it took place during the hours when the shelter was open. The work that had to do with the maintenance of the shelter also took place in the shelter, but it did not necessarily have to take place during the hours that the shelter was open. Other support activities such as cooking, shopping, and administrative work could be done by the volunteers in their homes or anywhere else that felt right. With this sort of flexibility, the shelters were able to provide volunteer opportunities of varying degrees of difficulty and of such a wide variety that they could appeal to a vast array of people with different strengths and experience levels. The shelters were also able to begin the process of integrating these people and socializing them into a community.

Create a System of Authority

For the association to ensure that all of its volunteers and external supporters were performing the necessary tasks for it to achieve its objectives, a system of authority that could direct the behavior of all of these people had to be created. This is the case for all would-be community-generating associations. When designing the authority system, Perlmutter suggests that all social architects need to decide whether their association should be centralized or decentralized. In associations that have developed a variety of volunteer jobs and that have a number of outside supporters, there can be different answers to this question that depend on which aspect of the work, or what sort of outside relationship, it applies to. The steps to be taken when creating the authority system are deciding on centralized authority or decentralized authority and establishing a behavioral code. I will explain some of the details of each.

Centralized Authority or Decentralized Authority?

In a voluntary community-generating institution this question of centralization or decentralization is likely to be an especially sensitive question. A balance needs to be struck between the need to ensure that all of the volunteers have freedom and spontaneity to enjoy their jobs and build relationships with other volunteers and clients and the organization's need to make sure that the jobs get done in a way that furthers its mission. This balance is often tenuous, as volunteers might be resistant to control over their activities and the institution must keep them content in order to perform the tasks that it was set up to perform. There will always be tension between the volunteer's need for freedom, self-expression, and self-development and the institution's need for authority; maintaining the right balance will require constant adjustment as different personalities come and go and as the work of the institution progresses. Conflict will inevitably result, and the way that the conflict is managed will either enhance or diminish the community.

Establishing a Behavioral Code

The shelter coordinators avoided the appearance of monitoring the volunteers by training them in what amounted to a mandatory code of behavior. The homeless people also had a behavioral code that was set for them by the Partnership for the Homeless and the drop-in centers and this included sobriety, cleanliness, and timeliness, which the shelters enforced. For the volunteers, their code included

- timeliness
- reliability
- firmness
- tolerance

With the volunteers working in pairs and with the homeless people, they all monitored each other. Because others dropped by the shelter to socialize, they were de facto monitors as well. Because the volunteers and the homeless people all monitored each other, the volunteer coordinators did not have to appear as the heavy. This way what would seem to be an issue that would demand a centralized solution actually was decentralized, in a way. When punishments had to be meted out, however, this was the exclusive responsibility of the coordinators. Just as the coordinators had the authority to refuse to admit a client to the shelter on any given evening, they also had the authority to dismiss a volunteer who was behaving in a manner antithetical to the well-being of the shelter. In fact, the volunteer coordinators found out that if they didn't dismiss those who were not living up to their obligations or commitments, then the rest of the shelter population protested.

While the authority system was relatively decentralized when it came to individual, interpersonal, and group work in the shelters, when it came to intergroup work, by which I mean work with other shelters, and work on the organizational level, the authority system was much more centralized. There was a large system that had been created to take care of these homeless people, so there had to be a systemwide authority structure and the question of centralization vs. decentralization also had to be answered on this high level. However decentralized a particular shelter might have been in its internal operations, there was no way that any shelter could be decentralized in its conduct of its external relations with the other components of the Partnership for the Homeless system. That meant that internal and external work had to be separated so that there could be a few select people who were in contact with the drop-in centers, the Partnership, DHS, and the external suppliers. These were most likely the shelter coordinators, but they didn't have to be. Furthermore, while the whole church shelter system itself was decentralized, as it was comprised of over 120 shelters, in order to keep all of the moving parts working in tandem, there had to be a few people at a central location whose job it was to oversee the whole system.

In this case, these were the paid employees of the Partnership for the Homeless, DHS, and the drop-in centers, with the employees of the Partnership playing the lead role. In determining what the authority structure would be like on this level, many of the same issues of control and freedom that had to be dealt with in the shelters had to be dealt with here. Because all of the shelters needed external support, and because the whole church shelter system was itself a component of the wider city response to homelessness, all of the shelters needed to be able to operate in a coordinated manner. At the same time, however, in order to entice churches to open shelters, each shelter needed to be relatively free to operate in the manner that it saw fit. This meant that the coordinators of the individual sites had to have the freedom to make many of their own decisions, but they had to accept that there would be boundaries on that freedom. Along with willingness to accept boundaries came access to those at the Partnership, DHS, and the drop-in centers and enough influence with these people so that volunteer coordinators could initiate discussions about making systemic change when they felt the need. In such discussions, the paid staff members at the Partnership, who were the only ones who could see the system as a whole and who were charged with maintaining its well-being, had the upper hand. The volunteer coordinators had to accept that. Not all of them did, and the Partnership has had to sever relationships with shelters because of this. Such actions were the rare exception, however, as most shelter coordinators were able to work with the staff of the Partnership to negotiate an authority structure that served the interests of the shelter system as a whole and the shelters as individual sites. As they developed this system, the shelters enhanced their ability to integrate the volunteers into a community and they began to develop their capacity as sites of moral development.

Develop a Means of Evaluation

With the tasks defined and with an authority system set up, the next thing that needs to be created is a means of evaluating the work of the people performing the various volunteer and support jobs. The key question to be answered when designing the evaluations is whether people should be evaluated by person-centered criteria or by performance-centered criteria. As with the authority system, the answer to this central question will likely be different for different aspects of the work, and in its various aspects, the nature of the work will drive the answer to this question. In designing the evaluation system, social architects must be careful to not mistakenly misdefine the work of the organization, as this will set them off in the wrong direction when creating an evaluation system. This is likely to be the case for any community-generating institution, and an evaluation system needs to be developed that can assess the ability of the institution to do its work. I say this because in the church homeless shelters, the uninitiated could look at them and decide that their work was to shelter homeless people, then design an evaluation system that would count how many people the churches were sheltering. Such a system would lead to a conclusion that the church shelters were doing a bad job, given their small size. Moreover, because the volunteers aren't finding any housing for their clients, an evaluation system that looked at the number of homeless people being rehoused would further denigrate the efforts of the church shelters. Such evaluations would not only miss the point, if they were used as guidelines to alter the nature of the services, they might cause a reconfiguration of the shelters in a way that would destroy their community-generating ability.

The fundamental point of the work of these shelters is that it is qualitative rather than quantitative, and the shelters aim to provide a high-quality voluntary experience as much as they aim to provide a high-quality environment for the homeless people. The church shelters need to make sure that they are attractive to volunteers and that they do a good job at volunteer recruitment and retention. They also need to develop a welcoming atmosphere for their homeless clients and work with their homeless clients to develop a social contract that they can all abide by. They then need to uphold that social contract. Despite the qualitative nature of the work, there still might be a way to quantify success. This is often the case with qualitative endeavors, but the point is to be sure not to count the wrong thing. The way to evaluate the success of the shelters is by seeing how many volunteers they have and by finding out whether the homeless clients would rather be there or at other shelters. The proof, in this instance, is in the pudding. This is an evaluation that is at once people centered and performance centered. It is performance centered in that it evaluates the ability of the shelters to perform their tasks by looking at their numbers, and it is people centered in that the high incidence of clients returning to these shelters night after night gives testament to the personal impact of the shelters on the lives of the clients and the volunteers.

Evaluation of the supporting institutions is also important, and although the Partnership has grown big enough so that the quantity of homeless people that it shelters has become important, the quality of its work is even more important than the quantity. Because the work quality that the paid staff of the Partnership is expected to deliver is different than the work quality that the volunteers are asked to deliver, the criteria for evaluating the paid staff will be different than the criteria for evaluating the volunteers. While the churches need to make themselves attractive to volunteers and clients, the Partnership needs to make sure that its shelter system is attractive to potential donors, that the shelters meet city codes, and that contractual obligations are met. It also needs to make sure that the shelters don't have empty beds, that the shelters are matched with appropriate drop-in centers, and that the shelters are provided with a homeless clientele that challenges them but does not overwhelm them. Because of this, there is a performance-centered focus in evaluating the work of the Partnership employees who support the shelters. It is such performance criteria, explicitly spelled out in job descriptions, that the executive director of the agency uses to evaluate the shelter support staff and it is the same sort of performance criteria that the Partnership's director of the shelter program uses to evaluate the employees.

Create a System of Rewards and Penalties

Once you have figured out how to evaluate the work of the association and its members, the next step is to figure out how to encourage the members and the outside supporters of the association to perform their tasks in a manner that will lead to a good evaluation. To do this a system of rewards, incentives, and punishments must evolve. Perlmutter uses the word *evolve* rather than *develop* when talking about the generation of the reward and penalty system, and the advantage of this is that it conveys the fact that the best rewards and punishments are those that arise organically. Perlmutter suggests that in creating this system the social architects should ask themselves what will motivate the people to perform in the desired manner and what is the best sort of punishment to deter undesirable performance?

As was the case with the other work areas, there will have to be different rewards and penalties for those involved in different aspects of the work, and in the case of the volunteer tasks, many of these jobs present their own obvious rewards and penalties. At first glance this would seem to relieve the social architects of some of the responsibility for creating a rewards system, as the volunteers are often motivated by spiritual and psychic gains. Many of the volunteers told me that what they got out of their work in the shelter was a sense of fulfillment that comes from being a part of an important pursuit; a feeling of camaraderie with their fellow volunteers; the opportunity to meet and become friends with people different from themselves; and the sense of doing God's will. In order for them to attain their desired spiritual state, however, the volunteers needed to find an appropriate setting, so creating this setting is an important aspect of creating a system of rewards. By the same token, denying the volunteers access to this setting is a major part of the punishment system. Creating this setting in which the volunteers can essentially self-provide rewards was just the start of creating the reward system at the church shelters, however, as volunteers often need more tangible rewards. This was especially so for the volunteers who did not interact with the homeless people face-to-face. So the Partnership developed volunteer recognition awards, they solicited citations from the mayor that they presented to the volunteers, employees of the Partnership spoke in front of congregations to laud the work of the volunteers in front of their fellow congregants, and the Partnership threw annual volunteer recognition dinners. They also treated the volunteers with respect and held annual membership meetings to ask the approval of the volunteers for the plans for the next year.

Punishments and penalties were also of the external strategic type and the internal tactical type. When things were not going well at a shelter the staff of the Partnership, or the leaders of the church, would meet with the shelter coordinator to find out what was causing the problems and to see what steps they could take to remedy the situation.

Sometimes, as was the case at Fifth Avenue Presbyterian, replacing the shelter coordinator was deemed to be the solution, and the old shelter coordinator was, in effect, fired for his or her inadequacy. On rare occasions the punishment was even more severe than that and the Partnership withdrew its support for the continued operation of the shelter.

These were all strategies that were important for the long-term health of the organization, but it was the rewards and punishments that the shelter coordinators developed that had the tactical day-to-day impact of making the shelters good community-generation sites. Coordinators used a mix of tangible and intangible rewards, with such tangible rewards as parties, end-of-year dinners, praise from the pulpit, and citations and certificates for outstanding service, and intangible rewards such as congratulations from the fellow volunteers and neighborhood respect and esteem. In neighborhood associations like the Sacred Heart shelter the intangible daily rewards and punishments carry out of the shelter and into the daily life of the volunteers more than they do in associations like the Fifth Avenue Presbyterian shelter. In neighborhood settings like Sacred Heart, the respect that an outstanding volunteer is given by his or her peers knows no bounds and it is as likely to be accorded at the grocery store as in the shelter. This makes these intangible rewards and punishments more potent motivators of desired actions, which is one of the reasons why it is easier to develop community with propinquity.[8]

The employees of the Partnership for the Homeless itself were also motivated by a mixture of psychic and material benefits and motivating them required a similar combination of rewards and penalties. Like many who work professionally in human services, employees of the Partnership aimed to relieve the suffering of their clientele and empower their volunteers. For people with this sort of motivation, long-term contact with their clientele and the volunteers was the basis of their job satisfaction and enabling or disabling this sort of contact was the basis of an appropriate reward and punishment system. So privileges like being able to spend more of the day out of the office and in the field with the clients, visiting churches, or visiting the drop-in centers are all important motivators for the paid staff. Such freedoms allow the staff to spend more time focused on the aspect of their jobs that matter to them, and it makes their jobs feel less corporate and regimented. Furthermore, those members of the Partnership staff who are in positions that bring them in direct contact with the homeless clientele are further motivated by being relieved of the paperwork required by city and state contracts. Agencies can create separate positions for record keepers and this can powerfully motivate their direct service employees.

While people who work in human services generally are willing to work for less so that they can be outside of the corporate world and gain the psychic satisfaction that comes from working to make the world a better place, even more than the volunteers, they are also motivated by material concerns. Pay raises, or the lack thereof, are always effective rewards and punishments, as are extra days off for exceptional service, good job reviews, and a promotion within the organization, or a bad job review and termination. For employees who have to spend time in the field after hours, allowing them to accumulate bonus time that they can add to their vacation time is another motivator and this privilege can be expanded or contracted as deemed appropriate. All of these rewards and punishments should be linked to performance criteria that is spelled out in the job descriptions, and the managers of the agency should have periodic meetings with the staff to evaluate the utility of the content of the job descriptions and to make the amendments that both parties feel are necessary.

Develop a System of Communication

To successfully carry out its mission an association must develop some method of sharing the information, ideas, and values that are relevant for its successful functioning. When sharing this information, however, the questions to consider are what information needs to be shared and how widespread the sharing should be. Just as knowledge is power, too much knowledge can disable, and the social architects will have to find a way of making sure the participants in the association know what they need to know while they are being shielded from information that is superfluous and potentially detrimental.

When operating a community-generating association, different types of information are necessary, and they will come from different sources. There is technical information, which pertains to the skills necessary for the delivery of the service; there is practical information, which pertains to the know-how for operating the shelter; and there is attitudinal information, or wisdom and common sense, which pertains to how to handle situations that arise in day-to-day operations.

In the church shelters the volunteers need such technical information as an understanding of what contagious diseases the homeless people might have, how these diseases might be spread in the shelter, and what the effective and ineffective means of protection are. They also need to know how to recognize signs of mental illness and they need to understand what appropriate and inappropriate responses are. This understanding can be gained with targeted training and everyone who will come in contact with the homeless people, even in a peripheral manner, should have access to this information. While those who are making the intake decisions for the shelters need to understand about the past and present drug and alcohol use and the mental and physiological illness histories of the homeless people, very little if any of this information needs to be disseminated to the individual volunteers. All the volunteers really need is the information that will help them do their jobs better, which in this instance is limited to whether or not the homeless individuals are staying clean and sober while they are in the shelters.

There are mountains of practical information that pertain to the administration of each of the shelters and the whole shelter system, much of which does not need to be widely shared either, as this would complicate people's roles in a way that they would likely find to be dissatisfactory. So shelter-specific information like how to keep records to get fuel and food reimbursement, and who to talk to at the drop-in center about a disagreeable client, only needs to be known by the few volunteers who have been specifically charged with carrying out those tasks. Likewise, only a few people need practical information that pertains to the operation of the shelter system, information such as who controls the bus schedule and how to alter it if need be, who the service providers are for homeless clients and how to get in contact with them, and who runs the drop-in centers and how to contact them.

What I call attitudinal information, or wisdom and common sense, needs to be as widespread as possible, both in its source and its dispersion. Cultivating and sharing this sort of information can be tricky because its sources are diffuse and they are of varying degrees of credibility. This makes it hard sometimes to distinguish wisdom and common sense from misinformation and prejudice. There is no foolproof way to deal with this difficulty, but by creating a situation in which there is a daily, ongoing discourse in which the volunteers continually learn more about their clients' lives and the clients are free to complain about maltreatment and to refuse at any time to come back, good judgment tends to win out as nontruths and half-truths are exposed for what they are, and wisdom is developed. In such settings the participants learn to give more weight to the voices of the wise veterans, to listen closely to the voices and actions of the clients, and to give the greatest weight of all to the voices of the coordinators. These veterans are the custodians of the discourse, and maintaining such people in an association is critical for the vitality of its community-generating ability. They are the ones, more than any others, who rein in the prejudice and the biases that can destroy community, and they frame the daily social interactions so that positive feelings result.

Communication in these settings is not just sharing knowledge, skill, and wisdom; it is also letting others know about successes and failures, building morale, and creating an inhospitable environment for prejudice. While the coordinators of the individual sites can play a large role in this, the paid staff of the agency and the social architects need to concern themselves with creating an environment in which these things can happen. Agencywide newsletters that trumpet successful approaches and awards ceremonies at annual volunteer celebrations are good vehicles for communicating and celebrating successes, just as disciplinary meetings with agency staff are effective ways of curbing undesired actions and behaviors in the shelters.

Two of the desired outgrowths of a discursive environment are the development of an esprit de corps among the volunteer corps and the development of symbols and rituals. Building esprit de corps is essential for building community, and symbols and rituals are indispensable for building a moral order. For the symbols and rituals to be effective in building a moral order they need to arise out of the daily work of the association and they need to be things that the participants can identify with and cherish. These, according to Perlmutter, should be things that embody the "wholeness, uniqueness and significance of the organization," and they should have an emotional tone.[9]

The key question in designing a group identity for the association is whether the focus of loyalty and affection should be the small groups within the association or the broader association itself. Who the volunteers become loyal to will depend almost entirely on who they interact with. Likewise, the level at which the volunteers interact will be the level at which the most effective and representative symbols and rituals will be developed. So if the social architects feel that the overall effort will be best served if the volunteers develop loyalty to the broader association, then they need to design the association in such a way that the volunteers interact across the broader association. This is an important consideration because once the interactive process is set in motion it, and its resultant effects, come to be seen as natural, especially to those who joined after the creation. It is very difficult to alter "natural" tendencies, so the social architects should consider beforehand what they think the ideal level of the focus of loyalty should be for the overall well-being of the association, and they should design the interactive opportunities so that they steer the affections of the participants to the level that they want. This way they will align the natural tendencies of the participants with the needs of the organization.

In case of the Partnership for the Homeless and its shelters, it was the church shelters that were deemed to be the ideal foci for the loyalty and affection of the volunteers, and it was at this level that meaningful symbols and rituals could best be developed. From what I saw in my time in the shelters, it was easier for the volunteers to become 219 loyal to small groups. Because there was very little opportunity for volunteers from different shelters to interact with each other, there was virtually no possibility that the volunteers would be more loyal and affectionate toward the Partnership for the Homeless as a whole rather than the individual shelter. On the other hand, the shelter co-ordinators often had to take steps to make sure that the volunteers didn't focus their loyalty on a subgroup within the shelter.

At Sacred Heart the volunteers worked in pairs such that they formed bonds with their partners. The responsibilities that came with these bonds were the primary level of allegiance in this shelter. The Sacred Heart volunteers watched out for their partners and felt an obligation to do their part of the bargain that the two of them had entered into. They developed their own ways of being together, which are the basis of rituals, and they had the strongest effect on the actions of each other. The shelter coordinators had to build on this level of allegiance and create opportunities to re-pose the volunteers' alle-giances and obligations they felt toward their partners to the next level. If they didn't do this, such subgroup allegiances would create contending identifications within the shelter, which might eventually lead to contending allegiances. The logical challenge, therefore, was to create opportunities for interaction with others. At Sacred Heart this was accomplished by first developing links among people who volun-teered on the same day and then developing shelterwide links. An ef-fect of the Sacred Heart system of day coordinators and phone trees and backups among the people who volunteered on the same day was that all of these volunteers got to know the other people they could turn to if they needed someone to stand in for them. Over time, this became the next level of allegiance for the volunteers and this larger group began to develop ways of being amongst themselves. Fortu-nately for the coordinators at Sacred Heart, very few of the volunteers kept strictly to any one day. From year to year most of the volunteers volunteered on various days and thus became a part of a number of different day groups. They also came down to the shelter to socialize on days when they weren't volunteering, and all of this led to the development of allegiances across the days and to the whole shelter volunteer corps. This took time, but once it happened, the volunteer corps at the shelter was at the point where amongst themselves they began developing ways of being that encompassed the entire volunteer corps. When this happened they began developing symbols and rituals that defined the entire shelter.

The rituals that the Sacred Heart volunteers have developed and the ones that they retain are those that make the work more enjoyable and effective. Some of these rituals are as simple as the regular routines that they and their clients have established for directing the events of the night. There are procedures for opening up the shelter, for the welcoming and the settling of the clients, for serving dinner, for washing up after dinner, for going to bed and for waking up, having breakfast and getting back on the bus to Manhattan. While the volunteers and the clients might think of the rituals in purely functionalist terms, from the community-generation perspective, they have important side effects that are much broader than the simple functions would lead one to imagine. It is out of ritualistic interactions that collective values are created and that moral orders start to form. For rituals to have a moral effect, Robert Wuthnow notes that the following must happen:

> When the ritual ends, its participants do not emerge emboldened and empowered simply from the experience of having been swept away in collective activity. The ritual must explicitly mandate a moral obligation for the individual participant, one that he or she can fulfill in service to the moral order that has been dramatized. This act of service demonstrates that the individual, too, can make a difference and has a moral responsibility to exercise choice. . . . Moral ritual not only dramatizes a connection between a symbolic event and collective values; it also creates an opportunity for the individual to exercise moral responsibility in relation to those values.[10]

At first these encounters can be unsettling for the volunteers, but as Clifford Geertz notes, prolonged encounters with others can lead to the growth of a powerful sensibility for the condition of others and an increased sense of what can be done about this condition.[11]

Not only do the rituals connect volunteers to the lives of their clients and build their moral sensibilities but they also connect volunteers to each other and build friendships. There are many volunteers, both past and present, who can't let a week go by without visits to the

shelter. These visits, to bring cakes, cookies, or Jell-O down to the shelter for people to share, play cards, or listen to stories have become
neighborhood rituals. They have now come to encompass the local
Girl Scout troop and the confirmation classes and when the shelter is
closed during the summer people sorely miss these times.

At Fifth Avenue Presbyterian, the volunteers were often allowed to
work singly and they could very easily have minimal interaction with
the other volunteers. So the allegiances that they were most likely to
build were to the homeless men in the shelter. Here the challenge of
creating a loyalty that encompasses the whole shelter has been a more
difficult one, as is evidenced by its history. This is a challenge that
Peter Saghir met by his newsletters that kept the volunteers up to date
on each other and on the homeless guests; by creating small teams
within the volunteers corps, like the hospital-visiting team and the
Homeless on the Steps program, in which otherwise isolated volunteers can work together and get to know each other; and by holding
all of those events organized by groups of volunteers and homeless
clients at the shelter so that people come and visit and spend more
time at the shelter getting to know each other than they would otherwise. These events are supplemented by open houses after the Sunday
service, when most of the volunteers are likely to be at the church
anyway, and by joint events with other volunteer groups. The shelter
coordinator's deliberate attempts to build an esprit de corps among
the shelter volunteers and help them develop their own rituals have
been succeeding. In urban settings, like that of Fifth Avenue Presbyterian, in which the volunteers do not live near the site, such deliberate
approaches are likely to be necessary, as the more organic development of group identity and rituals that took place at Sacred Heart just
won't happen.

Ensuring the Perpetuation of the Association

Communities take time to develop and in order to make sure that they
are given that time, a perpetuation system needs to be set up to make
sure that the organization continues to acquire an adequate quantity
and quality of the resources that it will need to operate successfully.
This can be conceived of as providing for community maintenance,

222   and when designing the perpetuation system, the designers need to think about the provision of human resources as well as nonhuman resources.

Providing for community maintenance is probably the hardest aspect of community generation. Not only do organizations tend to change over time and become more bureaucratic—what Van Til refers to as the Weber problem—but they also tend to become more oligopolistic—what Van Til refers to as the Michels problem. In addition to combating these problems, the social architect also needs to be concerned with prosaic questions such as where future members of the organization will come from, where revenue will come from, and where the sites will be located in the future.[12] They also need to think about who will be responsible for leading the organization in the future and for making sure that it doesn't get too bureaucratized or that it doesn't become too much of an oligopoly.

Because most volunteers are likely to be interested in direct service, procuring nonhuman resources is more likely to remain the territory of the paid staff at the agency's central office. That doesn't mean that the sites in the field won't play a role, and at the Partnership for the Homeless, the fact that the shelters are sited in churches and synagogues has been enormously beneficial for securing nonhuman resources for the agency. Not only is the Partnership relatively certain that these sites will continue as shelters for the foreseeable future but also these churches will likely continue to be reliable sources of donations. Though the Partnership has taken great pains to raise funds from private sources in order to prevent reliance on city contracts and avoid becoming an adjunct of the city over time, the fact that the agency has successfully won several large city contracts is a positive indicator of the Partnership's long-term financial viability. City contracts tend to be renewed and they tend to grow over time, and they bring a healthy measure of stability to the agency. Long-term relationships with private funders, such as banks that have to meet Community Reinvestment Act targets and foundations that support voluntary agencies, are also important to cultivate, and placing key executives from such places on the board of directors of the agency is always a good strategy for developing these relationships. Creating

paid positions in the agency so that there are staff members whose job
it is to secure financial resources is also a good way to ensure the
steady supply of resources to the agency.

As difficult a job as it may be, providing for the future supply of
nonhuman resources is much easier than providing for the future
supply of human resources. Of all the work processes, this is the one
that the shelters have been the least successful in attending to. It is a
process that is complicated and it can easily be overlooked, put off, or
attended to in such a way that it dooms the community-generating
capacity of the institution. However, this process cannot be ignored if
a community-generating institution is going to last. Securing human
resources is a job for all of the sites. In both of the shelters that I have
focused on, the most critical human resources have been the volunteer coordinators and a few other key veteran volunteers. Having effective volunteer coordinators and effective veteran volunteers is absolutely critical to the success of a community-generating association,
and finding such people and grooming equally capable replacements
is the only way that communities can ensure that they will continue
to function over an extended time period. While the functions of
community are things that, in the end, people have to self-provide,
inspired, dogged, hands-on leadership of the kind that takes success or
failure of the institution very personally is necessary for any association
to successfully generate a community. This was the kind of leadership
that Peter Saghir provided at Fifth Avenue Presbyterian, and when he
was succeeded by Kathleen McGuffin, she continued to successfully
operate the shelter as a community-generating institution.

When Margaret Shafer, the Fifth Avenue Presbyterian's associate
for outreach, reflected on what has made their shelter successful she
said, "When we have had a well-organized person as coordinator it
has worked well."[13] Sacred Heart was fortunate to start out with a trio
of such people. Of the two remaining coordinators, Jim Jones is about
to retire, leaving the leadership role solely on Virginia Brown's shoulders. These are very capable shoulders, and Jim referred to Virginia as
the fire behind the shelter.

One of the reasons the Sacred Heart shelter closes every summer is
so that Virginia can take a break. She has offered to train a replacement

224 coordinator, but no one has taken her up on this offer. Other than her annual summer breaks, the only time she has stepped back from her role as volunteer coordinator was in the fall of 1993 after her husband, brother, and son passed away in quick succession.[14] To take her place Jim found another woman who was also on the Parish Council. She became a co-coordinator in November of 1993 but by January Jim was asking Virginia to come back because he couldn't work with this woman. Virginia came back and she and Jim have been coordinating the shelter ever since.

Over the years Virginia and Jim have developed the rare sort of working relationship in which they can yell at each other one day and be back working side by side the next with no ill feelings. This sort of relationship is hard to come by but is critical if people are going to be able to work together through the trials of building and sustaining a community.

Because people who can be effective community leaders are hard to find, and because leading a community is hard work, social architects may be tempted to take the easy way out by dividing up the work and assigning it to a committee. Doing so, I feel, would be a tremendous error because it would rationalize this essentially charismatic position, thus stripping leadership of its essence. This could very easily be fatal to the community-generating capacity of the institution. While committees should exist to play a support role, and while leaders can emerge from committees, the committees themselves cannot be the actual leaders. Only dedicated, hardworking people can do that. The profound attachment that people like Virginia, Jim, and Peter bring to their work and the joy that they derive from it are infectious, and without their efforts neither shelter would have developed its community-generating capacity. Finding, training, and retaining people like them has to be a prime job of any social architect, because without them the associations will fall apart.

Conclusion

The type of association that results from these processes should be one that can take on an important social task and perform that task in such a way that it accomplishes community-generating functions in the lives of its members. I say that it should be able to, not that it will be able to, for the reasons that I said before—that success or failure in generating community hinges on the effort that the members of the association put forward. Though a major aspect of the work of the social architect is in attending to the efforts of the volunteers, this attention will not always be successful. Rather, community and community generation will always be works in progress, and the interrelationship between the workings of associations and the qualities and attitudes of the individual members will always be dynamic.

Though there is a cultural heritage in America that gives rise to the American Ethic and that venerates community associations, this ethic needs constant attention and nurturing. Creating organizations that can recruit people into membership and that can make it in their self-interest to remain will always be hard work. In America today, unless the requisite attention and nurturing are present, community-generating organizations will remain rare, and the ones that do get created will tend to lose their community-generating capacity as they either become community-serving organizations or fade away. The challenge, therefore, for those interested in generating and maintaining communities is to develop and maintain community-generating institutions.

This will always be a challenge, as institutions change, and in the years that I have been familiar with it, the changes at the Partnership for the Homeless have been significant following what seems to be a

226   standard trajectory that nonprofit, service delivery institutions tend to follow. When I first started working there, the Partnership was in the founding phase—the one in which a charismatic visionary creates an organization and attracts people who have a sense of calling to it and its work. This was Peter Smith and this sort of leader usually does not to like to have a board of directors that is independent. This sort of director is often uninterested in financial matters, but in this Peter differed from the norm. Not only was he very concerned with the fiscal health of the agency but he also preferred for the Partnership to get the majority of its funding from private donations because he did not want its work controlled by the sorts of restrictions that come with government contracts. As the organization got larger and Peter's health began to decline, the religious charities and Wall Street banks that backed the Partnership began to assert themselves. They demanded that the executive director be more accountable to board oversight, and they demanded that the board have more control over the organization's finances. In preparation for the day when Peter would no longer be in charge the board hired Joel Sesser to be the executive vice president and upon Peter's death in 1992, Joel became the executive director.

This transition marked the move into the second phase. With the charismatic leader gone, with a stronger board, and with an executive director who had been brought in to develop the administrative and fund-raising capacity of the agency, the Partnership entered its bureaucratic consolidation phase. Joel came to the Partnership from the Bowery Resources Center, a much older agency, and the knowledge that he had gained there was brought to bear on developing the bureaucratic capacity of the Partnership. Through the 1990s the agency moved to bigger offices, reorganized its money-losing programs, trimmed expenses, and successfully won more government contracts. As service delivery staff was cut from money-losing programs, staff was added in accounting, fund-raising, and administration. Despite this bureaucratic consolidation and the seeming succumbing of the agency to Van Til's Weber problem, many of the employees remained from the old days, especially in the shelter program, and they were still motivated to keep the programs running as they had before. The

shelters, too, retained their autonomy and kept operating in the manner that they had before.

Whereas Peter Smith seemed to be motivated by a complicated mix of responding to a social crisis and redeeming himself, Joel was more interested in organization building, and by the late 1990s he was looking for a new challenge. With his departure and with the hiring of Arnold Cohen in 1999, the Partnership entered a third phase, one of professionalization.

It is still too early to tell what the impact of the new leadership will be on the Partnership, and particularly on the shelter program, but indications are that it will be profound. In the time that he has been executive director, Cohen, who had previously been the executive director of Queens Legal Services and who like Peter is a lawyer, has gotten rid of all of the program directors who remained from the Peter Smith days and has replaced them with young lawyers and Ph.D.s. This means that people like Bill Appel and Brenda Griffin, who ran the shelter program for over 15 years, are no longer there and with their departure went the trusting relationships that they had built with city DHS employees, with partner agencies, and with the volunteers. The Partnership will have to work to rebuild these relationships.

Along with the personnel changes are program changes that have been made or that are in the offing. Among the changes that have already been made are the creation of a systematic program, called Transitions, that aims to help prepare the homeless people in the church shelters for independent living by doing such things as "assessing a client's readiness and individual needs, setting realistic goals, designing a plan to remove barriers to success, providing an array of supports and training, and developing an individualized program of follow-up and continued support after independence is achieved."[1] Other program changes include a support and advocacy program for homeless families with children and targeted outreach for older homeless adults and people with HIV/AIDS who are living on the streets. The most notable change from the point of view of this book, however, is that for the first time the Partnership plans to politicize its volunteers. With a planned program that they intend to call Our Voices Raised, the Partnership aims to begin "a community organizing effort to develop our volunteer community into an advocacy group that works on the systemic issues that affect our clients."[2]

In starting this program, the Partnership seems poised to try to tackle another of the problems that voluntary agencies typically face, one that Van Til refers to as the Marx problem. What Van Til meant by this was that voluntary agencies traditionally have a difficult time addressing inequities of social power as they are manifested institutionally. This is a problem that I addressed when I spoke about the mediating function of the shelters. As you may recall there are three aspects of mediation—connecting people to each other, to sources of meaning, and to sources of power—and the one that the Partnership, and almost any other mediating institution, has trouble with is the last one. Particularly problematic is the ability to connect people to those in power in such as way that the people in power are held accountable and will engage with the volunteers in deliberation and change their policies.

At best, the Partnership had moderate success with this aspect of mediation and when they were successful it was through the ability to persuade within the context of personal relationships. Peter Smith was good at this because of his personal relationships with many in the upper echelons of city government and within the judicial system. Over time, Bill Appel and Brenda Griffin built up a more limited version of these sorts of relationships with those in power and DHS and related social service agencies. Unfortunately these personal relationships often proved to be too weak to bring about changes in city policy that the volunteers and the staff of the Partnership thought were necessary, and with the changeover in staff at the Partnership, these personal relationships are no longer available.

In this situation, Our Voices Raised seems like an overdue development. The Partnership has been operating for nearly 20 years with a huge volunteer corps, yet it maintains such a low profile that it is unable to affect policy the way that some think it should. By organizing the volunteers into a more vocal group, the Partnership should be able to increase its ability to influence the actions of those in power, and it should be able to successfully deal with the Marx question. In making this change, however, the new leadership of the agency needs to think about the potential cost to other things that it does quite well. Community organizing, as it has traditionally been practiced, has been about finding an issue to politicize and mobilize people around, and the benefit of this move should be weighed against the costs.

Jim Jones's comments that he and Harold opened their shelter and worked with the Partnership because they wanted to stay away from politics is an important one to keep in mind. It was the apolitical nature of the Sacred Heart shelter that enabled it to attract support from people who would not have otherwise supported it, and this is what enabled the shelter to get people of all sorts of political persuasions to volunteer and get to know each other. When I asked Margaret Shafer what she thought about this point of view, she said, "I think that he [Jim] is right. We talk, and our senior pastor particularly talks a great deal about one of the characteristics of a big church is that is has big arms and it includes everybody—from liberal to conservative—and all stripes and colors."[3] At the Fifth Avenue Presbyterian shelter "every point of view is represented," and as Margaret notes, "we try not to talk about politics."[4] There were a myriad of other comments from volunteers who stated that they relish to opportunity to serve their fellow man without having too many other requirements put on them. They just did their jobs and over time it was in their self-interest to continue doing their jobs.

Whether or not the Partnership will be able to continue to attract such a large number of volunteers across such a broad spectrum and develop them into an advocacy group at the same time remains to be seen. In chasing after a solution to the Marx problem the directors of the Partnership should not forget that they seem to have already found a good solution to the Tocqueville problem, which in a large and diverse country such as ours might be at least as fundamental of a problem. In their church shelters they have created environments in which the American Ethic can be passed on to new generations and can be nourished in older generations. This is a precious thing, and it is not at all certain whether voluntary associations can function as community generators in our individualistic society while at the same time they try to be engines of dialectical change. Neither, however, is it certain that dialectical change is desirable.

Appendix: Research Methods

This book is an example of what Robert K. Yin calls an embedded case study—a method well suited for understanding and categorizing a complex system such as the Partnership and its network. Like all case studies, this one has five components: the questions; the propositions, if any; the units of analysis; the logic linking the data to the propositions; and the criteria for interpreting the findings. I will go through each of them to explain how I arrived at the conclusions that I did.[1]

I started developing the research questions shortly after beginning work at the Partnership for the Homeless in August 1991. With William F. Whyte's *Learning from the Field: A Guide from Experience* as my guide, I started exploring the shelters and what took place in them. I volunteered evenings and nights, I visited volunteers and their homeless clients, and I spoke at numerous services to recruit and reward volunteers. This was the participant observation phase of the research and, in addition to learning from the field, this was the time when I became accepted by the people that I was observing.[2]

Because recruitment was a central part of my work at the Partnership, I was very interested to learn from the existing volunteers why they started working with the homeless and particularly why they continued. Time and again the volunteers told me that they volunteered in these shelters because they felt as if they received more out of their voluntary efforts than they put in. Some of them even stated that they felt as if they got more out the shelters than did their homeless clients. Initially these statements made no sense to me, because it seemed that the only benefit that the volunteers were getting was the ability to feel good about themselves. For quite a while I ignored this statement, but I heard it repeated so often that I eventually started investigating.

Thus began the second phase of case study research that Yin identifies: the formulation of the propositions. I began by having conversations with 10 long-term volunteers. These were all taped and listening to them a number of times helped me conceptualize the questions that I used in the next step: in-depth interviews with 30 long-term volunteers. These interviews ranged in length from 45 minutes to 2 hours, and included in this group were volunteer shelter coordinators—such as Jim Jones and Virginia Brown at Sacred Heart, Chris Cleveland at Madison Avenue Baptist, and Rev. Erik Kolbell at Riverside Church—and some longtime volunteers who were not coordinators—such as Joe Pace and Pat and Gene Durant. During this phase I also interviewed former New York Mayor Ed Koch; Joel Sesser, the president of the Partnership for the Homeless; and Martha Johns, a board member of the Partnership and a vice president of the Federation of Protestant Welfare Agencies. These people all helped me to better understand the history of the Partnership and the nature of its relations to city agencies and to the big religious charities. Like the first set of conversations, all of these interviews were taped and I was able to listen to them again years later with a new set of ears.[3]

These interviews did not give me much insight into what it was that the volunteers were getting out of their work in the shelters. What I learned from them helped me to develop a questionnaire for subsequent interviews with the volunteers that did give me this insight. This next phase of figuring out how to interview the volunteers and assess what effect their voluntary experience was having on them was difficult because I could not find anyone who had done similar studies that had treated volunteers and the institutions that they formed in a systematic manner. As it turned out, there was good reason for this. Developing an understanding of the impact of volunteering on individual attitudes would require a longitudinal study in which the same volunteers were interviewed over and over again across many years, and no one had ever seemed to have the resources to do one. I did not have the resources for such a study either, so I devised what I called a virtual longitudinal study—one in which I surveyed new volunteers and veteran volunteers in the same shelters to see what differences of opinion there were between the two groups. With this framework set, shelter program director Bill Appel and I devised what we thought were a good series of questions that would help us to get a more detailed picture of how the shelters operated, what motivated the volunteers' actions, the scope of their actions, and what benefits accrued to them as a result. I then set out to pretest the questionnaire.

Over a period of a few months I mailed out about 50 written questionnaires, 20 of which were returned. These returned questionnaires gave me further insights into the impact that the volunteering was having on the volunteers and it helped me to theorize more about why people volunteered in the homeless shelters and what the impact of their activity was on them. During this theory formation phase, I did a lot of reading to form an interpretive context with which I could make sense of what the volunteers were telling me. This was one of a number of periods in which I went back and forth between literature and the findings to hone my theory of what was going on in these shelters. This pretest also indicated to me what parts of the questionnaire worked and what parts needed to be changed and, with this knowledge and with a clearer theory in mind, Bill Appel and I tinkered with the questionnaire to come up with better questions.

Once this questionnaire was done Bill phoned shelter coordinators around the city and asked permission for me to send them the questionnaire, which they would then pass on to their volunteers. Almost all of the shelter coordinators who were asked gave permission and I sent out about 400 questionnaires in late 1993 and early 1994. Because I was gathering information for the Partnership as well as for my research, the questionnaire was much longer than what I thought was needed. This made it harder for the volunteers to fill it out than I would have liked, and I think that this reduced the number of completed questionnaires that I received back. In the long run, however, these longer questionnaires proved to be a boon because of the amount of information that they gathered. Of these surveys 70 were completed by veteran volunteers and returned to me, and 30 were completed by new volunteers and returned. The veterans were all people who had been volunteering at their shelters for at least one year, and many of them had at that point been volunteering for 5 years or more. The new volunteers had all been volunteering less than one year. These completed questionnaires contained a wealth of information on the volunteers' views and opinions and with them in hand I began the stage of interpretation and theory testing.

From these surveys I learned why people began volunteering, why they continued, what they got out of volunteering, how the shelters were organized, what the shelters were good and not so good at doing, what the volunteers thought were the causes of homelessness, and what they thought some solutions to homelessness might be. I found that the veteran volunteers had views on some of these subjects that were different from those that the homeless advocates and other professionals in the field had and my initial hypothesis was that the volunteers' views were shaped by the experiences that they had in the shelters. Because this was not a true longitudinal study, however, I could not say so conclusively and the task then became figuring out what claims could validly be made with the results of the findings and what the next research steps should be.

Following graduate school I began teaching community development and in this new academic environment I began to read widely on the concept of community. From this new perspective I grasped that with my initial focus on the individuals I had missed the group phenomenon, which was that these homeless shelters had become the loci of communities. With this in mind I went back and I revisited my data to see what it said about community formation. The richest data that I had about this was from Sacred Heart, but as both I and the readers of a paper that I wrote about community formation at Sacred Heart realized, I would need more than one case if I was going to make any claims and develop and test any theories. So again with Bill Appel's help, I got in touch with some volunteer coordinators at other churches that had large groups of volunteers and I went back to New York in the fall of 2001 to do more interviews. I settled on Fifth Avenue Presbyterian as the second case because through some deliberate organizational changes they had turned a dying shelter with six volunteers into a thriving one. It seemed that comparing and contrasting the new organization at Fifth Avenue with the one at Sacred Heart would be illuminating and make for fruitful theorizing.

The conception that I had of what community generation at Sacred Heart looked like helped me to structure the new set of interviews that I conducted in the fall of 2001 at both Fifth Avenue Presbyterian and Sacred Heart, and this conception formed the basis of my theory of community generation. In my mind the key indicator of a vibrant community was that it had lots of members and that these people stayed involved with each other over an extended period of time. I also theorized that there was a relationship between the organizational structure of the shelter and the size and durability of the volunteer corps. With the findings from these new interviews I was able to refine my understanding of what was happening in the shelters, to better understand how these shelters worked to generate communities, and to develop a fuller definition of the type of community generation that goes on in these shelters. With close readings of the findings, and with integration of more pertinent literature, I was able to develop my conception of community generation and to break it down into discreet functions. These functions each became the subject of individual chapters, and in these chapters I discuss how each of the shelters performs these functions. It was from this standpoint that I developed guidelines for what a community-generation process should look like and how it could be replicated.

Notes

Introduction

1. Alexis de Tocqueville, *Democracy in America,* trans., ed., and with an introduction by Harvey C. Mansfield and Debra Winthrop (1835 and 1840; reprint, Chicago: University of Chicago Press, 2000), p. 502.

2. While Tocqueville was one of the earliest and is among the most famous commentators on this American characteristic, he wasn't the last. More recently Robert Bellah and his co-authors have written two well-received volumes that examine America's "Habits of the Heart" and they pay close attention to what they call *committed individualism* (Robert N. Bellah et al., *Habits of the Heart: Individualism and Commitment in American Life* [New York: Harper & Row, 1985]). This topic has also been examined recently by, among others, Herbert Gans in *Middle American Individualism: The Future of Liberal Democracy* (New York: Free Press, 1988); Harry Boyte in *Community Is Possible: Repairing America's Roots* (New York: Harper & Row, 1984); and Benjamin Barber in *Strong Democracy: Participatory Politics for a New Age* (Berkeley: University of California Press, 1984).

3. Among those who have looked into this relationship between participation in particular organizations and the ethics of their members are Seymour Mandelbaum in *Open Moral Communities* (Cambridge, Mass.: MIT Press, 2000); and Nancy L. Rosenblum in *Membership and Morals: The Personal Uses of Pluralism in America* (Princeton, N.J.: Princeton University Press, 1998). Neither of them, however, engaged in a sustained examination of volunteers and the institutions that they create.

4. This controversy was ignited by Robert D. Putnam in his *Bowling Alone: The Collapse and Revival of American Community* (New York: Simon & Schuster, 2000), and in his series of articles that led up to it.

5. Throughout the book I will refer to these simply as the church shelters. This is partially for brevity—it is much is easier than referring to them as the church and synagogue shelters—and partially because only six of the shelters are in synagogues.

6. In some of the larger Manhattan churches, the volunteer coordinators are paid, part-time staff.

7. This conception is derived from T. M. Scanlon, *What We Owe to Each Other* (Cambridge, Mass.: Harvard University Press, 1998).

8. This is the position that the communitarians take, with some of the leading communitarian voices being Barber, *Strong Democracy;* Alasdair MacIntyre, *After Virtue: A Study in Moral Theory* (South Bend, Ind.: University of Notre Dame Press, 1981); Amitai Etzioni, *The Spirit of Community: Rights, Responsibilities and the Communitarian Agenda* (New York: Crown Publishers, 1993); William Galston, *Liberal Purposes: Goods, Virtues, and Diversity in the Liberal State* (New York: Cambridge University Press, 1991).

9. This argument is drawn from Herve Varenne. See *Americans Together: Structured Diversity in a Midwestern Town* (New York: Teacher's College Press, 1977).

10. Michael Taylor, *Community, Anarchy and Liberty* (New York: Cambridge University Press, 1982), p. 26.

1. The Partnership for the Homeless

1. Jack Newfield and Paul DuBrul, *The Abuse of Power: The Permanent Government and the Fall of New York* (New York: Viking Press, 1977), p. 166.

2. Jack Newfield and Wayne Barrett, *City for Sale: Ed Koch and the Betrayal of New York* (New York: Harper & Row, 1988), p. 154.

3. Bruce Lambert, "Peter Smith Obituary," *New York Times,* 18 November 1992.

4. Ibid.

5. Ibid.

6. Bill Appel and Brenda Griffin interview, 15 October 2001.

7. Peter Smith died shortly after I started at the Partnership for the Homeless and before I began this research, so I was never able to interview him for this book.

8. Ed Koch interview, 16 December 1994.

9. Ibid.

10. Ibid.

11. Appel and Griffin interview.

12. Ibid.

13. Peter J. Wosh, "St. Paul's Chapel," in *The Encyclopedia of the City of New York,* ed. Kenneth T. Jackson (New Haven, Conn.: Yale University Press, 1995), p. 1037.

14. "Trinity Real Estate," http://www.trinityrealestate.org (accessed 29 October 2003).

15. Ibid.

16. "Battery Park City: Timeline," http://www.batteryparkcity.org/timeline.htm (accessed 29 October 2003).

17. Kim Hopper, "The Public Response to Homelessness in New York City: The Last Hundred Years," in *On Being Homeless: Historical Perspective,* ed. Rick Beard (New York: Museum of the City of New York, 1987), pp. 88–101.

18. Kenneth L. Kusmer, "The Underclass in Historical Perspective," in *On Being Homeless: Historical Perspective,* ed. Rick Beard (New York: Museum of the City of New York, 1987), p. 21.

19. Clara J. Hemphill and Raymond A. Mohl, "Poverty," in *The Encyclopedia of the City of New York,* ed. Kenneth T. Jackson (New Haven, Conn.: Yale University Press, 1995), p. 932.

20. Ibid.

21. See Michael B. Katz, *In the Shadow of the Poor House: A Social History of Welfare in America* (New York: Basic Books, 1986), especially chapter 3.

22. Ibid., p. 61.

23. Ibid.

24. Ibid., p. 63.

25. Alana J. Erickson, "Association for Improving the Condition of the Poor," in *The Encyclopedia of the City of New York,* ed. Kenneth T. Jackson (New Haven, Conn.: Yale University Press, 1995), p. 61.

2. In the Church Shelters

1. Newfield and Barrett, *City for Sale,* p. 117.

2. Jim Jones, Virginia Brown, and Virginia Brown Jr. interview, 9 September 1994.

3. *St. Anthony Messenger,* June 1997.

4. In recent years the Catholic Church has actually taken steps to reaffirm the fact that the priest is the sole authority in the parish. In August 1997, under the oversight of Pope John Paul II, a document titled *Instruction on Certain Questions Regarding the Collaboration of the Non-Ordained Faithful in the Sacred Ministry of Priest* stated that "directing, coordinating, moderating or governing the parish . . . are the competencies of a priest

alone." The Roman Catholic authors further proclaimed that "it is unlawful for the non-
ordained faithful to assume titles such as 'pastor,' 'chaplain,' 'coordinator,' 'moderator,' or
other such similar titles which can confuse their role and that of the pastor, who is always
a bishop or priest."

5. Jones, Brown, and Brown Jr. interview.

6. Ibid.

7. Ibid.

8. Ibid.

9. Ibid.

10. Ibid.

11. Ibid.

12. Ibid.

13. Ibid.

14. Ibid.

15. Charles Brecher and Raymond D. Horton, with Robert A. Cropf and Dean
Michael Mead, *Power Failure: New York City Politics and Policy since 1960* (New York: Oxford University Press, 1993), p. 57.

16. Jones, Brown, and Brown Jr. interview.

17. Ibid.

18. Ibid.

19. Ibid.

20. Ibid.

21. Appel and Griffin interview.

22. Ibid.

23. Jones, Brown, and Brown Jr. interview.

24. Ibid.

25. Ibid.

26. Ibid.

27. Ibid.

28. Ibid.

29. Ibid.

30. Ibid.

31. Virginia Brown interview, 18 October 2001.

32. Jones, Brown, and Brown Jr. interview.

33. Brown interview, 18 October 2001.

34. "Fifth Avenue Presbyterian Church—Architecture," http://www.fapc.org/
whoweare/architect.html (accessed 29 October 2003).

35. "Fifth Avenue Presbyterian Church—History," http://www.fapc.org/whoweare/
history.html (accessed 29 October 2003).

36. Margaret Shafer interview, 17 October 2001.

37. Ibid.

38. Ibid.

39. Peter Saghir interview, 10 January 2002.

40. Ibid.

41. Ibid.

42. Ibid.

43. Ibid.

44. Ibid.

45. Ibid.

46. Ibid.

47. Ibid.

48. Ibid.

49. Shafer interview, 17 October 2001.

50. Saghir interview.

51. Shafer interview, 17 October 2001.

52. Robin Finn, "In Search of 'Divine Justice' for the Homeless in Court," *New York Times,* 21 December 2001.

53. Jane Fritsch, "Church Lawsuit Tries to Stop Police from Ejecting Homeless," *New York Times,* 18 December 2001.

54. Shafer interview, 17 October 2001.

55. Ibid.

56. Ibid.

57. Peter Dobkin Hall, "Vital Signs: Organizational Population Trends and Civic Engagement in New Haven, Connecticut, 1850–1998," in *Civic Engagement in American Democracy,* ed. Theda Skocpol and Morris P. Fiorina (Washington, D.C.: Brookings Institution Press, and New York: Russell Sage Foundation Press, 1999), pp. 211–248.

58. Ibid., p. 232.

59. In fact there is the concept of the community of practice, which has been popularized by Etienne Wenger, Jean Lave, and others, and I will build on this concept in chapter 6 to illustrate how these two programs built communities through the daily practice of operating their shelters.

3. Why People Volunteer in Church Shelters and Why They Keep at It

1. Alexis de Tocqueville, *Democracy in America,* trans. Henry Reeve, rev. Francis Bowen, ed. Phillips Bradley (1835; reprint, New York: Vintage Books, 1990), 1:191.

2. Hauke Brunkhorst, "Action and Agency," in *The Blackwell Encyclopedia of Twentieth-Century Social Thought,* ed. William Outhwaite and Tom Bottomore (Cambridge, Mass.: Blackwell, 1993), p. 1.

3. Joe Pace interview, 4 March 1993.

4. Ibid.

5. Ibid.

6. Ibid.

7. Ibid.

8. Ibid.

9. Pat and Gene Durant interview, 14 April 1993.

10. Ibid.

11. Ibid.

12. Ibid.

13. Ibid.

14. Aristotle, *Ethics* (New York: E. P. Dutton & Co., 1963), p. 46.

15. An agent is an "acting subject," whose actions are "practical conclusions drawn from intentions and beliefs" (Brunkhorst, "Action and Agency," p. 1).

16. Morton Kole interview, spring 1994.

17. Virginia Brown interview, spring 1994.

18. Kate Coogan interview, spring 1994.

19. Ann Orstein interview, spring 1994.

20. Larry Whaler interview, spring 1994.

Schlesinger aptly labeled America as a nation of joiners, and Murray Hausknecht later reused that same phrase. See Arthur Schlesinger, "Biography of a Nation of Joiners," *American Historical Review* 50, no. 1 (1944): 1–25; and Murray Hausknecht, *The Joiners* (New York: Bedminster Press, 1962). The word *volunteer* comes from the Latin word *velle*, meaning "to will or wish." Thus, a volunteer is "one who enters into or offers himself for service of his own free will" (W. K. Kellogg Foundation, *Reaching Out: America's Volunteer Heritage* [Battle Creek, Mich.: W. K. Kellogg Foundation, 1990]).

22. The language about encumbered and unencumbered selves comes from Michael Sandel in *Liberalism and the Limits of Justice*. According to Sandel, liberals see American society as consisting of unencumbered selves—that is, people who act for their own self-referential reasons—while communitarians and others with a more collectivist visions see American society as consisting of encumbered selves—that is, people who act out of communal obligations and within institutional settings. See Michael Sandel, *Liberalism and the Limits of Justice* (New York: Cambridge University Press, 1982).

23. Only 10 of the new volunteers, or one-third of the sample, explained their decision to begin volunteering as primarily an exercise of their own agency, while 45 of the veterans, nearly two-thirds of the sample, explained their decision to begin volunteering as an exercise of free will.

24. Peter Cache survey, fall 1993; Steven Romeo survey, spring 1994.

25. George James survey, spring 1994.

26. Marie Ranga survey, spring 1994.

27. Craig Black interview, spring 1994.

28. Jane Toth interview, spring 1994.

29. Lee Pander interview, spring 1994.

30. Kathy Rich survey, spring 1994.

31. Eric Zale survey, fall 1993.

32. Bruce Cromwall survey, spring 1994.

33. Terri Anderson survey, spring 1994.

34. John Bartha survey, spring 1994.

35. Dan Marina survey, spring 1994; Sourabh Chatterjee survey, spring 1994.

36. Elmer Jang survey, spring 1994.

37. Donna Shane survey, fall 1993.

38. Clara Spence survey, spring 1994.

39. *Giving and Volunteering in the United States* (Washington, D.C.: Independent Sector, 1999). Other surveys on voluntarism include "Global Study Finds High Rate of Volunteerism," *Chronicle of Philanthropy*, 9 September 1999, source: Johns Hopkins Center for Civil Society Studies; and "Polls Show Americans Say Volunteering Is Important," *Chronicle of Philanthropy*, 23 April 1998, sources: United Parcel Service, National Commission on Philanthropy and Civic Renewal, and Lutheran Brotherhood.

40. *Giving and Volunteering in the United States* (Washington, D.C.: Independent Sector, 2001).

41. *Giving and Volunteering in the United States* (1999).

42. See Jon Van Til, *Mapping the Third Sector: Voluntarism in a Changing Social Economy* (New York: Foundation Center, 1988), pp. 26–31.

43. Ibid., p. 32.

44. Ira J. Cohen, "Theories of Action and Praxis," in *The Blackwell Companion to Social Theory*, 2nd ed., ed. Bryan S. Turner (Cambridge, Mass.: Blackwell, 2000), pp. 73–111.

45. Ibid., pp. 73–74.

46. Of course, a similar view of the degrees of encumbrance that people face in their decisions on how to act socially is not the only thing that these different schools of thought have in common. They also have common understandings of the effect that such issues as the role that morality or amorality, self-interest or communal obligation, and free will or cultural obligation and expectations and/or material determinism play in the decisions that people make on whether or not to volunteer.

47. See Sandel, *Liberalism and the Limits of Justice.* Leading examples of this approach include Friedrich Hayek, *The Road to Serfdom* (1944; reprint, Chicago: University of Chicago Press, 1976); John Rawls, *A Theory of Justice* (Cambridge, Mass.: Harvard University Press, 1971); and Robert Nozick, *Anarchy, State and Utopia* (New York: Basic Books, 1974).

48. Sandel, *Liberalism and the Limits of Justice,* p. 178.

49. Rawls, *A Theory of Justice.*

50. Barry Hindess, "Rational Choice Theory," in *The Blackwell Encyclopedia of Twentieth-Century Social Thought,* ed. William Outhwaite and Tom Bottomore (Cambridge, Mass.: Blackwell, 1993), pp. 542–543.

51. See Anthony Downs, *An Economic Theory of Democracy* (New York: Harper & Row, 1957); Mancur Olson, *The Logic of Collective Action: Public Goods and the Theory of Groups* (Cambridge, Mass.: Harvard University Press, 1965); Robert Axelrod, *The Evolution of Cooperation* (New York: Basic Books, 1984); and William Riker, *Liberalism against Populism: A Confrontation between the Theory of Democracy and the Theory of Social Choice* (San Francisco: W. H. Freeman, 1982). Rational actor theorists, a subset of the liberal approach, have a hard time accounting for volunteering, however, as rationally, people should free ride on the actions of others. Mancur Olson's selective incentives, which can either be positive (rewards) or negative (punishments), are oriented "selectively toward the individuals in the group" and "stimulate a rational individual . . . to act in a group oriented way," which goes a way toward dealing with this problem. With this concept, Olson added an interesting dimension to rational actor theory by recognizing that organized groups can impact the actions of individuals. He also recognized that small groups are likely to be more successful in providing these selective incentives than large ones. Nonetheless, his theory still does not account for the effect that human emotions and feelings might have on behavior. Though Olson sees the potential for group-oriented action, the action, as he understands it, isn't about the group, or about those whom the group might be serving. Instead, it is still about the self. Another rational choice theorist, Robert Axelrod, adds more depth to this framework by explaining that through success in playing tit-for-tat games in life, rational actors can learn to cooperate. The mere use of the word *cooperate* represents a subtle shift from self-orientation toward other orientation. But this is as far as the rational actor model gets.

52. According to this argument, doing good makes the altruist feel good, and feeling good is in his or her self-interest. See David Horton Smith, "Altruism, Volunteers, and Volunteerism," *Journal of Voluntary Action Research* 10, no. 1 (January–March 1981): 21–36. This is a viewpoint that a growing number of cognitive psychologists dispute. In her review of work on altruism, Kristen Renwick Monroe refers to the growing view among cognitive psychologists that altruists see themselves as different from self-interested individuals, and that they are motivated by factors other than self-interest. She calls this the cognitive aspect of altruism. See Kristen Renwick Monroe, "A Fat Lady in a Corset: Altruism and Social Theory," *American Journal of Political Science* 38, no. 5 (1994): 861–893. For more discussion on altruism see Jane Allen Piliavin and Hong-Wen Charng, "Altruism: A Review of Recent Theory and Research," *Annual Review of Sociology* 16 (1990): 27–65.

53. In this group I included Alexis de Tocqueville and Baron de Montesquieu, *The Spirit of the Laws* (1749; reprint, New York: Cambridge University Press, 1989).

54. Tocqueville, *Democracy in America,* trans. Henry Reeve, rev. Francis Bowen, ed. Phillips Bradley, 2:105.

55. According to it prime proponents, Gabriel Almond and Sidney Verba, a civic culture is "the specifically political orientations—attitudes toward the political system and its various parts, and attitudes toward the role of the self in the system." These values and attitudes are "the connecting link between micro-and macropolitics." See Gabriel A. Almond and Sidney Verba, *The Civic Culture: Political Attitudes and Democracy in Five Nations* (Princeton, N.J.: Princeton University Press, 1963), p. 33.

56. Some in the civic culture school, like Alex Inkeles, go so far as to identify the personality traits of "individual modernity" that they see as being key variables in explaining why the members of modern societies act as they do. See Alex Inkeles, *Exploring Individual Modernity* (New York: Columbia University Press, 1983).

57. See David Elkins and Richard Simeon, "A Cause in Search of Its Effect: What Does Political Culture Explain?" *Comparative Politics* 2, no. 2 (1979): 127–145.

58. I use the word *materialist* to stand in for the wide range of Marxists, most of whom no longer call themselves that, and post-Marxists. See Mark Kesselman, "Order or Movement: The Literature of Political Development as Ideology," *World Politics* 26, no. 1 (1973): 139–154.

59. Daniel Bell, "Communitarianism," in *The Stanford Encyclopedia of Philosophy* (Stanford, Calif.: Metaphysics Research Lab, Center for the Study of Language and Information, 2001, http://plato.stanford.edu/entries/communitarianism/ [accessed 29 October 2003]). Leading communitarians include Barber, *Strong Democracy;* MacIntyre, *After Virtue;* Sandel, *Liberalism and the Limits of Justice;* Charles Taylor, "Cross-Purposes: The Liberal-Communitarian Debate," in *Liberalism and the Moral Life,* ed. Nancy L. Rosenblum (Cambridge, Mass.: Harvard University Press, 1989); Michael Walzer, *Spheres of Justice: A Defense of Pluralism and Equality* (New York: Basic Books, 1983); Etzioni, *The Spirit of Community;* and Galston, *Liberal Purposes.*

60. Charles Taylor, "Atomism," in *Communitarianism and Individualism,* ed. Shlomo Avineri and Avner De-Shalit (New York: Oxford University Press, 1982), p. 50.

61. Sandel, *Liberalism and the Limits of Justice,* p. 172.

62. The communitarians have surged to the fore in recent years with an intellectual and political agenda that aims to counteract what they see as the destructive dominance of the liberal-individualist approach in American politics and law. To this end, Amitai Etzioni, a leading communitarian, created and edits the periodical *The Responsive Community,* which functions as the intellectual house organ for the American communitarian movement. Etzioni also directs the Institute for Communitarian Policy Studies, the leading communitarian think tank. The chief political problem that communitarians have identified and are trying to counter is what they see as the growing imbalance between rights, of which we have too many, and responsibilities, of which we have too few. Their favored response is a moratorium on new rights and enactment of new public policies to refocus Americans away from a focus on personal fulfillment and toward community, family, neighborhood, and civic institutions.

63. See Sidney Verba, Kay Lehman Schlozman, and Henry E. Brady, *Voice and Equality: Civic Voluntarism in American Politics* (Cambridge, Mass.: Harvard University Press, 1995).

64. Ibid., p. 271.

65. Ibid.

66. Ibid., p. 272.

67. Ibid., p. 273.

68. Others think this as well. See, for example, Daniel Bell, "'American Exceptionalism Revisited': The Role of Civil Society," *Public Interest* 95 (1989): 38–56; Theda Skocpol, "How Americans Became Civic," in *Civic Engagement in American Democracy*, ed. Theda Skocpol and Morris P. Fiorina (Washington, D.C.: Brookings Institution Press, and New York: Russell Sage Foundation Press, 1999), pp. 27–80.

69. Tocqueville, *Democracy in America*, trans. Henry Reeve, rev. Francis Bowen, ed. Phillips Bradley, 2:105.

70. This concept of the intersubjectivity of some types of social action is one that was examined in detail by Max Weber, and it is a concept that can clarify the relationship and the communications between the volunteers and the shelters in their recruitment and decision-making process. In *Economy and Society*, Weber noted that all rational social actions, which can more accurately be thought as social interaction, may be oriented in four ways: instrumentally rational, value rational, affectual, and traditional. While actual actions are more likely than not to be the outcome of a combination of these value orientations, Weber's concept illustrates the scope that a useful theory and terminology of voluntary action should have. When people are deciding to act in a certain way, like volunteering in a homeless shelter, a range of motivations—from self-interested instrumental calculations, to religious beliefs, to emotions, which may or may not be rational, to traditions—can come into play. While individuals may differ in their specific orientation, all of the decisions to volunteer were partly social and intersubjective. See also Jeffrey Alexander, "Formal and Substantive Voluntarism in the Work of Talcott Parsons: A Theoretical and Ideological Reinterpretation," *American Sociological Review* 43 (April 1978): 180.

71. Though volunteers offer their services of their own free will, and though these volunteers were expressing points of view that made it apparent that their decision to volunteer was in part an act of free will, the statements that they made about why they started volunteering indicate that other factors such as organizational membership, recruitment, social expectations, communal obligations, traditions, and values and attitudes played a role in their decisions.

72. Talcott Parsons, "Social Interaction," in *International Encyclopedia of the Social Sciences*, vol. 7, ed. David L. Sills (New York: Macmillan and Free Press, 1968), p. 439.

73. See David Sciulli, "Voluntaristic Action as a Distinct Concept: Theoretical Foundations of Societal Constitutionalism," *American Sociological Review* 51 (1986): 743–766.

74. Pace interview.

75. Durant interview.

76. Tocqueville, *Democracy in America*, trans., ed., and with an introduction by Harvey C. Mansfield and Debra Winthrop, p. 493.

77. Churches and church-based voluntary efforts in New York get a lot of help with their recruitment efforts. Full-time volunteer recruitment organizations such as the Mayor's Voluntary Action Center, Corporate Volunteers of New York, the Volunteer Referral Center, Family Matters, New York Cares, and the Retired Senior Volunteer Program all played a significant role in recruiting volunteers for the Partnership and for other voluntary agencies throughout the city. These organizations were established to recruit volunteers and match their abilities and desires with the service needs of voluntary agencies throughout the city.

Further recruitment assistance came from corporations in New York that sought to encourage volunteerism among their employees. For example, beginning in 1991 the J. Walter Thompson advertising agency began sponsoring community service days, and volunteers began coming to the Partnership for the Homeless to help in various ways; AT&T began a monthly volunteering project with the Partnership's furniture program in the summer of 1994; and in 1994 the Partnership negotiated with JP Morgan for a senior executive who was nearing retirement age to come to the Partnership "on loan" to build an endowment fund. Corporate volunteering is not a new phenomenon; the NYNEX Telephone Pioneers, formerly of AT&T, have been functioning as a volunteer recruitment and referral organization since 1947. What is new is the greater extent to which this is happening, and that corporate volunteer organizations are broadening their scope to help not just the local Little League and Fire Department but also social service organizations that are involved in such messy work as volunteering in homeless shelters. Without the efforts of volunteer referral and training organizations such as these, volunteering in the church shelters would be a much rarer phenomenon.

4. The Mediating Role of the Church Shelters

1. Jones, Brown, and Brown Jr. interview.
2. Ibid.
3. Ibid.
4. Ibid.
5. Peter L. Berger and Richard John Neuhaus, "Mediating Structures and the Dilemmas of the Modern Welfare State," in *To Empower People: From State to Civil Society,* 2nd ed., Peter L. Berger and Richard John Neuhaus (Washington, D.C.: American Enterprise Institute for Public Policy Research, 1996), p. 158.
6. Ibid., p. 3.
7. The subject of alienation is central to much of the critical literature on modernity. For Karl Marx, the foremost critic of the capitalist version of modernity, alienation was perhaps the fundamental condition of modern man and he discussed it widely. See Karl Marx, *The Economic and Philosophic Manuscripts of 1844, On the Jewish Question,* and *Capital.* Marx, of course, was not the only theorist of modernity who spoke to the issue of alienation. Following Marx, other Marxists took up the topic and spoke eloquently about the alienating effect that commodification had on modern life and about the transition of man from producer to consumer, even as far as his own culture was concerned. See Georg Lukacs, *History and Class Consciousness* (1923; reprint, Cambridge, Mass.: MIT Press, 1972); and Theodor Adorno and Max Horkheimer, *The Dialectic of Enlightenment* (New York: Continuum, 1976). Marxists, of course, were not the only authors on the subject. See also Emile Durkheim, *Suicide: A Study in Sociology* (1897; reprint, New York: Free Press, 1997).
8. See Howard M. Barr, ed., *Disaffiliated Man: Essays and Bibliography on Skid Row, Vagrancy and Outsiders* (Toronto: University of Toronto Press, 1970).
9. Max Weber, *Economy and Society: An Outline of Interpretive Sociology,* vol. 1, ed. Guenther Roth and Claus Wittich (1921–22; reprint, Berkeley: University of California Press, 1978).
10. Berger and Neuhaus, "Mediating Structures," p. 159.
11. See Daniel Bell, *The Cultural Contradictions of Capitalism* (New York: Basic Books, 1976).
12. See Robert N. Bellah, "Is Capitalism Compatible with 'Traditional Morality'?" (lecture delivered at the University of Southern California, August 23, 1983); and Robert N. Bellah et al., *Habits of the Heart: Individualism and Commitment in American Life* (New York: Harper & Row, 1985).

246   13. Berger and Neuhaus, "Mediating Structures," p. 159.

14. Ibid., p. 158.

15. See J. Philip Wogaman, "The Church as Mediating Institution: Theological and Philosophical Perspective," in *Democracy and Mediating Structures,* ed. Michael Novak, (Washington, D.C.: American Enterprise Institute for Public Policy Research, 1980), pp. 69–84.

16. Ibid., pp. 70–73.

17. Anne Walker interview, spring 1994.

18. Steven Romeo interview, spring 1994.

19. Wogaman, "The Church as Mediating Institution," pp. 70–71.

20. Saghir interview.

21. Jones, Brown, and Brown Jr. interview.

22. Shafer interview, 17 October 2001.

23. Ibid.

24. Saghir interview.

25. Shafer interview, 17 October 2001.

26. Saghir interview.

27. Ibid

28. Jones, Brown, and Brown Jr. interview.

29. Ibid.

30. Ibid.

31. Tocqueville, *Democracy in America*, trans. Henry Reeve, rev. Francis Bowen, ed. Phillips Bradley, 2:122.

32. Ibid., p. 123.

33. Ibid.

34. Jones, Brown, and Brown Jr. interview.

35. Ibid.

36. Ibid.

37. Ibid.

38. Ibid.

39. Ibid.

40. Ibid.

41. Shafer interview, 17 October 2001.

42. Saghir interview.

43. Ibid.

44. Shafer interview, 17 October 2001.

45. Wogaman, "The Church as Mediating Institution," pp. 71–72.

46. Brown interview, 18 October 2001.

47. Jones, Brown, and Brown Jr. interview.

48. Brown interview, 18 October 2001.

49. Ibid.

50. Ibid.

51. Ibid.

52. Ibid.

53. Ibid.

54. Ibid.

55. Ibid.

56. The Peninsula Hotel, which is across 55th Street and where rooms cost well in excess of $1,000 per night, asked Margaret how it should explain this "cardboard city" to its clientele. Some of the few residents that there were on the street have also grumbled in

letters to the editor that have been published in the *New York Times* about their block being turned into a "shantytown."

57. Bob Herbert, "Trumping Charity," *New York Times,* 20 December 2001.

58. Ibid.

59. Fritsch, "Church Lawsuit."

60. Ibid.

61. Jane Fritsch, "Judge Orders End to Rousting of Homeless Near Church," *New York Times,* 20 December 2001.

62. Fritsch, "Church Lawsuit."

63. Associated Press, "Church, New York City Clash over Homeless," 18 December 2001.

64. Fritsch, "Church Lawsuit."

65. Ibid.

66. Ibid.

67. Wogaman, "The Church as Mediating Institution," pp. 73–74.

68. Ibid., p. 77.

69. Ibid.

70. Tocqueville, *Democracy in America,* trans. Henry Reeve, rev. Francis Bowen, ed. Phillips Bradley, 2:303–304.

71. Seymour Martin Lipset, *The First New Nation: The United States in Historical and Comparative Perspective* (New York: W. W. Norton & Co., 1973), p. 144.

72. Garry Wills, *Under God: Religion and American Politics* (New York: Touchstone, 1990), p. 16.

73. George Gallup Jr. and Jim Castelli, *The People's Religion: American Faith in the 90s* (New York: Macmillan, 1989). Quoted in Wills, *Under God,* p. 16.

74. Ibid.

75. Durant interview.

76. George James interview, spring 1994.

77. Peter Cache interview, spring 1994.

78. Alfred Cecci interview, spring 1994.

79. Ginger More interview, spring 1994.

80. Steven Black interview, spring 1994.

81. Una Burden interview, spring 1994.

82. Timothy Gold interview, spring 1994.

83. Kenneth Rong interview, spring 1994.

84. Dan Marina interview, spring 1994.

85. Ibid.

86. Kathy Rich interview, spring 1994.

87. Frank J. Short interview, spring 1994.

88. Elmer Jang interview, spring 1994.

89. Lloyd Green interview, spring 1994.

90. Brenda Lane interview, spring 1994.

91. Susan Mayhew interview, spring 1994.

92. Bertha Rankin interview, fall 1993.

93. Antionette Marie Canelli interview, spring 1994.

94. Robert Nisbet, *The Quest for Community: A Study in the Ethics of Order and Freedom* (1953; reprint, San Francisco: ICS Press, 1990), p. xxvi.

95. Ferdinand Tonnies, *Community and Association (Gemeinschaft und Gesellschaft),* trans. and ed. Charles P. Lommis, with an introduction by John Samples (1887; reprint, New Brunswick, N.J.: Transaction Publishers, 1996).

248   96. Ibid.

97. Ibid.

98. Ernest Gellner explains the origins of the concept of the Iron Cage and its relationship to disenchantment in Weberian thought in the following manner: "This is Disenchantment: the Faustian purchase of cognitive, technological and administrative power, by the surrender of our previous meaningful, humanly suffused, humanly responsive, if often menacing and capricious world. That is abandoned for a more predictable, more amenable, but coldly indifferent and un-cozy world. The Iron Cage is not merely one of bureaucratic organization: it is also a conceptual one. It places constraints not merely on our conduct, but also on our vision." See Ernest Gellner, *Culture, Identity and Politics* (New York: Cambridge University Press, 1987), p. 153. Gellner goes on to note, correctly I believe, that the icy rationality of the modern world that is presupposed by the Iron Cage metaphor is not all that icy in reality, and he proposes a replacement metaphor, the rubber cage, to describe a world in which more efficient production leaves us more leisure time but in which our private lives remain cut off from production and are instead occupied with incoherent indulgence.

99. Jane Jacobs, *The Death and Life of Great American Cities* (New York: Vintage, 1961); and Herbert Gans, *The Urban Villagers* (New York: Free Press, 1962).

100. See Gans, *The Urban Villagers.*

101. Norman I. Fainstein and Susan S. Fainstein, "Mobility, Community and Participation: The American Way Out," in *Residential Mobility and Public Policy,* ed. W. A. V. Clark and Eric G. Moore, Urban Affairs Annual Reviews 19 (Beverly Hills, Calif.: Sage, 1980), pp. 242–262; Putnam, *Bowling Alone;* and J. M. Jasper, *Restless Nation: Starting Over in America* (Chicago: University of Chicago Press, 2000).

102. Robert D. Putnam, *Making Democracy Work: Civic Traditions in Modern Italy* (Princeton, N.J.: Princeton University Press, 1994); idem, "Bowling Alone: America's Declining Social Capital," *Journal of Democracy* 6, no. 1 (1994): 65–78; idem, "Tuning In, Tuning Out: The Strange Disappearance of Social Capital in America," *PS: Political Science and Politics,* December 1995, pp. 664–683; idem, "The Strange Disappearance of Civic America," *American Prospect* 24 (1996): 34–48; idem, *Bowling Alone;* Susan Crawford and Peggy Levitt, "Social Change and Civic Engagement: The Case of the PTA," in *Civic Engagement in American Democracy,* ed. Theda Skocpol and Morris P. Fiorina (Washington, D.C.: Brookings Institution Press, and New York: Russell Sage Foundation Press, 1999), pp. 249–296.

103. Putnam, "Tuning In, Tuning Out"; Marcella R. Ray, "Technological Change and Associational Life," in *Civic Engagement in American Democracy,* ed. Theda Skocpol and Morris P. Fiorina (Washington, D.C.: Brookings Institution Press, and New York: Russell Sage Foundation Press, 1999), pp. 297–329.

104. Michael Southworth and Balaji Parthasarathy, "The Suburban Public Realm I: Its Emergence, Growth, and Transformation of the American Metropolis," *Journal of Urban Design* 1, no. 3 (1996): 245–263; and Daniel Solomon, *Global City Blues* (Washington, D.C.: Island Press, 2003).

105. T. J. Glynn, "Psychological Sense of Community: Measures and Application," *Human Relations* 34 (1981): 789–818; and Andres Duany, Elizabeth Plater-Zyberk, and J. Speck, *Suburban Nation: The Rise of Sprawl and the Decline of the American Dream* (New York: North Point Press, 2000).

106. Nisbet, *The Quest for Community;* Daniel Bell, "The End of American Exceptionalism," *Public Interest* 41 (1975): 193–224.

107. Margaret Pender interview, spring 1994.

108. Pace interview.

110. Saghir interview.

111. Tocqueville, *Democracy in America,* trans., ed., and with an introduction by Harvey C. Mansfield and Debra Winthrop, p. 486.

112. Ibid.

113. Ibid.

114. Ibid., p. 487.

5. The Moral Effects of the Volunteer Experience

1. Joan Didion, *The White Album* (New York: Pocket Books, 1979), p. 11.

2. Suzy Nance interview, spring 1994.

3. Karl Barth, *Ethics,* ed. Dietrich Braun, trans. Geoffrey W. Bromley (New York: Seabury Press, 1981).

4. This conception of morality is lifted from Scanlon's publication *What We Owe to Each Other.* While this book includes *American Ethic* in the title, I prefer to use the term *morality* in this chapter rather than the seemingly more logical term, ethics. The explanation for this can be found in *The Oxford Dictionary of Philosophy,* where Simon Blackburn, in his entry under the heading "morality," notes that while morality and ethics amount to the same thing, "there is a usage that restricts morality to . . . notions such as duty, obligation, and principles of conduct, reserving ethics for . . . practical reasoning based on the notion of virtue" (Simon Blackburn, *The Oxford Dictionary of Philosophy* [New York: Oxford University Press, 1994]). So while this book is about an ethic, this chapter is about the principles of conduct that the volunteers develop, which then contribute to that ethic. Hence the chapter is not about the volunteers' ethics, rather it is about their morality, and more specifically it is about their sense of what they owe to their homeless clients.

5. Robert Wuthnow, *Meaning and Moral Order: Explorations in Cultural Analysis* (Berkeley: University of California Press, 1987), p. 66.

6. Stuart Hampshire, "The Reason Why Not," review of *What We Owe to Each Other,* by T. M. Scanlon, *New York Review of Books* 46 (1999): 21.

7. In the social sciences today, *morality* is seen as an old-fashioned word that has no place in value-neutral work. Blame for this can be laid at Max Weber's feet. Following the prevailing reading of *Science as Vocation,* social scientists now feel compelled to be value neutral in their work, in order to be more scientific. The problem with this approach, in my mind, is that value neutrality is impossible. For support on this view I turn to Isaiah Berlin, who stated that qualitative investigations that "are concerned with human affairs are committed to the use of moral categories and concepts which normal language incorporates" (Isaiah Berlin, "Historical Inevitability," in *Four Essays on Liberty* [New York: Oxford University Press, 1969], p. 115). When one is doing qualitative work, he notes, one cannot avoid using "normal language with all its associations and 'built in' moral categories" (ibid.). In fact, as Berlin points out, in qualitative work attempts to avoid using moral language invariably end up "adopt[ing] another moral category, not none at all" (ibid.). With morality and value-laden language unavoidable, the point, according to Berlin, is to avoid moralizing, not morality.

8. Jones, Brown, and Brown Jr. interview.

9. Durant interview.

10. Ibid.

11. Jones, Brown, and Brown Jr. interview.

12. Ibid.

13. Ibid.

14. Durant interview.

15. Ibid.

16. Ibid.

17. Saghir interview.

18. Pace interview.

19. Jones, Brown, and Brown Jr. interview.

20. Ibid.

21. Pierre Bourdieu, *Outline of a Theory of Practice* (New York: Cambridge University Press, 1977), p. 78.

22. Ibid.

23. Jones, Brown, and Brown Jr. interview.

24. Ibid.

25. Ibid.

26. Ibid.

27. In my interviews, I spoke with 70 veteran volunteers, each of whom had been volunteering for at least one year, and 30 new volunteers, each of whom had been volunteering for less than three months. The question "Why do you think people become homeless?" was only one of which the two groups answered differently.

28. Susan Mayhew interview, spring 1994.

29. Susan Monk survey, spring 1994.

30. Virginia Brown survey, fall 1993.

31. Margaret Panda survey, spring 1994.

32. K. Blanca survey, fall 1993.

33. Lloyd Green survey, fall 1993.

34. Michael Wheat survey, fall 1993.

35. Steven Black survey, fall 1993

36. Peter Beck survey, spring 1994

37. Donna Schmidt survey, spring 1994.

38. Terri Ecksen survey, spring 1994.

39. John Salmon survey, spring 1994.

40. Ruth Lengua survey, spring 1994.

41. Anish Mogul survey, spring 1994.

42. I surveyed 100 volunteers—70 of whom were veterans and 30 of whom were new. On the subject of why people became homeless the two groups of volunteers had distinctly different opinions. The new volunteers were quite divided in their opinions. In this group, 27 percent thought that people became homeless because of such societal reasons as the lack of low-skill jobs that paid a high enough wage to live in New York and the dearth of affordable housing; 47 percent thought that people became homeless for such nonsocietal reasons as behavior, drug and alcohol abuse, and lack of strong family support; and the remaining 26 percent thought that a mixture of personal reasons and structural reasons were to blame for homelessness. The veteran volunteers, however, were much less divided and much less prone to attribute the causes of homelessness to societal reasons. After volunteering for at least a year, only 14 percent of the veterans attributed homelessness to structural causes and 50 percent attributed homelessness to nonsocietal reasons, while 33 percent thought a mixture of societal and nonsocietal factors caused homelessness. A further 3 percent had no opinion. With experience, then, the volunteers were much less likely to think that homelessness was strictly society's fault and more likely to look to other factors.

43. Gertrude Himmelfarb, *Poverty and Compassion: The Moral Imagination of the*
Late Victorians (New York: Knopf, 1991), p. 5.

44. Monk survey.

45. Saghir interview.

46. Ibid.

47. See Pierre Bourdieu, "Forms of Capital," in *Handbook of Theory and Research for the Sociology of Education,* ed. J. C. Richards (New York: Greenwood Press, 1983), p. 248.

48. Saghir interview.

49. Joel Sesser interview, 13 December 1994.

50. Ibid.

51. Himmelfarb, *Poverty and Compassion,* p. 5.

52. Cited by Tom Bethell in *Rethinking Policy on Homelessness* (Washington, D.C.: Heritage Foundation, 1988), p. 2.

53. Jones, Brown, and Brown Jr. interview.

6. The Church Shelters as Community-Generating Institutions

1. Intentional and utopian communities, both of which are leading examples of the form that deliberate attempts at community formation take today, are place based.

2. See Benedict Anderson, *Imagined Communities* (New York: Verso, 1983); Melvin Webber, "Order in Diversity: Community without Propinquity," in *Cities and Space: The Future Use of Urban Land,* ed. Lowdon Wingo (Baltimore: Johns Hopkins University Press, 1963), pp. 25–54; Manuel Castells, *The Rise of Network Society* (New York: Blackwell, 1996), p. 22; and Robert Booth Fowler, "Community: Reflections on Definition," in *New Communitarian Thinking: Persons, Virtues, Institutions, and Communities,* ed. Amitai Etzioni (Charlottesville: University Press of Virginia, 1995), pp. 88–95. Fowler's vision that there are now many types of communities is a popular one. Seymour Mandelbaum, for example, though he sees communities as sentiments, also believes that there are three different types: open moral communities, contractual moral communities, and deep moral communities. See Mandelbaum, *Open Moral Communities,* p. 15.

3. Colin Bell and Howard Newby, *Community Studies: An Introduction to the Sociology of the Local Community* (New York: Praeger, 1972); and Chris Shore, "Community," in *The Blackwell Encyclopedia of Twentieth-Century Social Thought,* ed. William Outhwaite and Tom Bottomore (New York: Blackwell, 1993), p. 98.

4. Raymond Plant, "Community," in *The Blackwell Encyclopedia of Political Thought,* ed. David Miller (New York: Blackwell, 1986), p. 88.

5. William Galston, "Does the Internet Strengthen Community?" *National Civic Review* 89, no. 3 (2000): 193–202. In making this argument, Galston cites Daniel Yankelovich, Alan Ehrenhalt, Lawrence Freidman, and Alan Wolfe as authors who share this belief.

6. Bellah et al., *Habits of the Heart,* p.163.

7. Ibid.

8. Michael Taylor, *Community, Anarchy and Liberty,* p. 26; Thomas Bender, *Community and Social Change in America* (Baltimore: Johns Hopkins University Press, 1982).

9. See Etienne Wenger, *Communities of Practice: Learning, Meaning, and Identity* (New York: Cambridge University Press, 1988).

10. Michael Taylor, *Community, Anarchy and Liberty,* pp. 27–28.

11. Robert Nisbet, *The Quest for Community;* Putnam, "Bowling Alone"; idem, "Tuning In, Tuning Out"; idem, "The Strange Disappearance"; and idem, *Bowling Alone.*

12. Wenger, *Communities of Practice,* pp. 73–74.

13. While I am not aware of any theorist who has spoken about community in a manner that explains and accounts for the role that all of these functions play in community

generation, many have spoken about the ability of voluntary institutions to perform one or more of these. Theorists who have spoken about the mediating functions of community voluntary associations include Peter L. Berger and Richard John Neuhaus, *To Empower People: The Role of Mediating Structures in Public Policy* (Washington, D.C.: American Enterprise Institute for Public Policy Research, 1977); J. Philip Wogaman, "The Church as Mediating Institution: Theological and Philosophical Perspective" and "The Church as Mediating Institution: Contemporary American Challenge," in *Democracy and Mediating Structures: A Theoretical Inquiry,* ed. Michael Novak (Washington, D.C.: American Enterprise Institute for Public Policy Research, 1980), pp. 69–97; and Putnam, *Bowling Alone.* Theorists who have spoken about the socializing and educative functions of voluntary associations include Jean Jacques Rousseau, *The Social Contract* (1762; reprint, New York: Penguin, 1968); Alexis de Tocqueville, *Democracy in America;* Ernest Burgess, *The Function of Socialization in Social Evolution* (Chicago: University of Chicago Press, 1916); Carole Pateman, *Participation and Democratic Theory* (New York: Cambridge University Press, 1970); William Sullivan, "Institutions as the Infrastructure of Democracy," in *New Communitarian Thinking: Persons, Virtues, Institutions, and Communities,* ed. Amitai Etzioni (Charlottesville: University Press of Virginia, 1995), pp. 170–180; and Alan Wolfe, "Human Nature and the Quest for Community," in ibid., pp. 126–140. Theorists who have spoken about the integrative functions of voluntary associations include Bell, "The End of American Exceptionalism," and "'American Exceptionalism Revisited': The Role of Civil Society"; and Robert Dahl, *Dilemmas of Pluralist Democracy* (New Haven, Conn.: Yale University Press, 1982). Theorists who have spoken about the ability that voluntary associations have to serve as sites of moral development include Tocqueville, *Democracy in America;* Rousseau, *The Social Contract;* J. Donald Moon, "The Moral Basis of the Democratic Welfare State," in *Democracy and the Welfare State,* ed. Amy Guttman (Princeton, N.J.: Princeton University Press, 1988), pp. 27–52; Alan Wolfe, *Whose Keeper: Social Science and Moral Obligation* (Berkeley: University of California Press, 1989); Robert S. Ogilvie, "A Moral Argument in Favor of the Voluntary Provision of Social Services," *Berkeley Planning Journal* 13 (1999): 74–101; and Mandelbaum, *Open Moral Communities.*

14. Wenger, *Communities of Practice,* p. 74.

15. Michael Taylor, *Community, Anarchy and Liberty,* pp. 27–28.

16. Mandelbaum, *Open Moral Communities,* p. 15.

17. Jones, Brown, and Brown Jr. interview.

18. Saghir interview.

19. On this issue see Tocqueville, *Democracy in America;* Burgess, *The Function of Socialization;* Rousseau, *The Social Contract;* Pateman, *Participation and Democratic Theory;* Jane Mansbridge, *Beyond Adversary Democracy* (New York: Basic Books, 1980); Sullivan, "Institutions as the Infrastructure"; Wolfe, "Human Nature"; John Dryzek, *Deliberative Democracy and Beyond: Liberals, Critics, Contestations* (New York: Oxford University Press, 2000); and Mandelbaum, *Open Moral Communities.*

20. Wogaman, "The Church as Mediating Institution: Theological and Philosophical Perspective" and "The Church as Mediating Institution: Contemporary American Challenge."

21. On this issue see Berger and Neuhaus, *To Empower People;* Verba, Schlozman, and Brady, *Voice and Equality;* and Mandelbaum, *Open Moral Communities.*

22. William R. Freudenberg, "The Density of Acquaintanceship: An Overlooked Variable in Community Research?" *American Journal of Sociology* 92, no. 1 (1986): 27–63.

23. Berger and Neuhaus, *To Empower People.*

24. Bell, "The End of American Exceptionalism"; Berger and Neuhaus, *To Empower People;* Dahl, *Dilemmas of Pluralist Democracy;* and Putnam, *Making Democracy Work.*

25. See Max Weber, "Bureaucracy" and "The Types of Legitimate Domination," in *Economy and Society: An Outline of Interpretive Sociology,* ed. Guenther Roth and Claus Wittich (Berkeley: University of California Press, 1978), vol. 2, chapters 10 and 11.

26. Shafer interview, 17 October 2001.

27. Jones, Brown, and Brown Jr. interview.

28. For further discussion on this claim I refer you back to the Berlin reference in chapter 5 in which he notes that it is impossible to do away with moral claims in qualitative endeavors and attempts to do so do not rid one of morality but replace one morality with another. Morality is unavoidable—but what is avoidable and what should be avoided is moralizing. The volunteers are schooled to avoid moralizing.

29. On this issue see Dryzek, *Deliberative Democracy and Beyond;* and Mandelbaum, *Open Moral Communities.*

30. On this issue see Tocqueville, *Democracy in America;* Rousseau, *The Social Contract;* Moon, "The Moral Basis of the Democratic Welfare State"; Wolfe, *Whose Keeper;* Ogilvie, "A Moral Argument"; and Mandelbaum, *Open Moral Communities.*

31. Varenne, *Americans Together,* p.151.

32. Ibid., p. 66.

33. Ibid., p. 159.

34. Ibid.

35. Hall, "Vital Signs," p. 232.

7. Social Architecture

1. Robert N. Bellah et al., *The Good Society* (New York: Vintage, 1991), p. 5.

2. Tocqueville, *Democracy in America,* trans., ed., and with an introduction by Harvey C. Mansfield and Debra Winthrop, p. 488.

3. Douglas North, *Institutions, Institutional Change and Economic Performance* (New York: Cambridge University Press, 1990).

4. Wenger, *Communities of Practice,* p. 241.

5. Howard Perlmutter, *Toward a Theory and Practice of Social Architecture: The Building of Indispensable Institutions* (London: Tavistock, 1965). This phrase is meant for the art of building social institutions and not for the approach to architecture that maintains that building design should be guided by the way that people use buildings rather than by form or style.

6. In addition to the aforementioned works by Perlmutter and Wenger, see Chris Argyris and Donald A. Schon, *Organization Learning: A Theory of Action and Perspective* (Reading, Mass.: Addison-Wesley, 1978); Jean Lave and Etienne Wenger, *Situated Learning: Legitimate Peripheral Participation* (New York: Cambridge University Press, 1991); Seth Chaiklin and Jean Lave, eds., *Understanding Practice: Perspectives on Activity and Context* (New York: Cambridge University Press, 1995); John Seely Broan and Paul Duguid, "Organizational Learning and Communities of Practice: Toward a Unified View of Working, Learning, and Innovation," *Organizational Science* 2 (1996): 40–57; and Etienne Wenger, Richard McDermott, and William Snyder, *Cultivating Communities of Practice* (Boston: Harvard Business School Press, 2002).

7. See Chris Argyris and Edward Wright Bakke, *Organizational Structure and Dynamics* (New Haven, Conn.: Yale University Labor and Management Center, 1955).

8. This point is meant to engage Melvin Webber's note that we are in an age of community without propinquity. See Webber, "Order in Diversity."

254   9. Perlmutter, *Toward a Theory*, p. 24.

10. Wuthnow, *Meaning and Moral Order*, pp. 140–141.

11. Clifford Geertz, *Local Knowledge: Further Essays in Interpretive Anthropology* (New York: Basic Books, 1983), pp. 44–45.

12. Van Til, *Mapping the Third Sector*, pp. 59–63.

13. Shafer interview, 17 October 2001.

14. Jones, Brown, and Brown Jr. interview.

Conclusion

1. The Partnership for the Homeless, "Goals and Results," from http://www.guidestar.org/search/report/effective.jsp (accessed 30 October 2003).

2. Ibid.

3. Margaret Shafer interview, 25 October 2002.

4. Ibid.

Appendix

1. Robert K. Yin, *Case Study Research: Design and Methods* (Beverly Hills, Calif.: Sage, 1984). The research progressed, over a number of years, through the following phases: initial ideas, observation, conceptualization, interviewing, theory formation, survey writing and pretesting, survey rewriting, surveying, interpretation and theory testing, writing up the findings, reconceptualization, theory reformation with new literature, rewriting, critique, interviewing, interpretation and theory testing, writing. In a case study one is confronted by four potential threats to the validity of one's research: threats to construct validity, internal validity, external validity, and reliability. To mitigate against potential threats to construct validity I collected evidence from many sources—over the years that I worked at the Partnership for the Homeless I collected and analyzed numerous reports; attended endless meetings; read and wrote many meeting agendas; visited sites; read bylaws; interviewed staff, board members, and clients; and did hundreds of hours of direct participant observation—and I triangulated from them to reach my conclusions. As the research progressed key informants read what I was writing and I have incorporated their corrections. Given that this is primarily a descriptive and exploratory case study, internal validity in the research design is not a potential threat. External validity threats pertain to the attempts that you make as an author to generalize your findings and you have to be careful to establish which domains you can and cannot legitimately generalize to. In this book I generalize to a theoretical proposition—how to generate communities through voluntary action in certain types of institutions—rather than to a specific set of institutions. That is something that I wouldn't be able to do with this size of sample. As for reliability, the shelters are still there and are still operating, and I believe that someone replicating this study with the same methods would come to similar conclusions. The fact that there are many other studies that point in a similar direction gives me further confidence in the reliability of my findings.

2. William F. Whyte, *Learning from the Field: A Guide from Experience* (Beverly Hills, Calif.: Sage, 1984).

3. In quoting my interviewees I use pseudonyms except in the following cases: Ed Koch, Joel Sesser, Bill Appel, Brenda Griffin, Virginia Brown, Jim Jones, Peter Saghir, and Margaret Shafer.

Bibliography

Adorno, Theodor, and Max Horkheimer. *The Dialectic of Enlightenment.* New York: Continuum, 1976.

Alexander, Jeffrey. "Formal and Substantive Voluntarism in the Work of Talcott Parsons: A Theoretical and Ideological Reinterpretation." *American Sociological Review* 43 (April 1978): 180.

Almond, Gabriel A., and Sidney Verba. *The Civic Culture: Political Attitudes and Democracy in Five Nations.* Princeton, N.J.: Princeton University Press, 1963.

Anderson, Benedict. *Imagined Communities.* New York: Verso, 1983.

Argyris, Chris, and Edward Wright Bakke. *Organizational Structure and Dynamics.* New Haven, Conn.: Yale University Labor and Management Center, 1955.

Argyris, Chris, and Donald A. Schon. *Organization Learning: A Theory of Action and Perspective.* Reading, Mass.: Addison-Wesley, 1978.

Aristotle. *Ethics.* New York: E. P. Dutton & Co., 1963.

Associated Press. "Church, New York City Clash over Homeless." 18 December 2001.

Axelrod, Robert. *The Evolution of Cooperation.* New York: Basic Books, 1984.

Barber, Benjamin. *Strong Democracy: Participatory Politics for a New Age.* Berkeley: University of California Press, 1984.

Barr, Howard M., ed. *Disaffiliated Man: Essays and Bibliography on Skid Row, Vagrancy and Outsiders.* Toronto: University of Toronto Press, 1970.

Barth, Karl. *Ethics.* Edited by Dietrich Braun. Translated by Geoffrey W. Bromley. New York: Seabury Press, 1981.

Bell, Colin, and Howard Newby. *Community Studies: An Introduction to the Sociology of the Local Community.* New York: Praeger, 1972.

Bell, Daniel. "Communitarianism." In *The Stanford Encyclopedia of Philosophy.* Stanford, Calif.: Metaphysics Research Lab, Center for the Study of Language and Information, 2001, http://plato.stanford.edu/entries/communitarianism/.

Bell, Daniel. "'American Exceptionalism Revisited': The Role of Civil Society." *Public Interest* 95 (1989): 38–56.

———. *The Cultural Contradictions of Capitalism.* New York: Basic Books, 1976.

———. "The End of American Exceptionalism." *Public Interest* 41 (1975): 193–224.

Bellah, Robert N. "Civil Religion in America." *Daedalus* 96, no. 1 (1967): 1–21.

———. "Is Capitalism Compatible with 'Traditional Morality'?" Lecture delivered at the University of Southern California, 23 August 1983.

Bellah, Robert N., Richard Madsen, William M. Sullivan, Ann Swidler, and Steven M. Tipton. *The Good Society.* New York: Vintage, 1991.

———. *Habits of the Heart: Individualism and Commitment in American Life.* New York: Harper & Row, 1985.

———, eds. *Individualism and Commitment in American Life: Readings on the Themes of Habits of the Heart.* New York: Harper & Row, 1987.

Bender, Thomas. *Community and Social Change in America.* Baltimore: Johns Hopkins University Press, 1982.

Berger, Peter L., and Richard John Neuhaus. "Mediating Structures and the Dilemmas of the Modern Welfare State." In *To Empower People: From State to Civil Society,* 2nd ed., edited by Michael Novak, pp. 157–164. Washington, D.C.: American Enterprise Institute, 1996.

256   ———. *To Empower People: The Role of Mediating Structures in Public Policy.* Washington, D.C.: American Enterprise Institute for Public Policy Research, 1977.

Berlin, Isaiah. "Historical Inevitability." In *Four Essays on Liberty,* pp. 41–117. New York: Oxford University Press, 1969.

———. "Introduction." In *Four Essays on Liberty,* pp. ix–lxiii. New York: Oxford University Press, 1969.

———. "Political Ideas in the Twentieth Century." In *Four Essays on Liberty,* pp. 1–40. New York: Oxford University Press, 1969.

Bernstein, Nina. "Bloomberg and the Man on the Street." *New York Times,* 20 January 2002.

Bethell, Tom. *Rethinking Policy on Homelessness.* Washington, D.C.: Heritage Foundation, 1988.

Blackburn, Simon. *The Oxford Dictionary of Philosophy.* New York: Oxford University Press, 1994.

Bourdieu, Pierre. "Forms of Capital." In *Handbook of Theory and Research for the Sociology of Education,* edited by J. C. Richards, pp. 241–248. New York: Greenwood Press, 1983.

———. *Outline of a Theory of Practice.* New York: Cambridge University Press, 1977.

Boyte, Harry. *Community Is Possible: Repairing America's Roots.* New York: Harper & Row, 1984.

Brecher, Charles, and Raymond D. Horton, with Robert A. Cropf and Dean Michael Mead. *Power Failure: New York City Politics and Policy since 1960.* New York: Oxford University Press, 1993.

Broan, John Seely, and Paul Duguid. "Organizational Learning and Communities of Practice: Toward a Unified View of Working, Learning, and Innovation." *Organizational Science* 2 (1996): 40–57.

Brunkhorst, Hauke. "Action and Agency." In *The Blackwell Encyclopedia of Twentieth-Century Social Thought,* edited by William Outhwaite and Tom Bottomore, p. 1–3. Cambridge, Mass.: Blackwell, 1993.

Burgess, Ernest. *The Function of Socialization in Social Evolution.* Chicago: University of Chicago Press, 1916.

Burke, Edmund. *Reflections on the Revolution in France.* 1790. Reprint, New York: Doubleday, 1973.

Cardwell, Diane. "City to Appeal Court Order over Homeless at Church." *New York Times,* 18 January 2002.

Castells, Manuel. *The Rise of Network Society.* New York: Blackwell, 1996.

Chaiklin, Seth, and Jean Lave, eds. *Understanding Practice: Perspectives on Activity and Context.* New York: Cambridge University Press, 1995.

Cohen, Ira J. "Theories of Action and Praxis." In Bryan S. Turner, ed., *The Blackwell Companion to Social Theory,* 2nd ed., pp. 73–111. Cambridge, Mass.: Blackwell, 2000.

Crawford, Susan, and Peggy Levitt. "Social Change and Civic Engagement: The Case of the PTA." In *Civic Engagement in American Democracy,* edited by Theda Skocpol and Morris P. Fiorina, pp. 249–296. Washington, D.C.: Brookings Institution Press, and New York: Russell Sage Foundation Press, 1999.

Dahl, Robert. *Dilemmas of Pluralist Democracy.* New Haven, Conn.: Yale University Press, 1982.

Didion, Joan. *The White Album.* New York: Pocket Books, 1979.

Downs, Anthony. *An Economic Theory of Democracy.* New York: Harper & Row, 1957.

Dryzek, John. *Deliberative Democracy and Beyond: Liberals, Critics, Contestations.* New York: Oxford University Press, 2000.

Duany, Andres, Elizabeth Plater-Zyberk, and J. Speck. *Suburban Nation: The Rise of Sprawl*
and the Decline of the American Dream. New York: North Point Press, 2000.

Durkheim, Emile. *Suicide: A Study in Sociology.* 1897. Reprint, New York: Free Press, 1997.

Dworkin, Ronald. *Taking Rights Seriously.* Cambridge, Mass.: Harvard University Press, 1977.

Elkins, David, and Richard Simeon. "A Cause in Search of Its Effect: What Does Political Culture Explain?" *Comparative Politics* 2, no. 2 (1979): 127–145.

Erickson, Alana J. "Association for Improving the Condition of the Poor." In *The Encyclopedia of the City of New York,* edited by Kenneth T. Jackson, p. 61. New Haven, Conn.: Yale University Press, 1995.

Etzioni, Amitai. *The Spirit of Community: Rights, Responsibilities and the Communitarian Agenda.* New York: Crown Publishers, 1993.

Fainstein, Norman I., and Susan S. Fainstein. "Mobility, Community and Participation: The American Way Out." In *Residential Mobility and Public Policy,* edited by W. A. V. Clark and Eric G. Moore, pp. 242–262. Urban Affairs Annual Reviews 19. Beverly Hills, Calif.: Sage, 1980.

Finn, Robin. "In Search of 'Divine Justice' for the Homeless in Court." *New York Times,* 21 December 2001.

Fowler, Robert Booth. "Community: Reflections on Definition." In *New Communitarian Thinking: Persons, Virtues, Institutions, and Communities,* edited by Amitai Etzioni, pp. 88–95. Charlottesville: University Press of Virginia, 1995.

Freudenberg, William. R. "The Density of Acquaintanceship: An Overlooked Variable in Community Research?" *American Journal of Sociology* 92, no. 1 (1986): 27–63.

Fritsch, Jane. "Church Lawsuit Tries to Stop Police from Ejecting Homeless." *New York Times,* 18 December 2001.

———. "Judge Orders End to Rousting of Homeless Near Church." *New York Times,* 20 December 2001.

Gallup, George Jr., and Jim Castelli. *The People's Religion: American Faith in the 90s.* New York: Macmillan, 1989. Quoted in Wills, *Under God: Religion and American Politics.*

Galston, William. "Does the Internet Strengthen Community?" *National Civic Review* 89, no. 3 (2000): 193–202.

———. *Liberal Purposes: Goods, Virtues, and Diversity in the Liberal State.* New York: Cambridge University Press, 1991.

Gans, Herbert. *Middle American Individualism: The Future of Liberal Democracy.* New York: Free Press, 1988.

———. *The Urban Villagers.* New York: Free Press, 1962.

Geertz, Clifford. *Local Knowledge: Further Essays in Interpretive Anthropology.* New York: Basic Books, 1983.

Gellner, Ernest. *Culture, Identity and Politics.* New York: Cambridge University Press, 1987.

Giving and Volunteering in the United States. Washington, D.C.: Independent Sector, 1999.

Giving and Volunteering in the United States. Washington, D.C.: Independent Sector, 2001.

"Global Study Finds High Rate of Volunteerism." *Chronicle of Philanthropy,* 9 September 1999. Source: Johns Hopkins Center for Civil Society Studies.

Glynn, T. J. "Psychological Sense of Community: Measures and Application." *Human Relations* 34 (1981): 789–818.

Greenbaum, Sidney. "Agent." In *The Oxford Companion to the English Language,* edited by Tom McArthur, p. 26. New York: Oxford University Press, 1992.

Hall, Peter Dobkin. "Vital Signs: Organizational Population Trends and Civic Engagement in New Haven, Connecticut, 1850–1998." In *Civic Engagement in American Democracy,* edited by Theda Skocpol and Morris P. Fiorina, pp. 211–248. Washington, D.C.: Brookings Institution Press, and New York: Russell Sage Foundation Press, 1999.

Hampshire, Stuart. "The Reason Why Not." Review of T. M. Scanlon's *What We Owe to Each Other. New York Review of Books* 46 (22 April 1999): 21.

Hausknecht, Murray. *The Joiners.* New York: Bedminster Press, 1962.

Hayek, Friedrich. *The Road to Serfdom.* 1944. Reprint, Chicago: University of Chicago Press, 1976.

Hemphill, Clara J., and Raymond A. Mohl. "Poverty." In *The Encyclopedia of the City of New York,* edited by Kenneth T. Jackson, pp. 932–934. New Haven, Conn.: Yale University Press, 1995.

Herbert, Bob. "Trumping Charity." *New York Times,* 20 December 2001.

Himmelfarb, Gertrude. *Poverty and Compassion: The Moral Imagination of the Late Victorians.* New York: Knopf, 1991.

Hindess, Barry. "Rational Choice Theory." In *The Blackwell Encyclopedia of Twentieth-Century Social Thought,* edited by William Outhwaite and Tom Bottomore, pp. 542–543. Cambridge, Mass.: Blackwell, 1993.

Hopper, Kim. "The Public Response to Homelessness in New York City: The Last Hundred Years." In *On Being Homeless: Historical Perspective,* edited by Rick Beard, pp. 88–101. New York: Museum of the City of New York, 1987.

Inkeles, Alex. *Exploring Individual Modernity.* New York: Columbia University Press, 1983.

Jacobs, Jane. *The Death and Life of Great American Cities.* New York: Vintage, 1961.

Jasper, J. M. *Restless Nation: Starting Over in America.* Chicago: University of Chicago Press, 2000.

Katz, Michael B. *In the Shadow of the Poor House: A Social History of Welfare in America.* New York: Basic Books, 1986.

Kesselman, Mark. "Order or Movement: The Literature of Political Development as Ideology." *World Politics* 26, no. 1 (1973): 139–154.

Kusmer, Kenneth L. "The Underclass in Historical Perspective." In *On Being Homeless: Historical Perspective,* edited by Rick Beard, pp. 20–31. New York: Museum of the City of New York, 1987.

Lambert, Bruce. "Peter Smith Obituary." *New York Times,* 18 November 1992.

Lave, Jean, and Etienne Wenger. *Situated Learning: Legitimate Peripheral Participation.* New York: Cambridge University Press, 1991.

Lipset, Seymour Martin. *The First New Nation: The United States in Historical and Comparative Perspective.* New York: W. W. Norton & Co. , 1973.

Lukacs, Georg. *History and Class Consciousness.* 1923. Reprint, Cambridge, Mass.: MIT Press, 1972.

MacIntyre, Alasdair. *After Virtue: A Study in Moral Theory.* South Bend, Ind.: University of Notre Dame Press, 1981.

Mandelbaum, Seymour. *Open Moral Communities.* Cambridge, Mass.: MIT Press, 2000.

Mansbridge, Jane. *Beyond Adversary Democracy.* New York: Basic Books, 1980.

———. "The Rise and Fall of Self-Interest in the Explanation of Political Life." In *Beyond Self Interest,* edited by Jane Mansbridge, pp. 3–22. Chicago: University of Chicago Press, 1990.

McCormick, Pat. "Now Task Force on Voluntarism." *Ms.* 3 (February 1975): 73.

Milbrath, Lester W., and M. L. Goel. *Political Participation: How and Why Do People Get Involved in Politics?* 2nd ed. Lanham, Md.: University Press of America, 1977.

Monroe, Kristen Renwick. "A Fat Lady in a Corset: Altruism and Social Theory." *American Journal of Political Science* 38, no. 5 (1994): 861–893.

Montesquieu, Baron de. *The Spirit of the Laws.* 1749. Reprint, New York: Cambridge University Press, 1989.

Moon, J. Donald. "The Moral Basis of the Democratic Welfare State." In *Democracy and the Welfare State,* edited by Amy Guttman, pp. 27–52. Princeton, N.J.: Princeton University Press, 1988.

Newfield, Jack, and Wayne Barrett. *City for Sale: Ed Koch and the Betrayal of New York.* New York: Harper & Row, 1988.

Newfield, Jack, and Paul DuBrul. *The Abuse of Power: The Permanent Government and the Fall of New York.* New York: Viking Press, 1977.

Nisbet, Robert. *The Quest for Community: A Study in the Ethics of Order and Freedom.* 1953. Reprint, San Francisco: ICS Press, 1990.

North, Douglas. *Institutions, Institutional Change and Economic Performance.* New York: Cambridge University Press, 1990.

Nozick, Robert. *Anarchy, State and Utopia.* New York: Basic Books, 1974.

Ogilvie, Robert S. "A Moral Argument in Favor of the Voluntary Provision of Social Services." *Berkeley Planning Journal* 13 (1999): 74–101.

Olson, Mancur. *The Logic of Collective Action: Public Goods and the Theory of Groups.* Cambridge, Mass.: Harvard University Press, 1965.

Pateman, Carole. *Participation and Democratic Theory.* New York: Cambridge University Press, 1970.

Perlmutter, Howard. *Toward a Theory and Practice of Social Architecture: The Building of Indispensable Institutions.* London: Tavistock, 1965.

Piliavin, Jane Allen, and Hong-Wen Charng. "Altruism: A Review of Recent Theory and Research." *Annual Review of Sociology* 16 (1990): 27–65.

Plant, Raymond. "Community." In *The Blackwell Encyclopedia of Political Thought,* edited by David Miller, pp. 88–90. New York: Blackwell, 1986.

"Polls Show Americans Say Volunteering Is Important." *Chronicle of Philanthropy,* 23 April 1998. Sources: United Parcel Service, National Commission on Philanthropy and Civic Renewal, and Lutheran Brotherhood.

Putnam, Robert D. "Bowling Alone: America's Declining Social Capital." *Journal of Democracy* 6, no. 1 (1994): 65–78.

———. *Bowling Alone: The Collapse and Revival of American Community.* New York: Simon & Schuster, 2000.

———. *Making Democracy Work: Civic Traditions in Modern Italy.* Princeton, N.J.: Princeton University Press, 1994.

———. "The Strange Disappearance of Civic America." *American Prospect* 24 (1996): 34–48.

———. "Tuning In, Tuning Out: The Strange Disappearance of Social Capital in America." *PS: Political Science and Politics* (December 1995): 664–683.

Rawls, John. *A Theory of Justice.* Cambridge, Mass.: Harvard University Press, 1971.

Ray, Marcella R. "Technological Change and Associational Life." In *Civic Engagement in American Democracy,* edited by Theda Skocpol and Morris P. Fiorina, pp. 297–329. Washington, D.C.: Brookings Institution Press, and New York: Russell Sage Foundation Press, 1999.

Riker, William. *Liberalism against Populism: A Confrontation between the Theory of Democracy and the Theory of Social Choice.* San Francisco: W. H. Freeman, 1982.

Rosenblum, Nancy L. *Membership and Morals: The Personal Uses of Pluralism in America.* Princeton, N.J.: Princeton University Press, 1998.

Rousseau, Jean Jacques. *The Social Contract.* 1762. Reprint, New York: Penguin, 1968.

Sandel, Michael. *Liberalism and the Limits of Justice.* New York: Cambridge University Press, 1982.

Scanlon, T. M. *What We Owe to Each Other.* Cambridge, Mass.: Harvard University Press, 1998.

Schlesinger, Arthur. "Biography of a Nation of Joiners." *American Historical Review* 50, no. 1 (1944): 1–25.

Schneider, David, and Albert Deutsch. *The History of Public Welfare in New York State.* Chicago: University of Chicago Press, 1941.

Sciulli, David. "Voluntaristic Action as a Distinct Concept: Theoretical Foundations of Societal Constitutionalism." *American Sociological Review* 51 (1986): 743–766.

Shore, Chris. "Community." In *The Blackwell Encyclopedia of Twentieth-Century Social Thought,* edited by William Outhwaite and Tom Bottomore, p. 98–99. New York: Blackwell, 1993.

Skocpol, Theda. "How Americans Became Civic." In *Civic Engagement in American Democracy,* edited by Theda Skocpol and Morris P. Fiorina, pp. 27–80. Washington, D.C.: Brookings Institution Press, and New York: Russell Sage Foundation Press, 1999.

Smith, David Horton. "Altruism, Volunteers, and Volunteerism." *Journal of Voluntary Action Research* 10, no. 1 (January–March 1981): 21–36.

Solomon, Daniel. *Global City Blues.* Washington, D.C.: Island Press, 2003.

Southworth, Michael, and Balaji Parthasarathy. "The Suburban Public Realm I: Its Emergence, Growth, and Transformation of the American Metropolis." *Journal of Urban Design* 1, no. 3 (1996): 245–263.

Sullivan, William. "Institutions as the Infrastructure of Democracy." In *New Communitarian Thinking: Persons, Virtues, Institutions, and Communities,* edited by Amitai Etzioni, pp. 170–180. Charlottesville: University Press of Virginia, 1995.

Taylor, Charles. "Atomism." In *Communitarianism and Individualism,* edited by Shlomo Avineri and Avner De-Shalit, pp. 29–50. New York: Oxford University Press, 1992.

———. "Cross-Purposes: The Liberal-Communitarian Debate." In *Liberalism and the Moral Life,* edited by Nancy L. Rosenblum, pp. 159–182. Cambridge, Mass.: Harvard University Press, 1989.

Taylor, Michael. *Community, Anarchy and Liberty.* New York: Cambridge University Press, 1982.

Tocqueville, Alexis de. *Democracy in America.* 2 vols. Translated by Henry Reeve. Revised by Francis Bowen. Edited by Phillips Bradley. 1835. Reprint, New York: Vintage Books, 1990.

———. *Democracy in America.* Translated, edited, and with an introduction by Harvey C. Mansfield and Debra Winthrop. 1835 and 1840. Reprint, Chicago: University of Chicago Press, 2000.

———. "Memoir on Pauperism." In *Tocqueville and Beaumont on Social Reform,* pp. 1–27. 1835. Reprint, New York: Harper & Row, 1968.

Tonnies, Ferdinand. *Community and Association (Gemeinschaft und Gesellschaft).* Translated and edited by Charles P. Loomis. With an introduction by John Samples. 1887. Reprint, New Brunswick, N.J.: Transaction Publishers, 1996.

Van Til, Jon. *Mapping the Third Sector: Voluntarism in a Changing Social Economy.* New York: Foundation Center, 1988.

Varenne, Herve. *Americans Together: Structured Diversity in a Midwestern Town.* New York: Teacher's College Press, 1977.

Verba, Sidney, Kay Lehman Schlozman, and Henry E. Brady. *Voice and Equality: Civic Voluntarism in American Politics.* Cambridge, Mass.: Harvard University Press, 1995.

W. K. Kellogg Foundation. *Reaching Out: America's Volunteer Heritage*. Battle Creek, Mich.:
W. K. Kellogg Foundation, 1990.

Wakin, Daniel J. "Judge Says Homeless Can Stay, but Only on Church's Steps." *New York Times*, 5 January 2002.

Walzer, Michael. *Spheres of Justice: A Defense of Pluralism and Equality*. New York: Basic Books, 1983.

————. *What It Means to Be an American: Essays on the American Experience*. New York: Marsilio, 1996.

Webber, Melvin. "Order in Diversity: Community without Propinquity." In *Cities and Space: The Future Use of Urban Land*, edited by Lowdon Wingo, pp. 25–54. Baltimore: Johns Hopkins University Press, 1963.

Weber, Max. *Economy and Society: An Outline of Interpretive Sociology*. 2 vols. Edited by Guenther Roth and Claus Wittich. 1921–22. Reprint, Berkeley: University of California Press, 1978.

Wenger, Etienne. *Communities of Practice: Learning, Meaning, and Identity*. New York: Cambridge University Press, 1998.

Wenger, Etienne, Richard McDermott, and William Snyder. *Cultivating Communities of Practice*. Boston: Harvard Business School Press, 2002.

Whyte, William F. *Learning from the Field: A Guide from Experience*. Beverly Hills, Calif.: Sage, 1984.

Wills, Garry. *Under God: Religion and American Politics*. New York: Touchstone, 1990.

Wogaman, J. Philip. "The Church as Mediating Institution: Contemporary American Challenge." In *Democracy and Mediating Structures: A Theoretical Inquiry*, edited by Michael Novak, pp. 85–97. Washington, D.C.: American Enterprise Institute for Public Policy Research, 1980.

————. "The Church as Mediating Institution: Theological and Philosophical Perspective." In *Democracy and Mediating Structures*, edited by Michael Novak, pp. 69–84. Washington, D.C.: American Enterprise Institute for Public Policy Research, 1980.

Wolfe, Alan. "Human Nature and the Quest for Community." In *New Communitarian Thinking: Persons, Virtues, Institutions, and Communities*, edited by Amitai Etzioni, pp. 126–140. Charlottesville: University Press of Virginia, 1995.

————. *Whose Keeper: Social Science and Moral Obligation*. Berkeley: University of California Press, 1989.

Worth, Robert F. "Despite Suit Filed by Church, Police Rouse Homeless Squatters." *New York Times*, 19 December 2001.

Wosh, Peter J. "St. Paul's Chapel." In *The Encyclopedia of the City of New York*, edited by Kenneth T. Jackson, p. 1037. New Haven, Conn.: Yale University Press, 1995.

Wuthnow, Robert. *Meaning and Moral Order: Explorations in Cultural Analysis*. Berkeley: University of California Press, 1987.

Yin, Robert K. *Case Study Research: Design and Methods*. Beverly Hills, Calif.: Sage, 1984.

Index

Mitchell, Joseph, 10
Mœures, 1
Mohl, Raymond A., 238nn19,20
Monroe, James (President), 24
Monroe, Kristin Renwick, 242n52
Montesquieu, Baron de, 243n53
Moon, J. Donald, 251–252n13, 253n30
Moral crisis. *See* Crises of modernity, moral
Moral development. *See* Community generation functions, moral development
Moral imagination, 1
Moral obligation, 220, 249n4
Moral uplift, 28, 29
Morality, 6, 7, 28, 83, 146, 147, 159, 194, 242n46, 249nn4,7, 253n28
Morality plays, 7
Moravian Coffee Pot, 17, 122
Museum of Modern Art, 54
Mutual self-help, 29

National Organization of Women, 39
National Welfare Rights Organization, 30
Nehemiah plan, 25
Neighborhood Coalition, 17, 143
Neighborhood Guild, 29
Neuhaus, Richard John, 96, 97, 98, 136, 141, 145, 192, 193, 245nn5,6,10, 246n13–14, 251–252n13, 252nn21,23,24
New York Bible Society, 54
New York Board of Rabbis, 14, 179
New York Cares, 54, 81, 244n77
New York Catholic Protectory, 29
New York City Mission Society, 29
New York City Sanitation Department, 75
New York Police Department, 119, 128
New York Police Department's Homeless Outreach Squad, 18
New York Society for the Prevention of Pauperism, 28
New York State Financial Control Board, 12
New York Times, The, 10, 129, 168, 246–247n56
New York University (NYU), 11, 35, 57
Newby, Howard, 251n3
Newfield, Jack, 237n1 (Chapter 1), 238n2 (Chapter 1), 238n1

Nisbet, Robert, 137, 145, 175, 247n94, 248n106, 251n11
Nonprofit and Voluntary Sector Quarterly, 82
North, Douglas, 253n3
Nozick, Robert, 84, 242n47
NYNEX Telephone Pioneers, 244–245n77

Ogilvie, Robert S., 251–252n13, 253n30
Olivieri Center, 17
Olson, Mancur, 242n51
On the Jewish Question, 245n7
Open Door, 17
Open moral communities, 177, 251n2
Our Lady of Good Counsel. *See* Church and synagogue shelters, Our Lady of Good Counsel
Our Voices Raised, 227, 228

Parish Councils, 35–36
Parsons, Talcott, 90, 244nn70,72
Partnership for the Homeless (the Partnership), 2–8, 9–22, 23, 26, 35, 36, 39, 40, 42, 43, 51, 53, 54, 66, 69, 71, 72, 73, 74, 75, 79, 81, 91, 95, 99, 103, 118, 119, 120, 121, 123, 124, 125, 127, 128, 130, 141, 142, 144, 145, 155, 156, 167, 169, 178, 179, 182, 184, 188, 189, 190, 192, 193, 205, 208, 209, 210, 212, 213, 214, 215, 218, 219, 222, 225, 226, 227, 228, 229, 231, 232, 233, 238n7, 244–245n77, 254n1 (Conclusion), 254n1 (Appendix)
Pateman, Carole, 251–252n13, 252n19
Peninsula Hotel, 54, 246–247n56
Perlmutter, Howard, 201, 203, 207, 212, 218, 253nn5,6
Peter's Place, 18, 19, 63, 64
Piliavin, Jane Allen, 242n52
Plant, Raymond, 251n4
Plater-Zyberk, Elizabeth, 248n105
Plaza Hotel, 54
Plymouth Church of the Pilgrim. *See* Church and synagogue shelters, Plymouth Church of the Pilgrim
Political crisis. *See* Crises of modernity, political
Political development theory, 88
Poor laws, 27
Pope John XXIII, 35

Robert Ogilvie

is Assistant Professor in the Department of
City and Regional Planning at the University of
California, Berkeley, where he teaches classes in
community development and urban studies.
He holds a Ph.D. in political science from
Columbia University. He is the former director
of volunteers at the Partnership for the
Homeless in New York City.